The Light Eternal: J.M.W. Turner
by Jeremy Mark Robinson

Maurice Sendak and the Art of Children's Book Illustration
by L.M. Poole

Sex in Art: Pornography and Pleasure in Painting and Sculpture
by Cassidy Hughes

*Glorification: Religious Abstraction
In Renaissance and 20th Century Painting*
by Jeremy Mark Robinson

The Art of Andy Goldsworthy
by William Malpas

Andy Goldsworthy: Touching Nature
by William Malpas

Andy Goldsworthy In Close-Up
by William Malpas

The Art of Richard Long
by William Malpas

Constantin Brancusi: Sculpting the Essence of Things
by James Pearson

Alison Wilding: The Embrace of Sculpture
by Susan Quinnell

*The Erotic Object: Sexuality in Sculpture
From Prehistory to the Present Day*
by Susan Quinnell

*Land Art: A Complete Guide to Landscape, Environmental,
Earthworks, Nature, Sculpture and Installation Art*
by William Malpas

Land Art In Close-Up
by William Malpas

*Colourfield Painting: Minimal, Cool, Hard Edge, Serial
and Post-Painterly Abstract Art From the Sixties to the Present*
by Laura Garrard

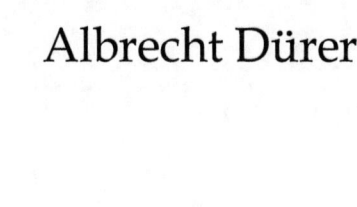

Albrecht Dürer

ALBRECHT DÜRER

T. STURGE MOORE

CRESCENT MOON

First published 1905. This edition © 2017.

Printed and bound in the U.S.A.
Set in Book Antiqua 10 on 14pt.
Designed by Radiance Graphics.

British Library Cataloguing in Publication data

ISBN-13 9781861716194 (Pbk)
ISBN-13 9781861716989 (Hbk)

CRESCENT MOON PUBLISHING
P.O. Box 1312, Maidstone, Kent, ME14 5XU
Great Britain, www.crmoon.com

CONTENTS

PART III

DÜRER AS A CREATOR

PART IV

DÜRER'S IDEAS

NOTE ON THE TEXT

The text is from *Albrecht Dürer* by T. Surge Moore, and published in 1905.

Footnotes are in square brackets, thus: [1].

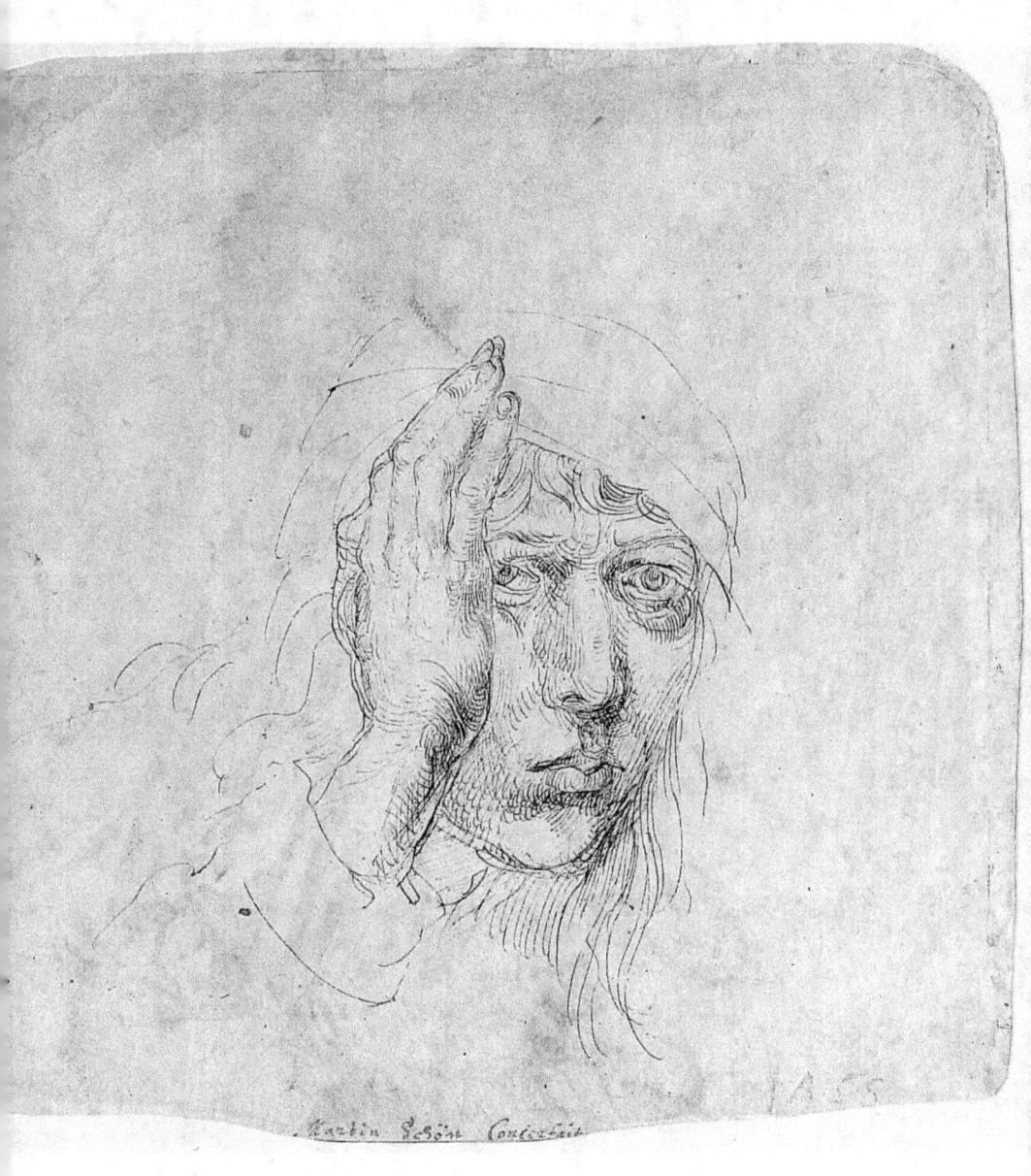

Albrecht Dürer, Self-Portrait, 1492, Erlangen

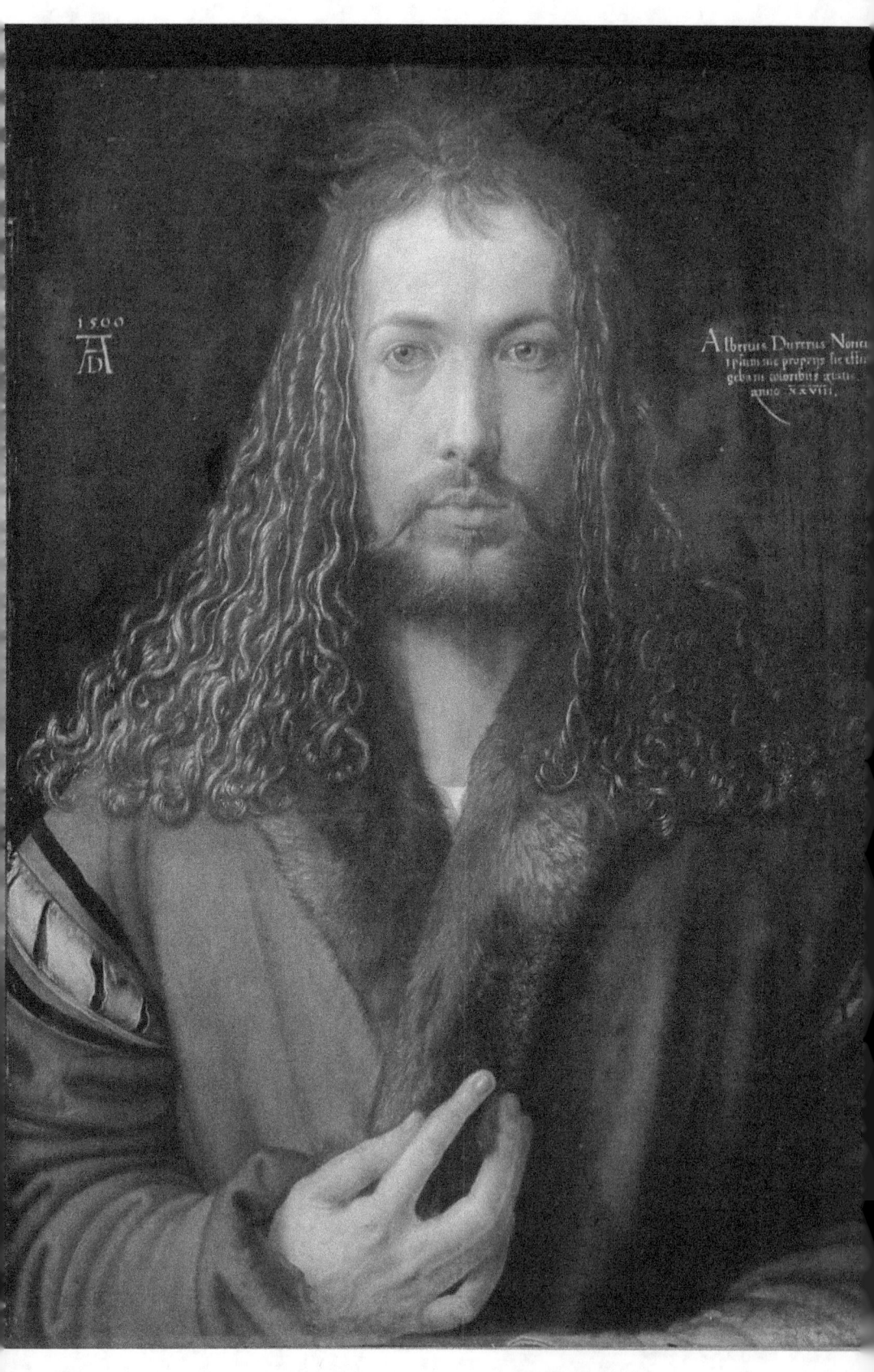

Albrecht Dürer, Self-Portrait, Munich

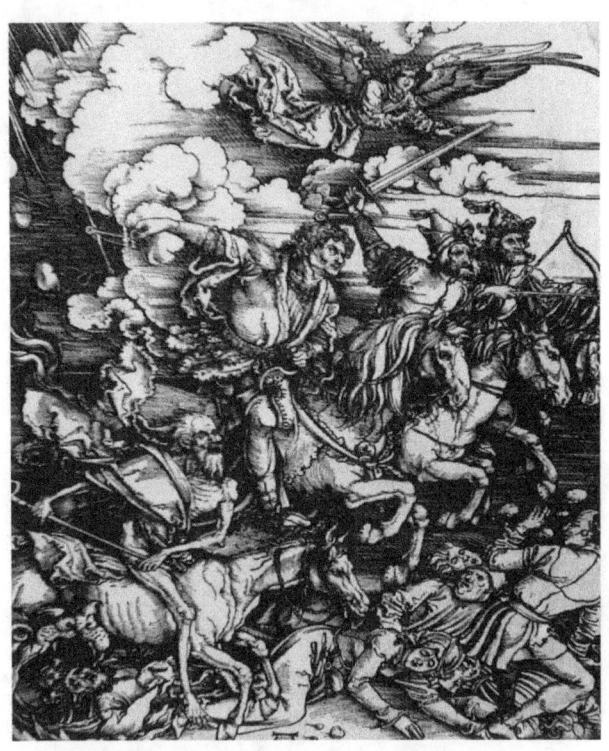

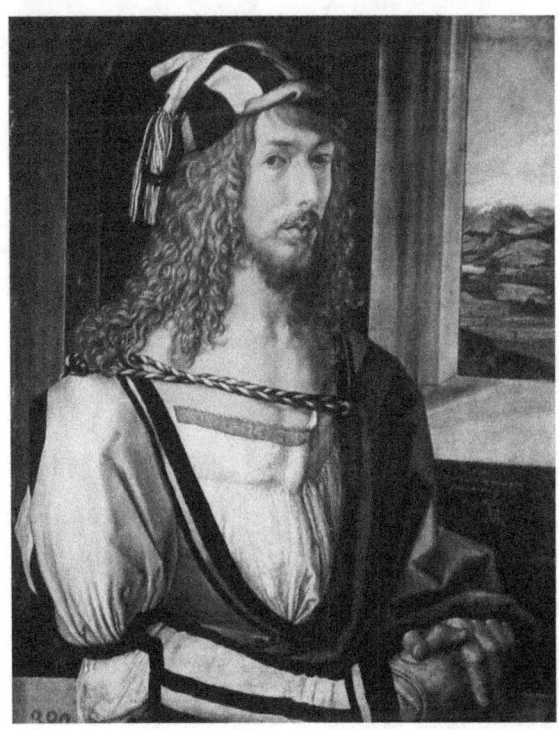

Albrecht Dürer

PREFACE

When the late Mr. Arthur Strong asked me to undertake the present volume, I pointed out to him that, to fulfil the advertised programme of the Series he was editing, was more than could be hoped from my attainments. He replied, that in the case of Dürer a book, fulfilling that programme, was not called for, and that what he wished me to attempt, was an appreciation of this great artist in relation to general ideas. I had hoped to benefit very largely by my editor's advice and supervision, but this his illness and death prevented. His great gifts and brilliant accomplishments, already darkened and distressed by disease, were all too soon to be utterly quenched; and I can but here express, not only my sense of personal loss in the hopes which his friendly welcome and generous intercourse had created and which have been so cruelly dashed by the event, but also that of the void which his disappearance has left in the too thin ranks of those who, filled with reverence and enthusiasm for the great traditions of the past, seem nevertheless eager and capable of grappling with the unwieldy present. Let and restricted had been the recognition of his maturing worth, and now we must do without both him and the impetus of his so nearly assured success.

The present volume, then, is not the result of new research; nor is it an abstract resuming historical and critical discoveries on its subject up to date. Of this latter there are several already before the British public; the former, as I said, it was not for me to attempt. Nor do I feel my book to be altogether even what it was intended to be; but am conscious that too much space has been given to the enumeration of Dürer's principal works and the events of his life without either being made exhaustive. Still, I hope that even these parts may be found profitable by those who are not already familiar with the subjects with which they deal. To those for whom these subjects are well known, I should like to point out that Parts I. and IV. and very much of Part III. embody my chief intention; that chapter 1 of Part I. finds a further illustration in division iii. of chapter 4, Part II.; and that division vi., chapter 1, Part II., should be taken as prefatory to chapter 1, Part IV.

Should exception be taken to the works chosen as illustrations, I would explain that the means of reproduction, the degree of reduction necessitated by the size of the page, and other outside considerations, have severely limited my choice. It is entirely owing to the extreme kindness of the Dürer Society – more especially of its courteous and enthusiastic secretaries, Mr. Campbell Dodgson and Mr. Peartree – that four copper-plates have so greatly enhanced the adequacy of the volume in this respect.

I have gratefully to acknowledge Sir Martin Conway's kindness in permitting me to quote so liberally from his "Literary Remains of Albrecht Dürer," by far the best book on this great artist known to me. Mr. Charles Eaton's translation of Thausing's "Life of Dürer," the "Portfolios of the Dürer Society," and Dr. Lippmanb "Drawings of Albrecht Dürer," are the only other works on my subject to which I feel bound to acknowledge my indebtedness. Lastly, I must express deep gratitude to my learned friend, Mr. Campbell Dodgson, for having so generously consented, by reading the proofs, to mitigate my defect in scholarship.

PART I

CONCERNING GENERAL IDEAS IMPORTANT TO THE COMPREHENSION OF DÜRER'S LIFE AND ART

CHAPTER I

THE IDEA OF PROPORTION

I

Ich hab vernomen wie der siben weysen aus kriechenland ainer gelert
hab das dymass in allen dingen sitlichen und naturlichen das pest
sey.

DÜRER, British Museum MS., vol. iv., 82a.

(I have heard how one of the Seven Sages of Greece taught that
measure is in all things, physical and moral, best.)

La souveraine habileté consiste à bien connaitre le prix des choses.

LA ROCHEFOUCAULD, III. 252.

(Sovereign skill consists in thoroughly understanding the value of
things.)

The attempt that the last quarter century has witnessed, to introduce the methods of science into the criticism of works of art, has tended, it seems to me, to put the question of their value into the background. The easily scandalous inquiries, "Who?" "When?" "Where?" have assumed an impertinent predominance. When I hear people very decidedly asserting that such a picture was painted by such an one, not generally supposed to be the author, at such a time, &c. &c., I often feel uneasy in the same way as one does on being addressed in a loud voice in a church or a picture gallery, where other persons are absorbed in an acknowledged and respected contemplation or study. I feel inclined to blush and whisper, for fear of being supposed to know the speaker too well. It is an awkward moment with me, for I am in fact very good friends with many such persons. "Sovereign skill consists in thoroughly understanding the value of things" – not their commercial value only, though that is sovereign skill on the Exchange, but their value for those whose chief riches are within them. The value of works of art is an intimate experience, and cannot be estimated by the methods of exact science as the weight of a planet can. There are and have been forgeries that are more beautiful, therefore more valuable, than genuine specimens of the class of work which they figure as. I feel that the specialist, with his special measure and point of view, often endangers the fair name and good repute of the real estimate; and that nothing but the dominion and diffusion of general ideas can defend us against the specialist and keep the specialist from being carried away by bad habits resulting from his devotion to a single inquiry.

There was one general idea, of the greatest importance in determining the true value of things, which preoccupied Dürer's mind and haunted his imagination: the idea of proportion. I propose therefore to attempt to make clear to myself and my readers what the idea of proportion really implies, and of what service a sense for proportion really is; secondly, to determine the special use of the term in relation to the appreciation of works of art; thirdly, in relation to their internal structure; – before proceeding to the special studies of Dürer as a man and an artist.

II

I conceive the human reason to be the antagonist of all known forces other than itself, and that therefore its most essential character is the hope and desire to control and transform the universe; or, failing that, to annihilate, if not the universe, at least itself and the consciousness of a monster fact which it entirely condemns. In this conception I believe myself to be at one with those by whom men have been most influenced, and who, with or without confidence in the support of unknown powers, have set themselves deliberately against the face of things to die or conquer. This being so, and man individually weak, it has been the avowed object of great characters – carrying with them the instinctive consent of nations – to establish current values for all things, according as their imagination could turn them to account as effective aids of reason: that is, as they could be made to advance her apparent empire over other elemental forces, such as motion, physical life, &c. This evaluation, in so far as it is constant, results in what we call civilisation, and is the only bond of society. With difficulty is the value of new acquisitions recognised even in the realm of science, until the imagination can place them in such a light as shall make them appear to advance reason's ends, which accounts for the reluctance that has been shown to accept many scientific results. Reason demands that the world she would create shall be a fact, and declares that the world she would transform is the real world, but until the imagination can find a function for it in reason's ideal realm, every piece of knowledge remains useless, or even an obstacle in the way of our intended advance. This applies to individuals just as truly as it does to mankind. And since man's reason is a natural phenomenon and does apparently belong to the class of elemental forces, this warfare against the apparent fact, and the fortitude and hope which its whole-hearted prosecution begets, appear as a natural law to the intelligence and as a command and promise to the reason.

The alternative between the will to cease and the will to serve reason, with which I start out, may not seem necessary to all. "Forgive their sin – and if not, blot me I pray thee out of thy book," was Moses' prayer; and to me it seems that only by lethargy can any soul escape from facing this alternative. The human mind in so far as it is active always postulates, "Let that which I desire come to pass, or let me cease!" Nor is there any diversity possible as to what really is desirable: Man desires the full and harmonious development of his faculties. As to how this end may most probably be attained, there is diversity enough to represent every possible blend of ignorance with knowledge, of lethargy with energy, of cowardice with courage.

"So endless and exorbitant are the desires of men, whether considered in their persons or their states, that they will grasp at all, and can form no scheme of perfect happiness with less."[1] So writes the most powerful of English prose-writers. And this hope and desire, which is reason, once thrown down, the most powerful among poets has brought from human lips this estimate of life –

"It is a tale
Told by an idiot, full of sound and fury,
Signifying nothing."

No one knows whether reason's object will or can be attained; but for the present each man finds confidence and encouragement in so far as he is able to imagine all things working together for the good of those who desire good – in short, for "reasonable beings."[2] The more he knows, the greater labour it is for him to imagine this; but the more he concentrates his faculties on doing good and creating good things, the more his imagination glows and shines and discovers to him new possibilities of success: the better he is able to find –

"Sermons in stones and good in everything;"
"And make a moral of the devil himself."

But how is it that reason can accept an imagination that makes what in a cold light she considers her enemy, appear her friend? All things impress the mind with two contradictory notions – their actual condition and their perfection. Even the worst of its kind impresses on us an idea of what the best would be, or we could not know it for the worst. Reason, then, seizes on this aspect of things which suggests their perfection, and awards them her attention in proportion as such aspect makes their perfection seem near, or as it may further her in transforming the most pressing of other evils. All life tends to affirm its own character; and the essential characteristic of man is reason, which labours to perfect all things that he judges to be good, and to transform all evil. Ultimate results are out of sight for all human faculties except the early-waking eyes of long-chastened hope; but reason loves this visionary mood, though she prefer that it be sung, and find that less lyrical speech brings on it something of ridicule; for such a rendering betrays, as a rule, faint desire or small power to serve her in those who use it.

The sense of proportion, then, is that fineness of susceptibility by which we appreciate in a given object, person, force, or mood, serviceableness in regard to reason's work; in other words, by which we estimate the capacity to transform the Universe in such a way that men may ultimately be enabled to give their hearty consent to its existence, which at present no man rationally can.

III

Now, art appeals to fine susceptibilities; for, as I have explained elsewhere,[3] the value of works of art depends on their having come as "real and intimate experiences to a large number of gifted men" – men who have some kinship to that "finely touched and gifted man, the [Greek *heuphnaes*] of the Greeks," to use the phrase of our greatest modern critic. And in so far as we are able to judge between works successfully making such an appeal, we must be governed by this sense of proportion, which measures how things stand in regard to reason; that is, not merely intellect, not merely emotion, but the alliance of both by means of the imagination in aid of man's most central demand – the demand for nobler life.

Perhaps I ought to point out before proceeding, that this position is not that of the writers on art most in view at the present day. It is the negation of the so-called scientific criticism, and also of the personal theory that reduces art to an expression of, and an appeal to, individual temperaments; it is the assertion of the sovereignty of the aesthetic conscience on exactly the same grounds as sovereignty is claimed for the moral conscience. Æsthetics deals with the morality of appeals addressed to the senses. That is, it estimates the success of such appeals in regard to the promotion of fuller and more harmonious life. Flaubert wrote:

> "Le génie n'est pas rare maintenant, mais ce que personne n'a plus et ce qu'il faut tacher d'avoir, c'est la conscience."

> ("Genius is not rare nowadays, but conscience is what nobody has and what one should strive after.")

To-day I am thinking of a painter. Painting is an art addressed primarily to the eye, and not to the intelligence, not to the imagination, save as these may be reached through the eye – that most delicate organ of infinite susceptibility, which teaches us the meaning of the word light – a word so often uttered with stress of ecstasy, of longing, of despair, and of every other shade of emotion, that the sound of it must soon be almost as powerful with the young heart, almost as immediate in its effect, as the break of day itself, gladdening the eyes and glorifying the earth. And how often is this joy received through the eye entrusted back to it for expression? For the eye can speak with varieties, delicacies, and subtle shades of motion far beyond the attainment of any other organ. "This art of painting is made for the eyes, for sight is the noblest sense of man,"[4] says Dürer; and again:

> "It is ordained that never shall any man be able, out of his own thoughts, to make a beautiful figure, unless, by much study, he hath well stored his mind. That then is no longer to be called his own; it is art acquired and learnt, which soweth, waxeth, and beareth fruit after its kind. Thence the gathered secret treasure of the heart is manifested openly in the work, and the new creature which a man createth in his heart, appeareth in the form of a thing."[5]

Yes, indeed, the function of art is far from being confined to telling us what we see, whatever some may pretend, or however naturally any small nature may desire to continue, teach, or regulate great ones. All so-called scientific methods of creating or criticising works of art are inadequate, because the only truly scientific statements that can be made about these inquiries are that nothing is certain – that no method ensures success, and that no really important quality can be defined; for what man can say why one cloud is more beautiful than another in the same sky, any more than he can explain why, of two men equally absorbed in doing their duty, one impresses him as being more holy than the other? The degrees essential to both kinds of judgment escape all definition; only the imagination can at times bring them home to us, only the refined taste or chastened conscience, as the case may be, witnesses with our spirit that its judgment is just, and bids us recognise a master in him who delivers it. As the expression on a face speaks to a delicate sense, often communicating more, other, and better than can be seen, so the proportion, harmony, rhythm of a painting may beget moods and joys that require the full resources of a well-stored mind and disciplined character in order that they may be fully relished – in brief, demand that maturity of reason which is the mark of victorious man.

Such being my conception, it will easily be perceived how anxious I must be to truly discern and express the relation between such objects as works of art by common consent so highly honoured, and at the same time so active in their effect upon the most exquisitely endowed of mankind. Especially since to-day caprice, humour and temperament are, by the majority of writers on art, acclaimed for the radical characteristic of the human creative faculty, instead of its perversion and disease; and it is thought that to be whimsical, moody, or self-indulgent best fits a man both to create and appraise works of art, whereas to become so really is the only way in which a man capable of such high tasks can with certainty ruin and degrade his faculties. Precious, surpassingly precious indeed, must every manifestation of such faculty before its final extinction remain, since the race produces comparatively few endowed after this kind.

Perhaps a sufficient illustration of this prevalent fallacy may be drawn from Mr. Whistler's "Ten O'Clock," where he speaks of art:

> "A whimsical goddess, and a capricious, her strong sense of joy tolerates no dulness, and, live we never so spotlessly, still may she turn her back upon us."

> "As from time immemorial, she has done upon the Swiss in their mountains."

Here is no proof of caprice, save on the witty writer's part; for men who fast are not saved from bad temper, nor have the kindly necessarily discreet tongues. The Swiss may be brave and honest, and yet dull. Virtue is her own reward, and art her own. Virtue rewards the saint, art the artist; but men are rewarded for attention to morality by some measure of joy in virtue, for attention to beauty by some measure of joy in works of art. Between the artist and the Philistine is no great gulf fixed, in the sense that the witty "master of the butterfly" pretends to assume, but an infinite and gentle decline of persons representing every possible blend of the virtues and faults of these two types. Again, an artist is miscalled "master of art." "Where he is, there she appears," is airy impudence. "Where she wills to be, there she chooses a man to serve her," would not only have been more gallant but more reasonable; for that "The wind bloweth where it listeth, and thou hearest the sound thereof, but canst not tell whence it cometh and whither it goeth: so is every one that is born of the spirit," and that "many are called, few chosen," are sayings as true of the influence which kindleth art as of that which quickeneth to holiness. Art is not dignified by being called whimsical – or capricious. What can a man explain? The intention, behind the wind, behind the spirit, behind the creative instinct, is dark. But man is true to his own most essential character when, if he cannot refrain from prating of such mysteries, he qualifies them as hope would have him, with the noblest of his virtues; not when he speaks of the unknown, in whose hands his destiny so largely rests, slightingly, as of a woman whom he has seduced because he despised her – calling her capricious because she answered to his caprice, whimsical, because she was as flighty as his error. It is not art's function to reward virtue. But, caprices and whimseys being ascribed to a goddess, it will be natural to expect them in her worshipper; and Mr. Whistler revealed the limitations of his genius by whimseys and caprice. Though it was in their relations to the world that this goddess and her devotee claimed freedoms so far from perfect, yet this, their avowed characteristic abroad, I think in some degree disturbed their domestic relations, Though others have underlined the absurdity of this theory by applying themselves to it with more faith and less sense, I have chosen to quote from the "Ten O'Clock," because I admire it and accept most of the ideas about art advanced therein. The artist who wrote it was able, in Dürer's phrase, "to prove" what he wrote "with his hand." Most of those who have elaborated what was an occasional unsoundness of his doctrine into ridiculous religions are as unable to create as they are to think; there is no need to record names which it is wisdom to forget. But it may be well to point out that Mr. Whistler does not succeed in glorifying great artists when he declares that beauty "to them was as much a matter of certainty and triumph as is to the astronomer the verification of the result, foreseen with the light granted to him alone." No, he only sets up a false analogy; for the true parallel to the artist is the saint, not the astronomer; both are convinced, neither understands. Art is no more the reward of intelligence than of virtue. She permits no caprice in her own realm. Loyalty is the only virtue she insists on, loyalty in regard to her servant's experience of beauty; he may be immoral in every other way and she not desert him; but let him turn Balaam and declare beauty absent where he feels its presence – though in doing this he hopes to advance virtue or knowledge, she needs no better than an ass to rebuke him. Nothing effects more for anarchy than these notions that art derives from individual caprice, or defends virtue, or demonstrates knowledge; for they are all based on those flattering hopes of the unsuccessful, that chance, rules both in life and art, or that it is possible to serve two masters.

Doctrines often repeated gain easy credence; and, since art demands leisure in order to be at all enjoyed, ideas about it, in so fatiguing a life as ours has become, take men off their guard, when their habitual caution is laid to sleep, and, by an over-easiness, they are inclined to spoil both their sense of distinction and their children. Yes, they consent to theatres that degrade them, because they distract and amuse; and read journals that are smart and diverting at the expense of dignity and truth – in the same way as they smile at the child whom reason bids them reprove, and with the like tragic result; for they become incapable of enjoying works of art, as the child is incapacitated for the best of social intercourse. To prophesy smooth things to people in this condition, and flatter their dulness, is to be no true friend; and so the modern art-critic and journalist is often the insidious enemy of the civilisation he contents.

Nothing strikes the foreigner coming to England more than our lack of general ideas. Our art criticism is no exception; it, like our literature and politics, is happy-go-lucky and delights in the pot-shot. We often hear this attributed admiringly to "the sporting instinct." "If God, in his own time, granteth me to write something further about matters connected with painting, I will do so, in hope that this art may not rest upon use and wont alone, but that in time it may be taught on true and orderly principles, and may be understood to the praise of God and the use and pleasure of all lovers of art."[6]

Our art is still worse off than our trade or our politics, for it does not even rest upon use and wont, but is wholly in the air. Yet the typical modern aesthete has learnt where to take cover, for, though destitute of defence, he has not entirely lost the instinct for self-preservation; and, when he finds the eye of reason upon him, he immediately flies to the diversity of opinions. But Dürer follows him even there with the perfect good faith of a man in earnest.

"Men deliberate and hold numberless differing opinions about beauty, and they seek after it in many different ways, although ugliness is thereby rather attained. Being then, as we are, in such a state of error, I know not certainly what the ultimate measure of true beauty is, and cannot describe it aright. But glad should I be to render such help as I can, to the end that the gross deformities of our work might be and remain pruned away and avoided, unless indeed any one prefers to bestow great labour upon the production of deformities. We are brought back, therefore, to the aforesaid judgment of men, which considereth one figure beautiful at one time and another at another....

"Because now we cannot altogether attain unto perfection, shall we therefore wholly cease from learning? By no means. Let us not take unto ourselves thoughts fit for cattle. For evil and good lie before men, wherefore it behoveth the rational man to choose the good."[7]

* 28

A man may see, if he will but watch, who is more finely touched and gifted than himself. In all the various fields of human endeavour, on such men he should try to form himself; for only thus can he enlarge his nature, correct his opinions. Something he can learn from this man, something from that, and it is rational to learn and be taught. Are we to be cattle or gods? "Is it not written in your law, I said, 'Ye are gods?'" Reason demands that each man form himself on the pattern of a god, and God is an empty name if reason be not the will of God. Then he whom reason hath brought up may properly be called a son of God, a son of man, a child of light. But it is easier to bob to such phrases than to understand them. However, their mechanical repetition does not prevent their having meant something once, does not prevent their meaning being their true value. It is time we understood our art, just as it is time we understood our religion. Docility, as I have pointed out elsewhere, is one of the marks of genius. Dürer's spirit is the spirit of the great artist who will learn even from "dull men of little judgment."

> "Let none be ashamed to learn, for a good work requireth good counsel. Nevertheless, whosoever taketh counsel in the arts, let him take it from one thoroughly versed in those matters, who can prove what he saith with his hand. Howbeit any one may give thee counsel; and when thou hast done a work pleasing to thyself, it is good for thee to show it to dull men of little judgment that they may give their opinion of it. As a rule they pick out the most faulty points, whilst they entirely pass over the good. If thou findest something they say true, thou mayst thus better thy work."[8]

Those who are thoroughly versed in art are the great artists; we have guides then, and we have a way – the path they have trodden – and we have company, the gifted and docile men of to-day whom we see to be improving themselves; and, in so far as we are reasonable, a sense of proportion is ours, which we may improve; and it will help us to catch up better and yet better company until we enjoy the intimacy of the noblest, and know as we are known. Then: "May we not consider it a sign of sanity when we regard the human spirit as ... a poet, and art as a half written poem? Shall we not have a sorry disappointment if its conclusion is merely novel, and not the fulfilment and vindication of those great things gone before?"[9] For my own part, those appear to me the grandest characters who, on finding that there is no other purchase for effort but only hope, and that they can never cease from hope but by ceasing to live, clear their minds of all idle acquiescence in what could never be hoped, and concentrate their energies on conquering whatever in their own nature, and in the world about them, militates against their most essential character – reason, which seeks always to give a higher value to life.

IV

When we speak of the sense of proportion displayed in the design of a building, many will think that the word is used in quite a different sense, and one totally unrelated to those which I have been discussing. But no; life and art are parallel and correspond throughout; ethics are the Esthetics of life, religion the art of living. Taste and conscience only differ in their provinces, not in their procedure. Both are based on instinctive preferences; the canon of either is merely so many of those preferences as, by their constant recurrence to individuals gifted with the power of drawing others after them, are widely accepted.

The preference of serenity to melancholy, of light to darkness, are among the most firmly established in the canon, that is all. The sense of proportion within a design is employed to stimulate and delight the eye. Ordinary people may fear there is some abstruse science about this. Not at all; it is as simple as relishing milk and honey, and its development an exact parallel to the training of the palate to distinguish the flavours of teas, coffees and wines. "Taste and see" is the whole business. There are many people who have no hesitation in picking out what to their eye is the wainscot panel with the richest grain: they see it at once. So with etchings; if people would only forget that they are works of art, forget all the false or ill-understood standards which they have been led to suppose applicable, and look at them as they might at agate stones; or choose out the richest in effect: the most suitable for a gay room, or a hall, or a library, as though they were patterned stuffs for curtains; they would come a thousand times nearer a right appreciation of Dürer's success than by making a pot-shot to lasso the masterpiece with the tangle of literary rubbish which is known as art criticism.

The harmonies and contrasts of juxtaposed colours or textures are affected by quantity, and a sense of proportion decides what quantities best produce this effect and what that. The correctness or amount of information to be conveyed in the delineation of some object, in relation to the mood which the artist has chosen shall dominate his work, is determined by his sense of proportion. He may distort an object to any extent or leave it as vague as the shadow on a wall in diffused light, or he may make it precise and particular as ever Jan Van Eyck did; so only that its distortion or elaboration is so proportioned to the other objects and intentions of his work as to promote its success in the eyes of the beholder.

There are no fallacies greater than the prevalent ones conveyed by the expressions "out of drawing" or "untrue to nature." There is no such thing as correct drawing or an outside standard of truth for works of art.

"The conception of every work of art carries within it its own rule and method, which must be found out before it can be achieved." "Chaque oeuvre à faire a sa poétique en soi, qu'il faut trouver," said Flaubert. Truth in a work of art is sincerity. That a man says what he really means – shows us what he really thinks to be beautiful – is all that reason bids us ask for. No science or painstaking can make up for his not doing this. No lack of skill or observation can entirely frustrate his communicating his intention to kindred natures if he is utterly sincere. An infant communicates its joy. It is probable that the inexpressible is never felt. Stammering becomes more eloquent than oratory, a child's impulsiveness wiser than circumlocutory experience. When a single intention absorbs the whole nature, communication is direct and immediate, and makes impotence itself a means of effect-iveness. So the naïveties of early art put to shame the purposeless parade of prodigious skill. Wherever there is communication there is art; but there are evil communications and there is vicious art, though, perhaps, great sincerity is incompatible with either. For an artist to be deterred by other people's demands means that he is not artist enough; it is what his reason teaches him to demand of himself that matters, though, doubtless, the good desire the approval of kindred natures.

A work of art addresses the eye by means of chosen proportions; it may present any number of facts as exactly as may be, but if it offend the eye it is a mere misapplication of industry, or the illustration of a scientific treatise out of place; and those that choose ribbons well are better artists than the man that made it. Or again it may overflow with poetical thought and suggestion, or have the stuff to make a first-rate story in it; but, if it offend the eye, it is merely a misapplication of imagination, invention or learning, and the girl who puts a charming nosegay together is a better artist than he who painted it. On the other hand, though it have no more significance than a glass of wine and a loaf of bread, if the eye is rejoiced by gazing on the paint that expresses them, it is a work of art and a fine achievement. Still, it may be as fanciful as a fairy-tale, or as loaded with import as the Crucifixion; and, if it stimulates the eye to take delight in its surfaces over and above mere curiosity, it is a work of art, and great in proportion as the significance of what it conveys is brought home to us by the very quality of the stimulus that is created in return for our gaze. For painting is the result of a power to speak beautifully with paint, as poetry is of a power to express beautifully by means of words either simple things or those which demand the effort of a welltrained mind in order to be received and comprehended. The mistake made by impressionists, luminarists, and other modern artists, is that a true statement of how things appear to them will suffice; it will not, unless things appear beautiful to them, and they render them beautifully. It will not, because science is not art, because knowledge is a different thing from beauty. A true statement may be repulsive and degrading; whereas an affirmation of beauty, whether it be true or fancied, is always moving, and if delivered with corresponding grace is inspiring – is a work of art and "a joy for ever." For reason demands that all the eye sees shall be beautiful, and give such pleasure as best consists with the universe becoming what reason demands that it shall become. This demand of reason is perfectly arbitrary? Yes, but it is also inevitable, necessitated by the nature of the human character. It is equally arbitrary and equally inevitable that man must, where science is called for, in the long run prefer a true statement to a lie. From art reason demands beautiful objects, from science true statements: such is human nature; for the possession of this reason that judges and condemns the universe, and demands and attempts to create something better, is that which differentiates human life from all other known forces – is that by which men may be more than conquerors, may make peace with the universe; for

"A peace is of the nature of a conquest;
For then both parties nobly are subdued
And neither party loser."

Of such a nature is the only peace that the soul can make with the body – that man can make with nature – that habit can make with instinct – that art can make with impulse. In order to establish such a peace the imagination must train reason to see a friend in her enemy, the physical order. For, as Reynolds says of the complete artist:

"He will pick up from dunghills, what, by a nice chemistry, passing through his own mind, shall be converted into pure gold, and under the rudeness of Gothic essays, he will find original, rational, and even sublime inventions."[10]

It is not too much to say that the nature both of the artist and of the dunghills is "subdued" by such a process, and yet neither is a "loser." Goethe profoundly remarked that the highest development of the soul was reached through worship first of that which was above, then of that which was beneath it. This great critic also said, "Only with difficulty do we spell out from that which nature presents to us, the DESIRED word, the congenial. Men find what the artist brings intelligible and to their taste, stimulating and alluring, genial and friendly, spiritually nourishing, formative and elevating. Thus the artist, grateful to the nature that made him, weaves a second nature – but a conscious, a fuller, a more perfectly human nature."

CHAPTER II

THE INFLUENCE OF RELIGION ON THE CREATIVE IMPULSE

I

There are some artists of whom one would naturally write in a lyrical strain, with praise of the flesh, and those things which add to its beauty, freshness, and mystery – fair scenes of mountain, woodland, or sea-shore; blue sky, white cloud and sunlight, or the deep and starry night; youth and health, strength and fertility, frankness and freedom. And, in such a strain, one would insist that the fondness and intoxication which these things quicken was natural, wise, and lovely. But, quite as naturally, when one has to speak of Dürer, the mind becomes filled with the exhilaration and the staidness that the desire to know and the desire to act rightly beget; with the dignity of conscious comprehension, the serenity of accomplished duty with all the strenuousness and ardour of which the soul is capable; with science and religion.

It is natural to refer often to the towering eminence of these virtues in Michelangelo; both he and Dürer were not only great artists, and active and powerful minds, but men imbued with, and conservative of, piety. And it seems to me, if we are to appreciate and sympathise deeply with such men, we must try to understand the religion they believed in; to estimate, not only what its value was supposed to be in those days, but what value it still has for us. Surely what they prized so highly must have had real and lasting worth? Surely it can only be the relation of that value to common speech and common thought which has changed, not its relation to man's most essential nature? Therefore I will first try to arrive at a general notion of the real worth of their ideas, – that is, the worth that is equally great from their point of view and ours.

The whole of that period, the period of the so belauded Renascence, had within it (or so it seems to me) an incurable insufficiency, which troubles the affections of those who praise or condemn it; so that they show themselves more passionate than those who praise or condemn the art and life of ancient Greece. This insufficiency I believe to have been due to the fact that Christian ideas were more firmly rooted in, than they were understood by, the society of those days. And to-day I think the same cause continues to propagate a like insufficiency, a like lack of correspondence between effort and aim. Certain ideas found in the reported sayings of Jesus have so fastened upon the European intellect that they seem well-nigh inseparable from it. We are told that the effort of the Greek, of Aristotle, was to "submit to the empire of fact." The effort of the Jew was very similar; for the prophets, what happened was the will of God, what will happen is what God intends. Now it is noteworthy that Aristotle did not wish to submit to ignorance, though it and the causes which produce it and preserve it in human minds are among the most horrible and tremendous of facts; and it is the imperishable glory of the prophets, that, whatever the priest the king, the Sadducee or Pharisee might do, *they* could not rest in or abide the idea that God's will was ever evil; no inconsistency was too glaring to check their indignation at Eastern fatalism which quietly supposed that as things went wrong it was their nature to do so; – vanity, vanity, all is vanity! – or that if men did wrong and prospered, it was God's doing, and showed that they had pleased Him with sacrifices and performances.

II

'Wherever poetry, imagination, or art had been busy, there had appeared, both in Judea and Greece, some degree of rebellion against the empire of fact. When Jesus said: "The kingdom of heaven is within you," he recognised that the human reason was the antagonist of all other known forces, and he declared war on the god of this world and prophesied the downfall of – the empire of the apparent fact; – not with fume and fret, not with rant and rage, as poets and seers had done, but mildly affirming that with the soul what is best is strongest, has in the long run most influence; that there is one fact in the essential nature of man which, antagonist to the influence of all other facts, wields an influence destined to conquer or absorb all other influences. He said: "My Father which is in heaven, the master influence within me, has declared that I shall never find rest to my soul until I prefer His kingdom, the conception of my heart, to the kingdoms of earth and the glory of the earth." 'We have seen that Dürer describes the miracle; the work of art, thus:

"The secret treasure which a man conceived in his heart shall appear as a thing" (see page 10).

And we know that he prized this, the master thing, the conception of the heart, above everything else.

Much learning is not evil to a man, though some be stiffly set against it, saying that art puffeth up. Were that so, then were none prouder than God who hath formed all arts, but that cannot be, for God is perfect in goodness. The more, therefore, a man learneth, so much the better doth he become, and so much the more love doth he win for the arts and for things exalted.

The learning Dürer chiefly intends is not book-learning or critical lore, but knowledge how to make, by which man becomes a creator in imitation of God; for this is of necessity the most perfect knowledge, rivalling the sureness of intuition and instinct.

III

"Heaven and earth shall pass away, but my words shall not pass away." Every one knows how anxious great artists become for the preservation of their works, how highly they value permanence in the materials employed, and immunity from the more obvious chances of destruction in the positions they are to occupy. Michelangelo is said to have painted cracks on the Sistina ceiling to force the architect to strengthen the roof. When Jesus made the assertion that his teaching would outlast the influence of the visible world of nature and the societies of men – the kingdoms of earth and the glory of the earth – he did no more than every victorious soul strives to effect, and to feel assured that it has in some large degree effected; the difference between him and them is one of degree. It may be objected that different hearts harbour and cherish contradictory conceptions. Doubtless; but does the desire to win the co-operation and approval of other men consist with the higher developments of human faculties? Is it, perhaps, essential to them? If so, in so far as every man increases in vitality and the employment of his powers, he will be forced to reverence and desire the solidarity of the race, and consequently to relinquish or neglect whatever in his own ideal militates against such solidarity. And this will be the case whether he judge such eccentric elements to be nobler or less noble than the qualities which are fostered in him by the co-operation of his fellows. Jesus, at any rate, affirmed that the law of the kingdom within a man's soul was: "Love thy neighbour as thyself"; and that obedience to it would work in every man like leaven, which is lost sight of in the lump of dough, and seems to add nothing to it, yet transforms the whole in raising up the loaf; or as the corn of wheat which is buried in the glebe like a dead body, yet brings forth the blade, and nourishes a new life.

So he that should follow Jesus by obeying the laws of the kingdom, by loving God (the begetter or fountainhead of a man's most essential conception of what is right and good) and his neighbour, was assured by his mild and gracious Master that he would inherit, by way of a return for the sacrifices which such obedience would entail, a new and better life. (Follow me, I laid down my life in order that I might take it again. He that findeth his life shall lose it; and he that loseth his life *for* my *sake* – as I did, in imitation of me – shall find it.) For in order to make this very difficult obedience possible, it was to be turned into a labour of love done for the Master's sake. As Goethe said:

"Against the superiority of another, there is no remedy
but love."

Is it not true that the superiority of another man humiliates, crushes and degrades us in our own eyes, if we envy it or hate it instead of loving it? while by loving it we make it in a sense ours, and can rejoice in it. So Jesus affirmed that he had made the superiority of the ideal his; so that he was in it, and it was in him, so that men who could no longer fix their attention on it in their own souls might love it in him. He was their master-conception, their true ideal, acting before them, captivating the attention of their senses and emotions. This is what a man of our times, possessed of rare receptivity and great range of comprehension, considered to be the pith of Jesus' teaching. Matthew Arnold gave much time and labour to trying to persuade men that this was what the religion they professed, or which was professed around them, most essentially meant. And he reminded us that the adequacy of such ideas for governing man's life depended not on the authority of a book or writings by eye-witnesses with or without intelligence, but on whether they were true in experience. He quoted Goethe's test for every idea about life, "But is it true, is it true for me, now?" "Taste and see," as the prophets put it; or as Jesus said, "Follow me." For an ideal must be followed, as a man woos a woman; the pursuit may have to be dropped, in order to be more surely recovered; an ideal must be humoured, not seized at once as a man seizes command over a machine. This *secret of success was* was only to be won by the development of a temper, a spirit of docility. To love it in an example was the best, perhaps the only way of gaining possession of it.

IV

As we are placed, what hope can we have but to learn? and what is there from which we might not learn? An artist is taught by the materials he uses more essentially than by the objects he contemplates; for these teach him "how," and perfect him in creating, those only teach him "what," and suggest forms to be created. But for men in general the "what" is more important than the "how"; and only very powerful art can exhilarate and refine them by means of subjects which they dislike or avoid.

Every seer of beauty is not a creator of beautiful things; and in art the "how" is so much more essential than the "what," that artists create unworthy or degrading objects beautifully, so that we admire their art as much as we loathe its employment; in nature, too, such objects are met with, created by the god of this world. A good man, too, may create in a repulsive manner objects whose every association is ennobling or elevating.

"The kingdom of heaven is within you," but hell is also within.

> "Hell hath no limits, nor is circumscribed
> In one self place; for where we are is hell
> And where hell is, must we for ever be:
> And, to conclude, when all the world dissolves,
> And every creature shall be purified,
> All places shall be hell that are not heaven,"

as Marlowe makes his Mephistophilis say: and the best art is the most perfect expression of that which is within, of heaven or of hell. Goethe said:

> "In the Greeks, whose poetry and rhetoric was simple and positive, we encounter expressions of approval more often than of disapproval. With the Romans, on the other hand, the contrary holds good; and the more corrupted poetry and rhetoric become, the more will censure grow and praise diminish."

I have sometimes thought that the difference between classic and more or less decadent art lies in the fact that by the one things are appreciated for what they most essentially are – a young man, a swift horse, a chaste wife, &c. – by the other for some more or less peculiar or accidental relation that they hold to the creator. Such writers lament that the young are not old, the old not young, prostitutes not pure, that maidens are cold and modest or matrons portly. They complain of having suffered from things being cross, or they take malicious pleasure in pointing that crossness out; whereas classical art always rebounds from the perception that things are evil to the assertion of what ought to be or shall be. It triumphs over the Prince of Darkness, and covers a multitude of sins, as dew or hoar frost cover and make beautiful a dunghill. Dunghills exist; but he who makes of Macbeth's or Clytemnestra's crimes an elevating or exhilarating spectacle triumphs over the god of this world, as Jesus did when he made

✳ 41

the most ignominious death the symbol, of his victory and glory. Little wonder that Albert Dürer, and Michelangelo found such deep satisfaction in Him as the object of their worship – his method of docility was next-of-kin to that of their art. Respect and solicitude create the soul, and these two pre-eminently docile passions preside over the soul's creation, whether it be a society, a life, or a thing of beauty.

V

Here, when art was still religion, with a simple, reverent heart,
Lived and laboured Albrecht Dürer, the Evangelist of Art.

These jingling lines would scarcely merit consideration but that they express a common notion which has its part of truth as well as of error. Let us examine the first assertion (that art has been religion.) Baudelaire, in his *Curiosités Esthétiques* says: *La première affaire d'un artiste est de substituer l'homme à la nature et de protester contre elle.* ("The first thing for an artist is to substitute man for nature and to protest against her.") The beginners and the smatterers are always "students of nature," and suppose that to be so will suffice; but when the understanding and imagination gain width and elasticity, life is more and more understood as a long struggle to overcome or humanise nature by that which most essentially distinguishes man from other animals and inanimate nature. Religion should be the drill and exercise of the human faculties to fit them and maintain them in readiness for this struggle; the work of art should be the assertion of victory. A life worthy of remembrance is a work of art, a life worthy of universal remembrance is a masterpiece: only the materials employed differentiate it from any other work of art. The life of Jesus is considered as such a masterpiece. Thus we can say that if art has never been religion, religion has always been and ever will be an art.

Now let us examine the second assertion that Dürer was an evangelist. What kind of character do we mean to praise when we say a man is an evangelist? Two only of the four evangelists can be said to reveal any ascertainable personality, and only St. John is sufficiently outlined to stand as a type; but I do not think we mean to imply a resemblance to St. John. The bringer of good news, the evangelist par excellence, was Jesus. He it was who made it evident that the sons of men have power to forgive sins. Victory over evil possible – this was the good news. No doubt every sincere Christian is supposed to be a more or less successful imitator of Jesus; and as such, Dürer may rightly be called an evangelist. But more than this is I think, implied in the use of the word; an evangelist is, for us above all a bringer of good news in something of the same manner as Jesus brought it, by living among sinners for those sinners' sake, among paupers for those paupers' sake; to see a man sweet, radiant, and victorious under these circumstances, is to see an evangelist. Goethe's final claim is that, "after all, there are honest people up and down the world who have got light from my books; and whoever reads them, and gives himself the trouble to understand me, will acknowledge that he has acquired thence a certain inward freedom"; and for this reason I have been tempted to call him the evangelist of the modern world. But it is best to use the word as I believe it is most correctly employed, and not to yield to the temptation (for tempting it is) to call men like Dürer and Goethe evangelists. They are teachers who charm as well as inform us, as Jesus was; but they are not evangelists in the sense that he was, for they did not deal directly with human life where it is forced most against its distinctive desire for increase in nobility, or is most obviously degraded by having betrayed it.'[11]

VI

I have often heard it objected that Jesus is too feminine an ideal, too much based on renunciation and the effort to make the best of failure. No doubt that as women are, by the necessity of their function, more liable to the ship-wreck of their hopes, the bankruptcy of their powers, they have been drawn to cling to this hope of salvation in greater numbers, and with more fervour; so that the most general idea of Jesus may be a feminine one. It does not follow that this is the most correct or the best: every object, every person will appear differently to different natures. And it still remains true that there have been a great many men of very various types who have drawn strength and beauty from the contemplation and reverence of Jesus. That this ideal is too much based on making the best of failure is an objection that makes very little impression on me, for I think I perceive that failure is one of the most constant and widespread conditions of the universe, and even more certainly of human life.

VII

It remains now to see in what degree these ideas were felt or made themselves felt through the Romanism and Lutheranism of the Renascence period. Perhaps we English shall best recognise the presence of these ideas, the working of this leaven – this docility, the necessary midwife of 'genius, who transforms the difficult tasks which the human reason sets herself into labours of love – in an Englishman; so my first example shall be taken from Erasmus' portrait of Dean Colet.

It was then that my acquaintance with him began, he being then thirty, I two or three months his junior. He had no theological degree, but the whole University, doctors and all, went to hear him. Henry VII took note of him, and made him Dean of St. Paul's. His first step was to restore discipline in the Chapter, which had all gone to wreck. He preached every saint's day to great crowds. He cut down household expenses, and abolished suppers and evening parties. At dinner a boy reads a chapter from Scripture; Colet takes a passage from it and discourses to the universal delight. Conversation is his chief pleasure, and he will keep it up till midnight if he finds a companion. Me he has often taken with him on his walks, and talks all the time of Christ. He hates coarse language, furniture, dress, food, books, all clean and tidy, but scrupulously plain; and he wears grey woollen when priests generally go in purple. With the large fortune which he inherited from his father, he founded and endowed a school at St. Paul's entirely at his own cost – masters, houses, salaries, everything.

He is a man of genuine piety. He was not born with it. He was naturally hot, impetuous and resentful – indolent, fond of pleasure and of women's society – disposed to make a joke of everything. He told me that he had fought against his faults with study, fasting and prayer, and thus his whole life was in fact unpolluted with the world's defilements. His money he gave all to pious uses, worked incessantly, talked always on serious subjects, to conquer his disposition to levity; not but what you could see traces of the old Adam when wit was flying at feast or festival. He avoided large parties for this reason. He dined on a single dish, with a draught or two of light ale. He liked good wine, but abstained on principle. I never knew a man of sunnier nature. No one ever more enjoyed cultivated society; but here, too, he denied himself, and was always thinking of the life to come.

His opinions were peculiar, and he was reserved in expressing them for fear of exciting suspicion. He knew how unfairly men judge each other, how credulous they are of evil, how much easier it is for a lying tongue to stain a reputation than for a friend to clear it. But among his friends he spoke his mind freely.

He admitted privately that many things were generally taught which he did not believe, but he would not create a scandal by blurting out his objections. No book could be so heretical but he would read it, and read it carefully. He learnt more from such books than he learnt from dogmatism and interested orthodoxy.[12]

Some may wonder what Colet could have found to say about Christ which could not only interest but delight the young and witty Erasmus; and may judge that at any rate to-day such a subject is sufficiently fly-blown. The proper reflection to make is, "A rose by any other name would smell as sweet."

Whether we say Christ or Perfection does not matter, it is what we mean which is either enthralling or dull, fresh or fusty; "there's nothing in a name."

"When Colet speaks I might be listening to Plato," says Erasmus in another place, at a time when he was still younger and had just come from what had been a gay and perhaps in some measure a dissolute life in Paris: not that it is possible to imagine Erasmus as at any time committing great excesses, or deeply sinning against the sense of proportion and measure.

Success is the only criterion, as in art, so in religion: the man that plucks out his eye and casts it from him, and remains the dull, greedy, distressful soul he was before, is a damned fool; but the man who does the same and becomes such that his younger friends report of him, "I never knew a sunnier nature," is an artist in life, a great artist in the sense that Christ is supposed to have been a great master; one who draws men to him, as bees are drawn to flowers. Colet drew the young Henry the Eighth as well as Erasmus. "The King said: 'Let every man choose his own doctor. Dean Colet shall be mine!'" Though no doubt charlatans have often fascinated young scholars and monarchs, yet it is peculiarly impossible to think of Colet as a charlatan.

Next let us take a sonnet and a sentence from Michelangelo:

> Yes! hope may with my strong desire keep pace,
> And I be undeluded, unbetrayed;
> For if of our affections none finds grace
> In sight of heaven, then, wherefore hath God made
> The world which we inhabit? Better plea
> Love cannot have than that in loving thee
> Glory to that eternal peace is paid,
> Who such divinity to thee imparts,
> As hallows and makes pure all gentle hearts.
> His hope is treacherous only whose love dies
> With beauty, which is varying every hour;
> But in chaste hearts, uninfluenced by the power
> Of outward change, there blooms a deathless flower,
> That breathes on earth the air of paradise.[13]

It is very remarkable how strongly the conviction of permanence, and the preference for the inward conception over external beauty are expressed in this fine sonnet; and also that the reason given for accepting the discipline of love is that experience shows how it "hallows and makes pure all gentle hearts." In such a love poem – the object of which might very well have been Jesus – I seem to find more of the spirit of his religion, whereby he binds his disciples to the Father that ruled within him, till they too feel the bond of parentage as deeply as himself and become sons with him of his Father; – more of that binding power of Jesus is for me expressed in this fine sonnet than in Luther's Catechism. The religion that enables a great artist to write of love in this strain, is the religion of docility, of the meek and lowly heart. For Michelangelo was not a man by nature of a meek and lowly heart, any more than Colet was a man naturally saintly or than Luther was a man naturally refined. But because Michelangelo thus prefers the kingdom of heaven to external beauty, one must not suppose that he, its arch high-priest, despised it. Nobody had a more profound respect for the thing of beauty, whether it was the creation of God or man. He said:

> "Nothing makes the soul so pure, so religious, as the endeavour to create something perfect; for God is perfection, and whoever strives for perfection, strives for something that is God-like."

Now we can perceive how the same spirit worked in a great artist, not at Nuremberg or London, but at Rome, the centre of the world, where a Borgia could be Pope.

IX

Erasmus, the typical humanist, the man who loved humanity so much that he felt that his love for it might tempt him to fight against God, travelled from the one world to the other; passed from the society of cardinals and princes to the seclusion of burgher homes in London, or to chat with Dürer at Antwerp. He belonged perhaps to neither world at heart; but how greatly his love and veneration of the one exceeded his admiration and sense of the practical utility of the other, a comparison of his sketch of Colet with such a note as this from his New Testament makes abundantly plain:

> "I saw with my own eyes Pope Julius II. at Bologna, and afterwards at Rome, marching at the head of a triumphal procession as if he were Pompey or Cæsar. St. Peter subdued the world with faith, not with arms or soldiers or military engines. St. Peter's successors would win as many victories as St. Peter won if they had Peter's spirit."

But we must not forget that the book in which these notes appeared was published with the approval of a Pope, and that he and others sought its author for advice as to how to cope best with their more hot-headed enemy Martin Luther. We must also remember that we are told that Colet "was not very hard on priests and monks who only sinned with women. He did not make light of impurity, but thought it less criminal than spite and malice and envy and vanity and ignorance. The loose sort were at least made human and modest by their very faults, and he regarded avarice and arrogance as blacker sins in a priest than a hundred concubines." This spirit was not that of the Reformation which came to stop, yet it existed and was widespread at that time; it was I think the spirit which either formed or sustained most of the great artists. At any rate it both formed and sustained Albert Dürer. Yet the true nature of these ideas, derived from Jesus, could not be understood even by Colet, even by Erasmus. For them it was tradition which gave value and assured truth to Christ's ideas, not the truth of those ideas which gave value to the traditions and legends concerning him. The value of those ideas was felt, sometimes nearer, sometimes further off; it was loved and admired; their lives were apprehended by it, and spent in illustrating and studying it, as were also those of Albert Dürer and Michelangelo. To understand the life and work of such men, we must form some conception of the true nature and value of those ideas, as I have striven to do in this chapter. Otherwise we shall merely admire and love them, as they admired and loved Jesus; and it has now become a point of honour with educated men not only to love and admire, but to make the effort to understand. Even they desired to do this. And I think we may rejoice that the present time gives us some advantage over those days, at least in this respect.

X

And lastly, in order to bring us back to our main subject, let us quote from a stray leaf of a lost MS. Book of Dürer's, which contains the description of his father's death.

> ... desired. So the old wife helped him up, and the night-cap on his head had suddenly become wet with drops of sweat. Then he asked to drink, so she gave him a little Reinfell wine. He took a very little of it, and then desired to get into bed again and thanked her. And when he had got into bed he fell at once into his last agony. The old wife quickly kindled the candle for him and repeated to him S. Bernard's verses, and ere she had said the third he was gone. God be merciful to him! And the young maid, when she saw the change, ran quickly to my chamber and woke me, but before I came down he was gone. I saw the dead with great sorrow, because I had not been worthy to be with him at his end.
>
> And thus in the night before S. Matthew's eve my father passed away, in the year above mentioned (Sept. 20, 1502) – the merciful God help me also to a happy end – and he left my mother an afflicted widow behind him. He was ever wont to praise her highly to me, saying what a good wife she was, wherefore I intend never to forsake her. I pray you for God's sake, all ye my friends, when you read of the death of my father, to remember his soul with an "Our Father" and an "Ave Maria"; and also for your own sake, that we may so serve God as to attain a happy life and the blessing of a good end. For it is not possible for one who has lived well to depart ill from this world, for God is full of compassion. Through which may He grant us, after this pitiful life, the joy of everlasting salvation – in the name of the Father, the Son, and the Holy Ghost, at the beginning and at the end, one Eternal Governor. Amen.

The last sentences of this may seem to share in the character of the vain repetitions of words with which professed believers are only too apt to weary and disgust others. They are in any case commonplaces: the image has taken the place of the object; the Father in heaven is not considered so much as the paternal governor of the inner life as the ruler of a future life and of this world. The use of such phrases is as much idolatry as the worship of statue and picture, or as little, if the words are repeated, as I think in this case they were, out of a feeling of awe and reverence for preceding mental impressions and experiences, and not because their repetition in itself was counted for righteousness. Their use, if this was so, is no more to be found fault with than the contemplation of pictures or statues of holy personages in order to help the mind to attend to their ensample, or the reading of a poem, to fill the mind with ennobling emotions. Idolatry is natural and right in children and other simple souls among primitive peoples or elsewhere. It is a stage in mental development. Lovers pass through the idolatrous stage of their passion just as children cut their teeth. It is a pity to see individuals or nations remain childish in this respect just as much as in any other, or to see them return to it in their decrepitude. But a temper, a spirit, an influence cannot easily be apprehended apart from examples and images; and perhaps the clearest reason is only the exercise of an infinitely elastic idolatry, which with sprightly efficiency finds and worships good in everything, just as the devout, in Dürer's youth, found sermons in stones, carved stones representing saint, bishop, or Virgin. And Dürer all his life long continued to produce pictures and engravings which were intended to preach such sermons.

Goethe admirably remarks:

"*Superstition* is the poetry of life; the poet therefore suffers no harm from being *superstitious*." (Aberglaube.)

Superstition and idolatry are an expenditure of emotion of a kind and degree which the true facts would not warrant; poetry when least superstitious is a like exercise of the emotions in order to raise and enhance them; superstition when most poetical unconsciously effects the same thing.

This glimpse he gives of the way in which death visited his home, and how the visitation impressed him, is coloured and glows with that temper of docility which made Colet school himself so severely, and was the source of Michelangelo's so fervent outpourings. And all through the accounts which remain of his life, we may trace the same spirit ever anew setting him to school, and renewing his resolution to learn both from his feelings and from his senses.

XI

As I took a sentence from Michelangelo, I will now take a sentence from Dürer, one showing strongly that evangelical strain so characteristic of him, born of his intuitive sense for human solidarity. After an argument, which will be found on page 306, he concludes: "It is right, therefore, for one man to teach another. He that doeth so joyfully, upon him shall much be bestowed by God."[14] These last words, like the last phrases of my former quotation from him, may stand perhaps in the way of some, as nowadays they may easily sound glib or irreverent. But are we less convinced that only tasks done joyfully, as labours of love, deserve the reward of fuller and finer powers, and obtain it? When Dürer thought of God, he did not only think of a mythological personage resembling an old king; he thought of a mind, an intention, "for God is perfect in goodness." Words so easily come to obscure what they were meant to reveal; and if we think how the notion of perfect goodness rules and sways such a man's mind, we shall not wonder that he did not stumble at the omnipotency which revolts us, cowed as we are by the presence of evil. The old gentleman dressed like a king; – this was not the part of his ideas about God which occupied Dürer's mind. He accepted it, but did not think about it: it filled what would otherwise have been a blank in his mind and in the minds of those about him. But he was constantly anxious about what he ought to do and study in order to fulfil the best in himself, and about what ought to be done by his town, his nation, and the civilisation that then was, in order to turn man's nature and the world to an account answerable to the beauty of their fairer aspects. God was the will that commanded that "consummation devoutly to be wished." Obedience to His law revealed in the Bible was the means by which this command could be carried out; and to a man turning from the Church as it then existed to the newly translated Bible texts, the commands of God as declared in those texts seemed of necessity reason itself compared with the commands of the Popes; were, in fact, infinitely more reasonable, infinitely more akin to a good man's mind and will. Luther's revolt is for us now characterised by those elements in it which proved inadequate – were irrational; but then these were insignificant in comparison with the light which his downright honesty shed on the monstrous and amazingly irrational Church. This huge closed society of bigots and worldlings which arrogated to itself all powers human and divine, and used them according to the lusts and intemperance of an Alexander Borgia, a Julius II., and a Leo X., was that farce perception of which made Rabelais shake the world with laughter, and which roused such consuming indignation in Luther and Calvin that they created the gloomy puritanical asylums in which millions of Germans, English, and Americans were shut up for two hundred years, as Matthew Arnold puts it. But Dürer was not so immured: even Luther at heart neither was himself, nor desired that others should be, prevented from enjoying the free use of their intellectual powers. It was because he was less perspicacious than Erasmus that he did not see that this was what he was inevitably doing in his wrath and in his haste.

XII

Erasmus was, perhaps, the man in Europe who at that time displayed most docility; the man whom neither sickness, the desire for wealth and honour, the hope to conquer, the lust to engage in disputes, nor the adverse chances that held him half his life in debt and necessitous straits, and kept him all his life long a vagrant, constantly upon the road – the man in whom none of these things could weaken a marvellous assiduity to learn and help others to learn. He it was who had most kinship with Dürer among the artists then alive; for Dürer is very eminent among them for this temper of docility. It is interesting to see how he once turned to Erasmus in a devout meditation, written in the journal he kept during his journey to the Netherlands. His voice comes to us from an atmosphere charged with the electric influence of the greatest Reformer, Martin Luther, who had just disappeared, no man knew why or whither; though all men suspected foul play. In his daily life, by sweetness of manner, by gentle dignity and modesty, Dürer showed his religion, the admiration and love that bound his life, in a way that at all times and in all places commands applause. The burning indignation of the following passage may in times of spiritual peace or somnolence appear over-wrought and uncouth. We must remember that all that Dürer loved had been bound by his religion to the teaching and inspiration of Jesus, and had become inseparable from it. All that he loved – learning, clear and orderly thought, honesty, freedom to express the worship of his heart without its being turned to a mockery by cynical monk, priest, or prelate; – these things directly, and indirectly art itself, seemed to him threatened by the corruption of the Papal power. We must remember this; for we shall naturally feel, as Erasmus did, that the path of martyrdom was really a short cut, which a wider view of the surrounding country would have shown him to be likely to prove the longest way in the end. Indeed the world is not altogether yet arrived where he thought Erasmus could bring it in less than two years. And Luther himself returned to the scene and was active, without any such result, a dozen years and more.

Oh all ye pious Christian men, help me deeply to bewail this man, inspired of God, and to pray Him yet again to send us an enlightened man. Oh Erasmus of Rotterdam, where wilt thou stop? Behold how the wicked tyranny of worldly power, the might of darkness, prevails. Hear, thou knight of Christ! Ride on by the side of the Lord Jesus. Guard the truth. Attain the martyr's crown. Already indeed art thou a little old man, and myself have heard thee say that thou givest thyself but two years more wherein thou mayest still be fit to accomplish somewhat. Lay out the same well for the good of the Gospel, and of the true Christian faith, and make thyself heard. So, as Christ says, shall the Gates of Hell in no wise prevail against thee. And if here below thou wert to be like thy master Christ, and sufferest infamy at the hands of the liars of this time, and didst die a little sooner, then wouldst thou the sooner pass from death unto life and be glorified in Christ. For if thou drinkest of the cup which He drank of, *with Him shalt thou reign and judge with justice those who* HAVE *dealt unrighteously.* Oh! Erasmus! cleave to this, that God Himself may be thy praise, even as it is written of David. For thou mayest, yea, verily thou mayest overthrow Goliath. Because God stands by the Holy Christian Church, even as He alone upholds the Roman Church, according to His godly will. May He help us to everlasting salvation, who is God the Father, the Son, and Holy Ghost, one eternal God! Amen!!

"With Him shalt thou reign and judge with justice those that have dealt unrighteously." This will seem to many a mere cry for revenge; and so perhaps it was. Still it may have been, as it seems to me to have been, uttered rather in the spirit of Moses' "Forgive their sin – and if not, blot me, I pray Thee, out of Thy book"; or the "Heaven and earth shall pass away, but my words shall not pass away" of Jesus. If the necessity for victory was uppermost, the opportunity for revenge may scarcely have been present to Dürer's mind.

It is now more generally recognised than in Luther's day that however sweet vengeance may be, it is not admirable, either in God or man.

The total impression produced by Dürer's life and work must help each to decide for himself which sense he considers most likely. The truth, as in most questions of history, remains for ever in the balance, and cannot be ascertained.

XIII

I have called docility the necessary midwife of Genius, for so it is; and religion is a discipline that constrains us to learn. The religion of Jesus constrains us to learn the most difficult things, binds us to the most arduous tasks that the mind of man sets itself, as a lover is bound by his affection to accomplish difficult feats for his mistress' sake. Such tasks as Michelangelo and Dürer set themselves require that the lover's eagerness and zest shall not be exhausted; and to keep them fresh and abundant, in spite of cross circumstances, a discipline of the mind and will is required. This is what they found in the worship of Jesus. The influence of this religious hopefulness and self-discipline on the creative power prevents its being exhausted, perverted, or embittered; and in order that it may effect this perfectly, that influence must be abundant not only within the artist, as it was in Michelangelo and Dürer, but in the world about them.

This, then, is the value of religious influence to creative art: and though we to-day necessarily regard the personages, localities, and events of the creed as coming under the category of "things that are not," we may still as fervently hope and expect that the things of that category may "bring to nought the things that are," including the superstitious reverence for the creed and its unprovable statements; for has not the victory in human things often been with the things that were not, but which were thus ardently desired and expected? To inquire which of those things are best calculated to advance and nourish creative power, and in what manner, should engage the artist's attention far more than it has of late years. For what he loves, what he hopes, and what he expects would seem, if we study past examples, to exercise as important an influence on a man's creative power as his knowledge of, and respect for, the materials and instruments which he controls do upon his executive capacity.

The universe in which man finds himself may be evil, but not everything it contains is so: then it must for ever remain our only wisdom to labour to transform those parts which we judge to be evil into likeness or conformity to those we judge to be good: and surely he who neglects the forces of hope and adoration in that effort, neglects the better half of his practical strength? The central proposition of Christianity, that this end can only be attained by contemplation and imitation of an example, is, we shall in another place find, maintained as true in regard to art by Dürer, and by Reynolds, our greatest writer on aesthetics. These great artists, so dissimilar in the outward aspects of their creations, agree in considering that the only way of advancement open to the aspirant is the attempt to form himself on the example of others, by imitating them not slavishly or mechanically, but in the same spirit in which they imitated their forerunners: even as the Christian is bound to seek union with Christ in the same spirit or way in which Jesus had achieved union with his Father – that is, by laying down life to take it again, in meekness and lowliness of heart. Docility is the sovran help to perfection for Dürer and Reynolds, and more or less explicitly for all other great artists who have treated of these questions.

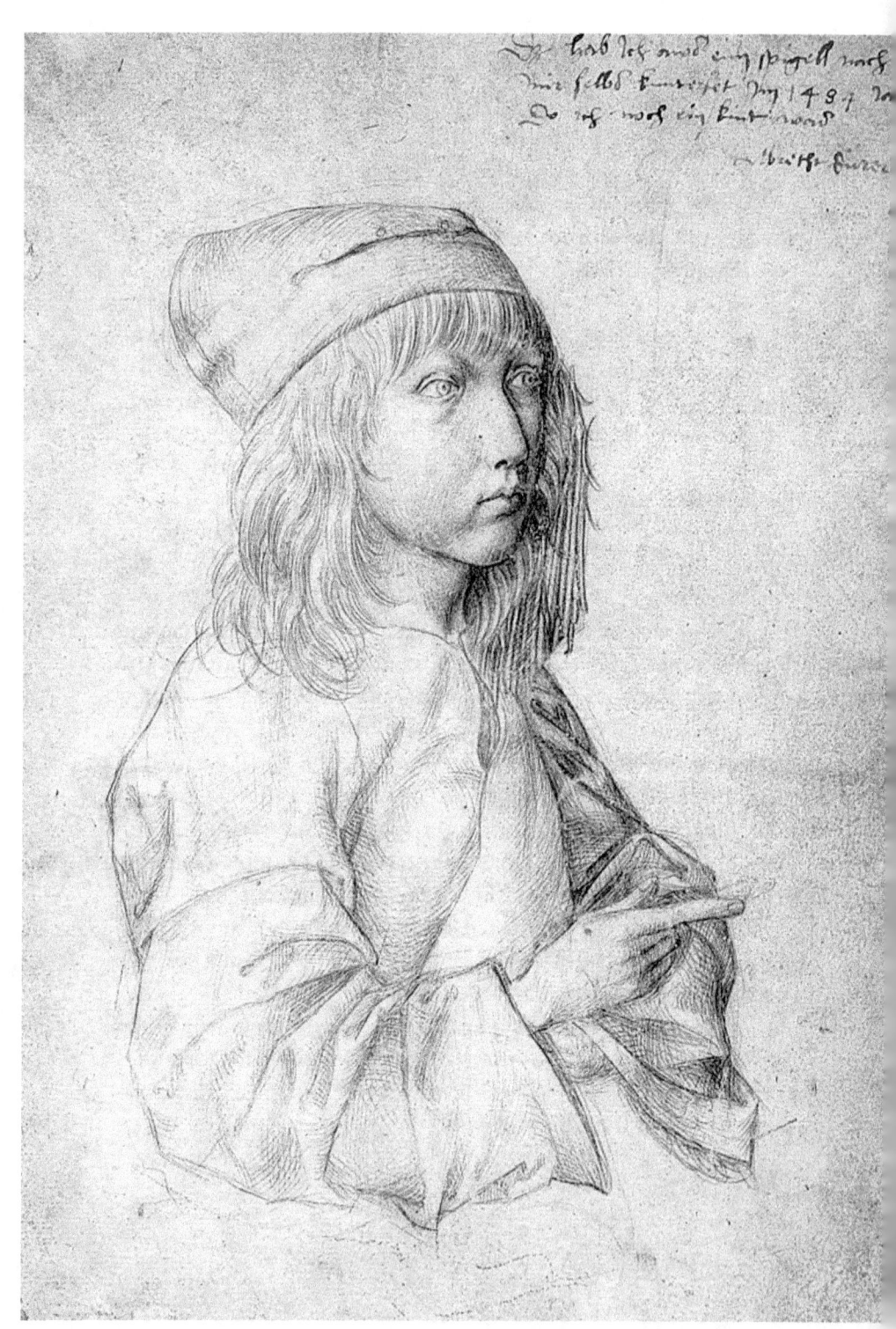

Albrecht Dürer, Self-Portrait At the Age of Thirteen, 1484, Vienna

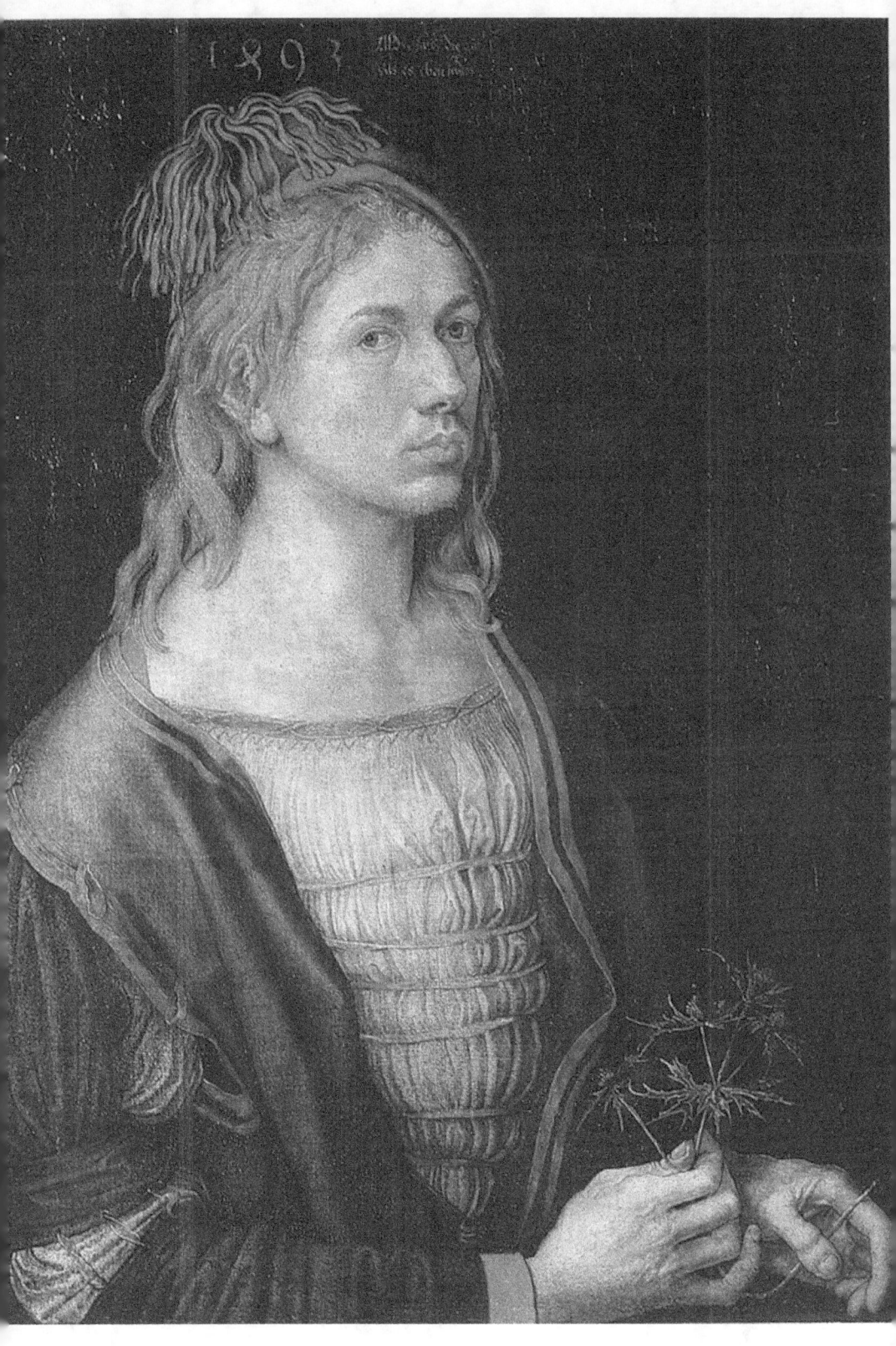

Albrecht Dürer, Self-Portrait, 1493 Louvre, Paris

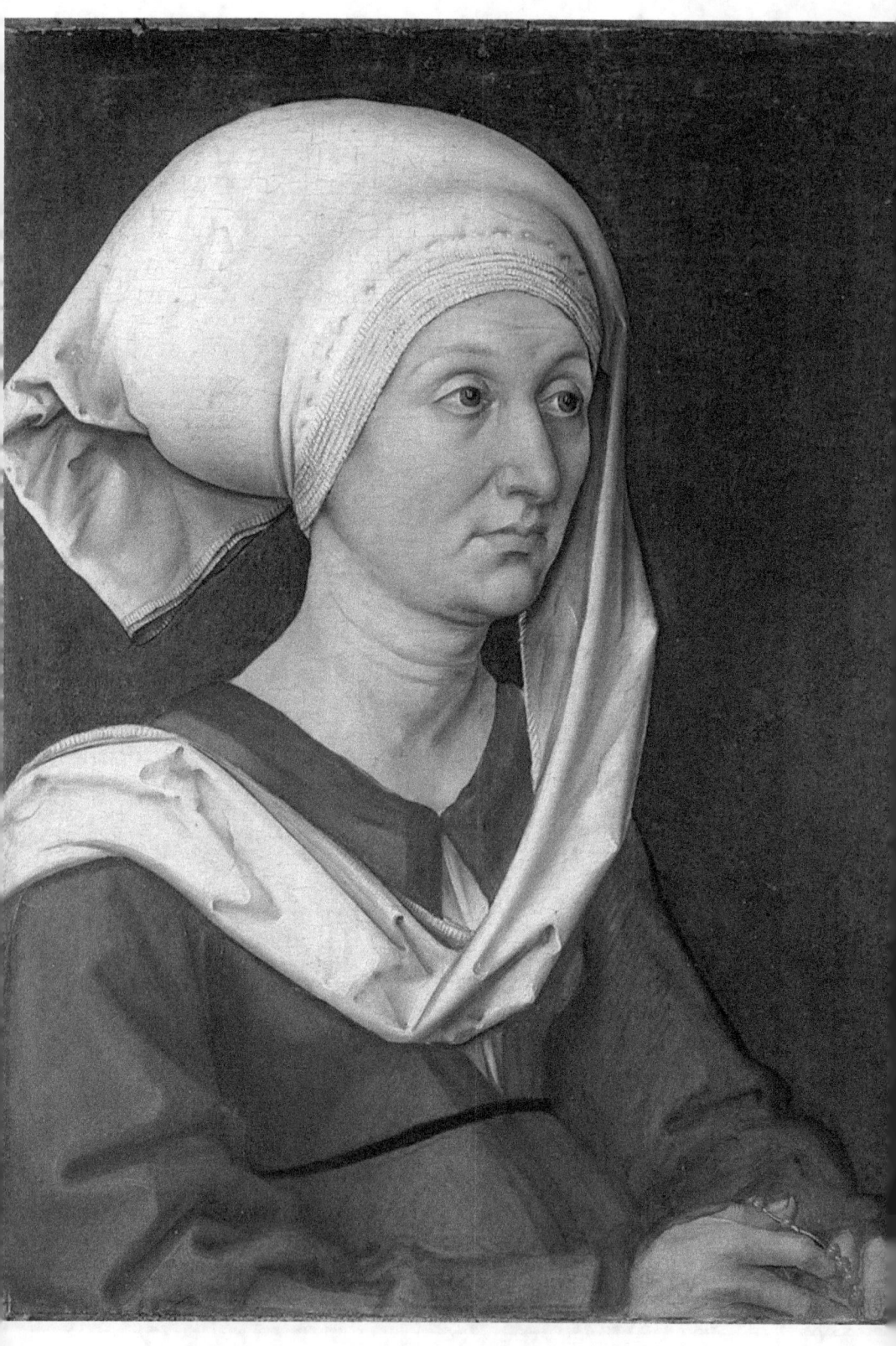

Albrecht Dürer, Portrait of His Mother, 1490, Nuremburg

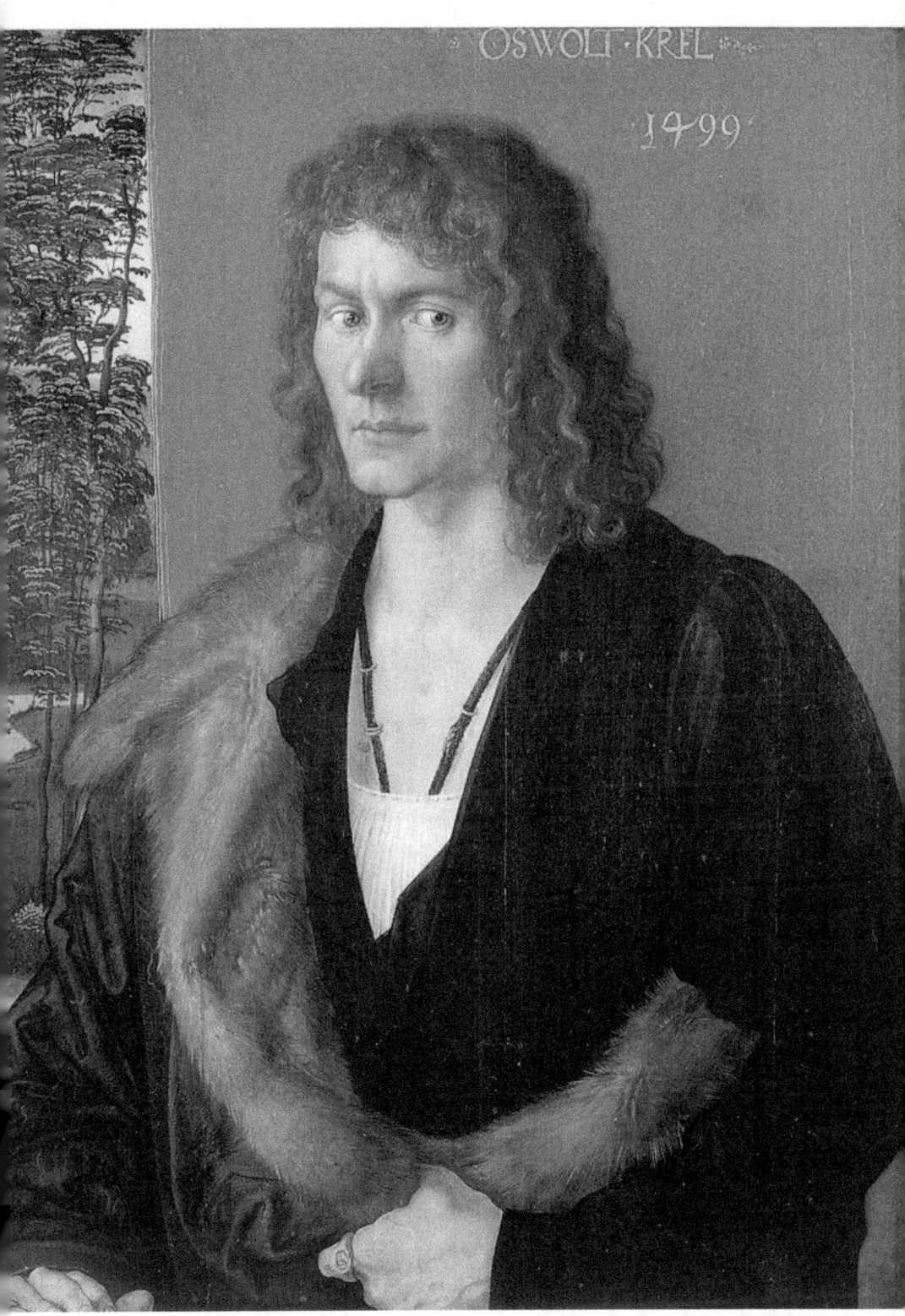

Albrecht Dürer, Oswolt Krel, 1499

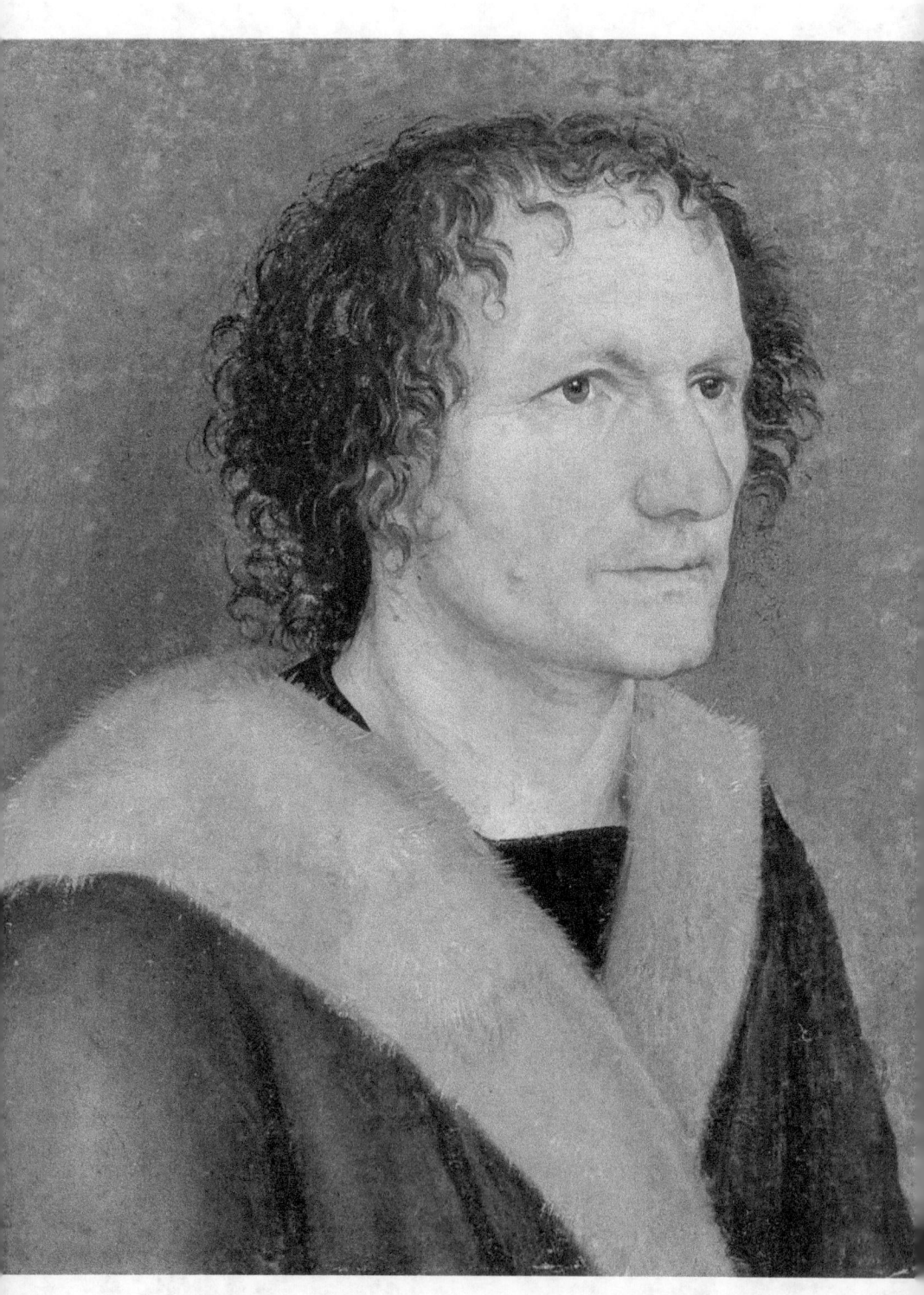
Albrecht Dürer, Männliches Porträt vor grünem Grund, 1497

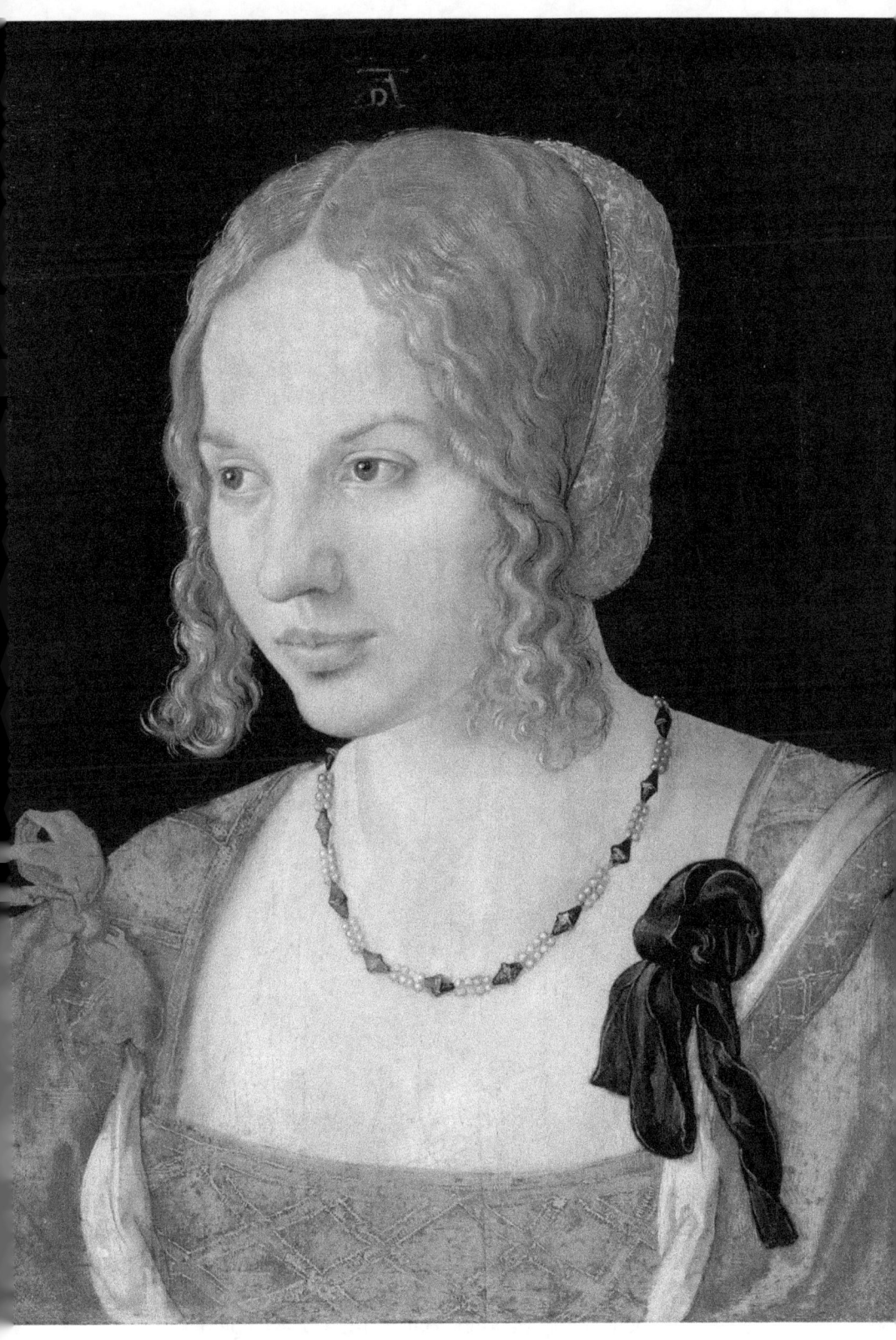

Albrecht Dürer, Portrait of a Young Woman, 1505, Vienna

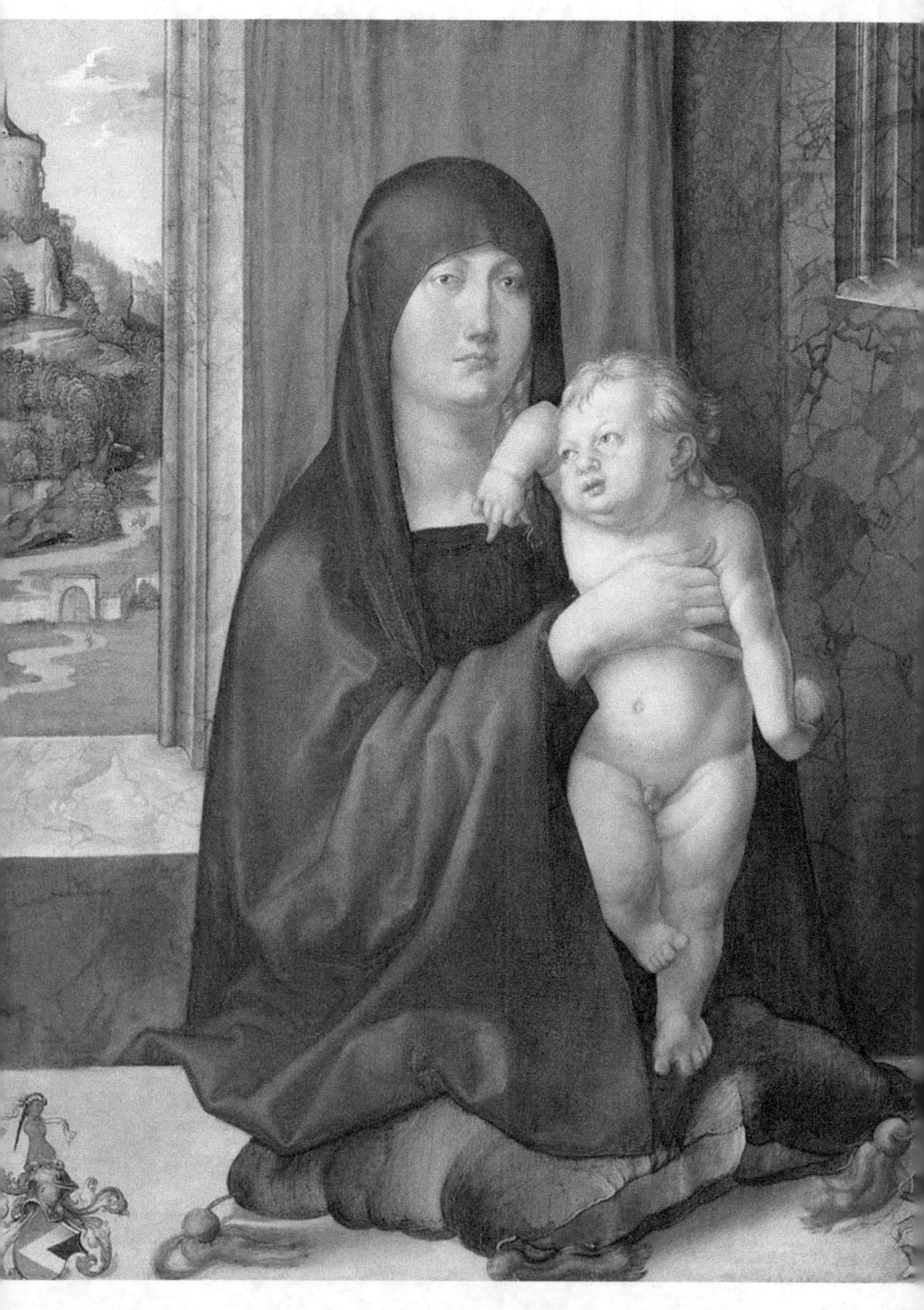

Albrecht Dürer, Madonna Haller, 1499, Washington, DC

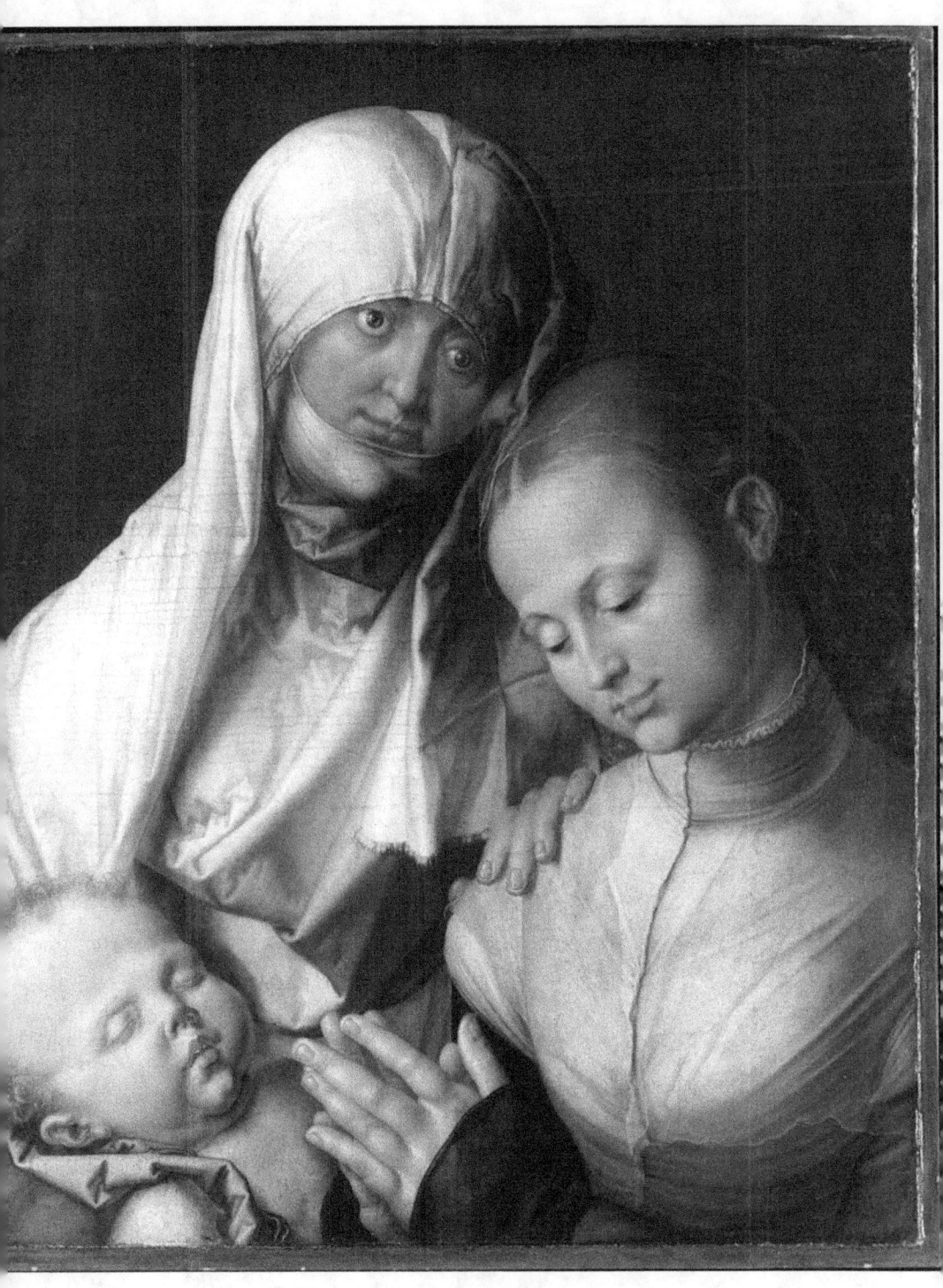

Albrecht Dürer, Virgin and Child, 1518,
Metropolitan Museum of Art, New York City

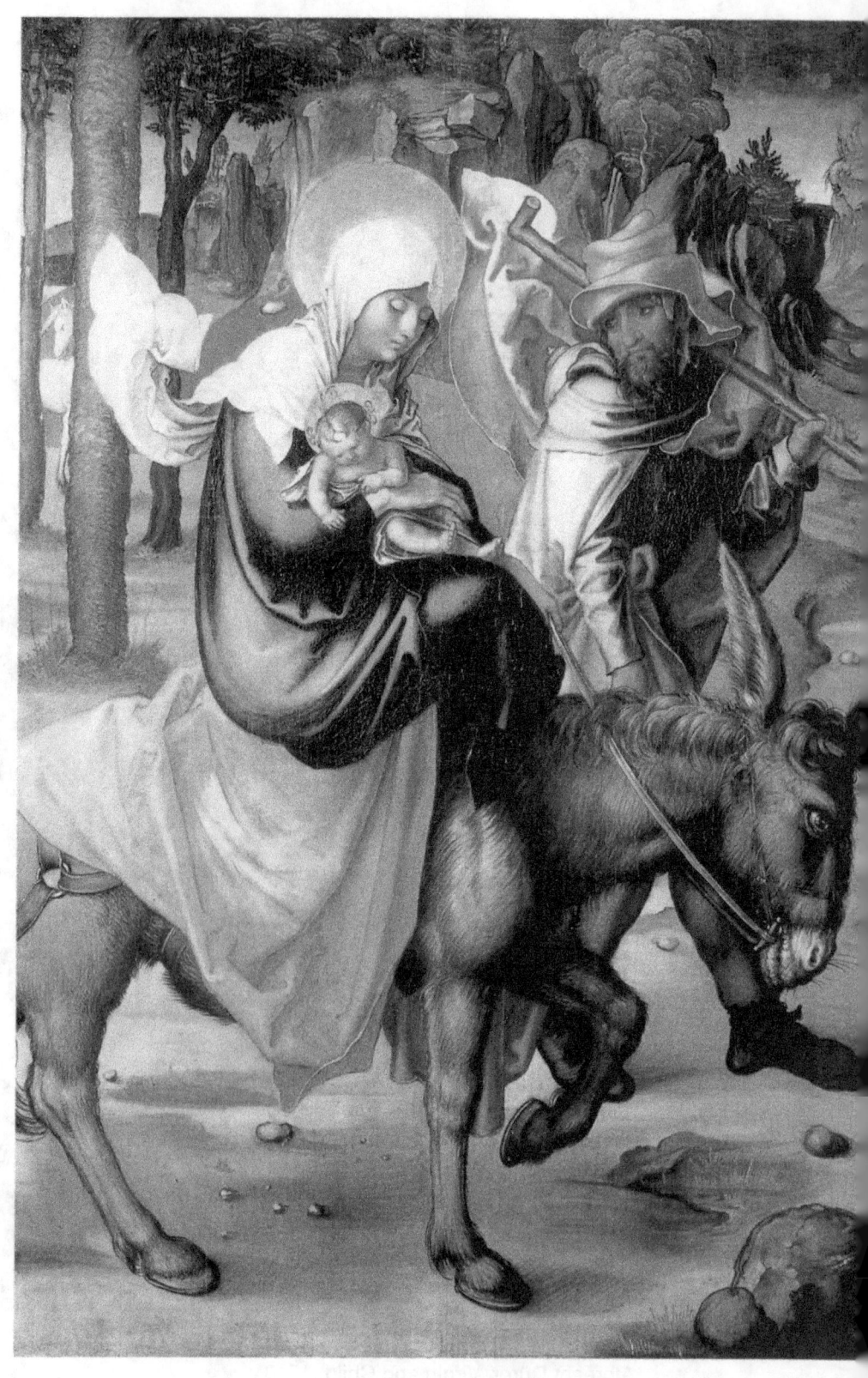

Albrecht Dürer, The Seven Sorrows of Mary, Munich

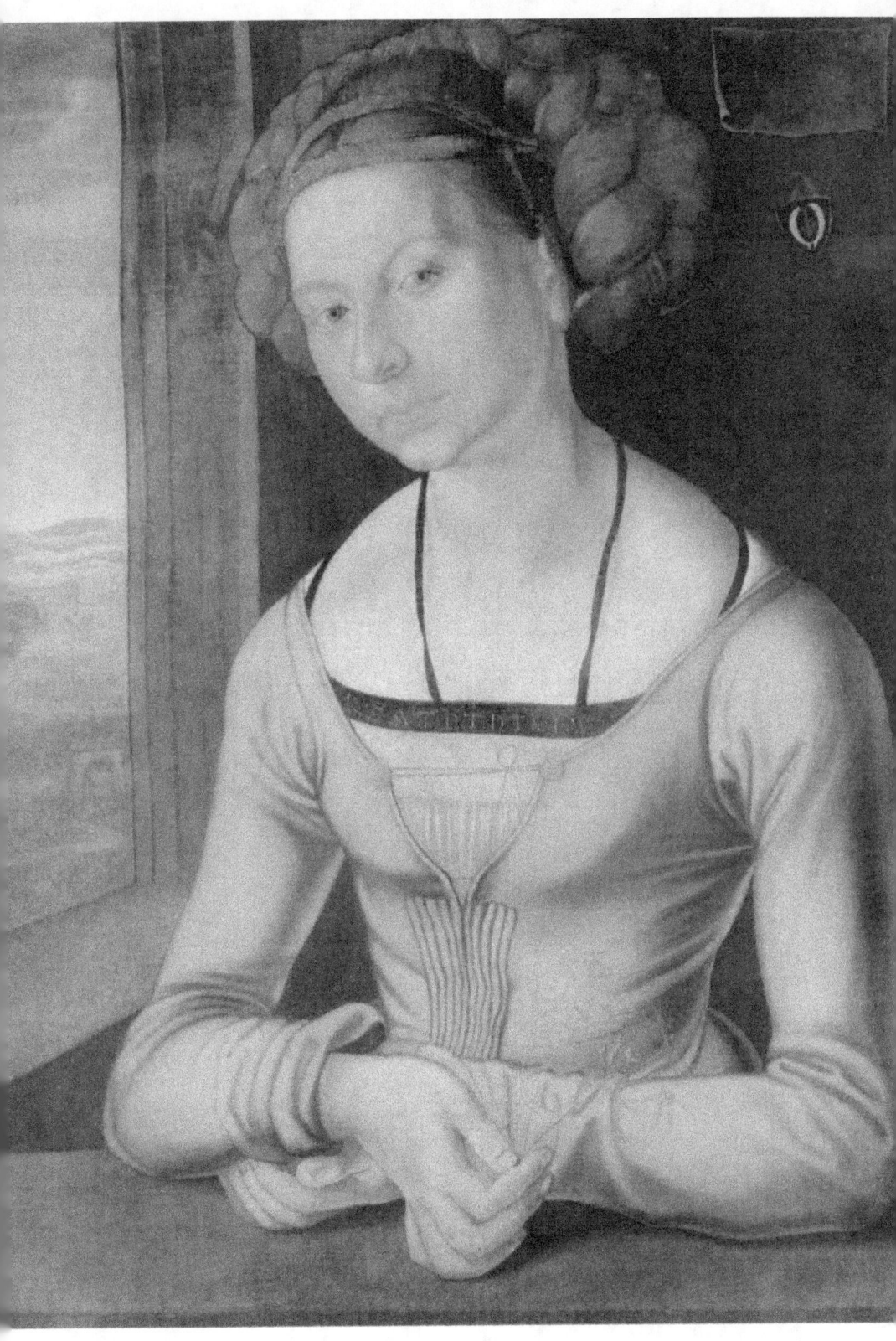

Albrecht Dürer, Young Woman With Braided Hair, 1497, Berlin

PART II

DÜRER'S LIFE IN RELATION TO THE TIMES IN WHICH HE LIVED

CHAPTER I

DÜRER'S ORIGIN, YOUTH
AND EDUCATION

I

Who was Dürer? He has told us himself very simply, and more fully than men of his type generally do; for he was not, like Montaigne, one whose chief study was himself. Yet, though he has done this, it is not easy for us to fully understand him. It is perhaps impossible to place oneself in the centre of that horizon which was of necessity his and belonged to his day, a vast circle from which men could no more escape than we from ours; this cage of iron ignorance in which every human soul is trapped, and to widen and enlarge which every heroic soul lives and dies. This cage appeared to his eyes very different from what it does to ours; yet it has always been a cage, and is only lost sight of at times when the light from within seems to flow forth, and with its radiant sapphire heaven of buoyancy and desire to veil the eternal bars. It is well to remind ourselves that ignorance was the most momentous, the most cruel condition of his life, as of our own; and that the effort to relieve himself of its pressure, either by the pursuit of knowledge, or by giving spur and bridle to the imagination that it might course round him dragging the great woof of illusion, and tent him in the ethereal dream of the soul's desire, was the constant effort and resource of his days.

II

At the age of fifty-three he took the pen and commenced:

In the year 1524, I, Albrecht Dürer the younger, have put together from my father's papers the facts as to whence he was, how he came hither, lived here, and drew to a happy end. God be gracious to him and us! Amen.

Like his relatives, Albrecht Dürer the elder was born in the kingdom of Hungary, in a little village named Eytas, situated not far from a little town called Gyula, eight miles below Grosswardein; and his kindred made their living from horses and cattle. My father's father was called Anton Dürer; he came as a lad to a goldsmith in the said little town and learnt the craft under him. He afterwards married a girl named Elizabeth, who bare him a daughter, Katharina, and three sons. The first son he named Albrecht; he was my dear father. He too became a goldsmith, a pure and skilful man. The second son he called Ladislaus; he was a saddler. His son is my cousin Niklas Dürer, called Niklas the Hungarian, who is settled at Köln. He also is a goldsmith, and learnt the craft here in Nürnberg with my father. The third son he called John. Him he set to study, and he afterwards became a parson at Grosswardein, and continued there thirty years.

So Albrecht Dürer, my dear father, came to Germany. He had been a long time with the great artists in the Netherlands. At last he came hither to Nürnberg in the year, as reckoned from the birth of Christ, 1455, on S. Elogius' day (June 25). And on the same day Philip Pirkheimer had his marriage feast at the Veste, and there was a great dance under the big lime tree. For a long time after that my dear father, Albrecht Dürer, served my grandfather, old Hieronymus Holper, till the year reckoned 1467 after the birth of Christ. My grandfather then gave him his daughter, a pretty upright girl, fifteen years old, named Barbara; and he was wedded to her eight days

✳ 70

before S. Vitus (June 8). It may also be mentioned that my grandmother, my mother's mother, was the daughter of Oellinger of Weissenburg, and her name was Kunigunde.

And my dear father had by his marriage with my dear mother the following children born – which I set down here word for word as he wrote it in his book:

Here follow eighteen items, only one of which, the third, is of interest.

3. Item, in the year 1471 after the birth of Christ, in the sixth hour of the day, on S. Prudentia's day, a Tuesday in Rogation Week (May 21), my wife bare me my second son. His godfather was Anton Koburger, and he named him Albrecht after me, &c. &c.

All these, my brothers and sisters, my dear father's children, are now dead, some in their childhood, others as they were growing up; only we three brothers still live, so long as God will, namely: I, Albrecht, and my brother Andreas and my brother Hans, the third of the name, my father's children.

This Albrecht Dürer the elder passed his life in great toil and stern hard labour, having nothing for his support save what he earned with his hand for himself, his wife and his children, so that he had little enough. He underwent moreover manifold afflictions, trials, and adversities. But he won just praise from all who knew him, for he lived an honourable, Christian life, was a man of patient spirit, mild and peaceable to all, and very thankful towards God. For himself he had little need of company and worldly pleasures; he was also of few words, and was a God-fearing man.

III

We shall, I think, often do well, when considering the superb ostentation of Dürer's workmanship, with its superabundance of curve and flourish, its delight in its own ease and grace, to think of those young men among his ancestors who made their living from horses on the wind-swept plains of Hungary. The perfect control which it is the delight of lads brought up and developing under such conditions to obtain over the galloping steed, is similar to the control which it gratified Dürer to perfect over the dashing stroke of pen or brush, which, however swift and impulsive, is yet brought round and performs to a nicety a predetermined evolution. And the way he puts a little portrait of himself, finely dressed, into his most important pictures, may also carry our thoughts away to the banks of the Danube where it winds and straggles over the steppes, to picture some young horse-breeder, whose costume and harness are his only wealth; who rides out in the morning as the cock-bustard that, having preened himself, paces before the hen birds on the plains that he can scour when his wings, which are slow in the air, join with his strong legs to make nothing of grassy leagues on leagues. And first, this life with its free sweeping horizon, and the swallow-like curves of its gallops for the sake of galloping, or those which the long lashes of its whips trace in deploying, and which remind us of the lithe tendrils in which terminate Dürer's ornamental flourishes; this life in which the eye is trained to watch the lasso, as with well-calculated address it swirls out and drops over the frighted head of an unbroken colt; – this life is first pent up in a little goldsmith's shop, in a country even to-day famous for the beauty and originality of its peasant jewelry: and here it is trained to follow and answer the desire of the bright dark eyes of girls in love; – in love, where love and the beauty that inspires it are the gifts of nature most guarded and most honoured, from which are expected the utmost that is conceived of delicacy in delight by a virile and healthy race. "A pure and skilful man." Patient already has this life become, for a jeweller can scarcely be made of impatient stuff; patient even before the admixture of German blood when Albert the elder married his Barbara Holper. The two eldest sons were made jewellers; but the third, John, is set to study and becomes a parson, as if already learning and piety stood next in the estimation of this life after thrift, skill and the creation of ornament. And Germany boasts of this life beyond that of any of her sons; but her blood was probably of small importance to the efficiency that it attained to in the great Albert Dürer. The German name of Dürer or Thürer, a door, is quite as likely to be the translation, correct or otherwise, of some Hungarian name, as it is an indication that the family had originally emigrated from Germany. In any case, a large admixture by intermarriage of Slavonic blood would correspond to the unique distinction among Germans, attained in the dignity, sweetness and fineness which signalised Dürer. Of course, in such matters no sane man looks for proof; but neither will he reject a probable suggestion which may help us to understand the nature of an exceptional man.

IV

Dürer continues to speak of his childhood:

> And my father took special pleasure in me, because he saw that I was diligent to learn. So he sent me to school, and when I had learnt to read and write he took me away from it, and taught me the goldsmith's craft. But when I could work neatly, my liking drew me rather to painting than to goldsmith's work, so I laid it before my father; but he was not well pleased, regretting the time lost while I had been learning to be a goldsmith. Still he let it be as I wished, and in 1486 (reckoned from the birth of Christ) on S. Andrew's day (November 30) my father bound me apprentice to Michael Wolgemut, to serve him three years long. During that time God gave me diligence, so that I learnt well, but I had much to suffer from his lads.
>
> When I had finished my learning my father sent me off, and I stayed away four years till he called me back again. As I had gone forth in the year 1490 after Easter (Easter Sunday was April 11), so now I came back again in 1494 as it is reckoned after Whitsuntide (Whit Sunday was May 18).

Erasmus tells us that German disorders were "partly due to

the natural fierceness of the race, partly to the division into so many separate States, and partly to the tendency of the people to serve as mercenaries." That there were many swaggerers and bullies about, we learn from Dürer's prints. In every crowd these gentlemen in leathern tights, with other ostentatious additions to their costume, besides poniards and daggers to emphasise the brutal male, strut straddle-legged and self-assured; and of course raw lads and loutish prentices yielded them the sincerest flattery. We can well understand that the model boy, to whom "God had given diligence," with his long hair lovely as a girl's, and his consciousness of being nearly always in the right, had much to suffer from his fellow prentices. Besides, very likely, he already consorted with Willibald Pirkheimer and his friends, who were the aristocrats of the town. And though he may have been meek and gentle, there must have appeared in everything he did and was an assertion of superiority, all the more galling for its being difficult to define and as ready to blush as the innocent truth herself.

V

It is much argued as to where Dürer went when his father "sent him off." We have the direct statement of a contemporary, Christopher Scheurl, that he visited Colmar and Basle; and what is well nigh as good, for a visit to Venice. For Scheurl wrote in 1508: *Qui quum nuper in Italiam rediset, tum a Venetis, tum a Bononiensibus artificibus, me saepe interprete cansalutatus est alter Apelles.*

> "When he lately *returned* to Italy, he was often greeted as a second Apelles, by the craftsmen both of Venice and Bologna (I acting as their interpreter)."

Before we accept any of these statements it is well to remember how easily quite intimate friends make mistakes as to where one has been and when; even about journeys that in one's own mind either have been or should have been turning-points in one's life. For they will attribute to the past experiences which were never ours, or forget those which we consider most unforgettable. No one who has paid attention to these facts will consider that historians prove so much or so well as they often fancy themselves to do. In the present case what is really remarkable is, that none of these sojournings of the young artist in foreign art centres seem to have produced such a change in his art as can now be traced with assurance. At Colmar he saw the masterpieces and the brothers of the "admirable Martin," as he always calls Schongauer. At Basle there is still preserved a cut wood-block representing St. Jerome, on the back of which is an authentic signature; there is besides a series of uncut wood-blocks, the designs on which it is easy to imagine to have been produced by the travelling journeyman that Dürer then seemed to the printers and painters of the towns he passed through. By those processes by which anything can be made of anything, much has been done to give substantiality to the implied first visit to Venice. There are drawings which were probably made there, representing ladies resembling those in pictures by Carpaccio as to their garments, the dressing of their hair, and the type of their faces. Of course it is not impossible that such a lady or ladies may have visited Nuremberg, or been seen by the young wanderer at Basle or elsewhere. And the resemblance between a certain drawing in the Albertina and one of the carved lions in red marble now on the Piazzetta de' Leoni does not count for much, when we consider that there is nothing in the workmanship of these heads to suggest that they were done after sculptured originals; – the manes, &c., being represented by an easy penman's convention, as they might have been whether the models were living or merely imagined. Nor is there any good reason for dating the drawings of sites in the Tyrol, supposed to have been sketched on the road, rather this year than another. Lastly, the famous sentence in a letter written from Venice during Dürer's authenticated visit there, in 1506, may be construed in more than one sense. The passage is generally rather curtailed when quoted.

> He (Giovanni Bellini) is very old, but is still the best painter of them all. The thing that pleased me so well eleven years ago, pleases me now no more; if I had not seen it for myself, I should never have believed any one who told me. You must know, too, that there are many better painters here than Master Jacob (Jacopo de' Barbari) is abroad; yet Anton Kolb would swear an oath that no better painter than Jacob lives.

If "the thing that pleased so well eleven years before" was a picture or pictures by Master Jacob or by Andrea Mantegna, as is usually supposed, the phrase, "If I had not seen it for myself I should never have believed any one who told me" is extremely strange. It is not usual to expect to change one's opinion of a work of art by hearsay, or to imagine others, when they have not done so, predicting with assurance that we shall change a decided opinion upon the merits of a work of art; yet one of these two suppositions seems certainly to be implied. I do not say that it is impossible to conceive of either, only that such cursory reference to such conceptions is extremely strange. Again, if work by Jacopo de' Barbari is referred to, it might very well have been seen elsewhere than at Venice eleven years ago; and indeed the last sentence in the passage might be taken to imply as much. To me at least the truth appears to be that these hints, which we may well have misunderstood, point to something which the imagination is only too delighted to entertain. It is a charming dream – the young Dürer, just of age, trudging from town to town, designing wood-blocks for a printer here, questioning the brothers of the "admirable Martin" there, or again painting a sign in yet another place, such as Holbein painted for the schoolmaster at Basle; and at last arriving in Venice – Venice untouched as yet by the conflicting ideals that were even then being brought to birth anew: Mediaeval Venice, such as we see her in the pictures of Gentile Bellini and Carpaccio. One painting of real importance in the work of Dürer remains to us from this period: the greatest of modern critics has described it and its effect on him in a way which would make any second attempt impertinent.

I consider as invaluable Albrecht Dürer's portrait of himself painted in 1493, when he was in his twenty-second year. It is a bust half life-size, showing the two hands and the forearms. Crimson cap with short narrow strings, the throat bare to below the collar bone, an embroidered shirt, the folds of the sleeves tied underneath with peach-coloured ribbons, and a blue-grey, fur-edged cloak with yellow laces, compose a dainty dress befitting a well-bred youth. In his hand he significantly carries a blue *eryngo*, called in German "Mannstreu." He has a serious, youthful face, the mouth and chin covered with an incipient beard. The whole splendidly drawn, the composition simple, grand and harmonious; the execution perfect and in every way worthy of Dürer, though the colour is very thin, and has cracked in some places.

Such is the figure which we may imagine making its way among the crowd in Gentile Bellini's Procession of the "True Cross" before St. Mark's, with eyes all wonder and lips often consciously imprisoning the German tongue, which cannot make itself understood. How comes he so finely dressed, the son of the modest Nuremberg goldsmith? Has he won the friendship of some rich burgher prince at Augsburg, or Strasburg, or Basle? Has he been enabled to travel in his suite as far as Venice? Or has he earned a large sum for painting some lord's or lady's portrait, which, if it were not lost, would now stand as the worthy compeer of this splendid portrait of the "true man" far from home; true to that home only, or true to Agnes Frey? – for some suppose the sprig of eryngo to signify that he was already betrothed to her. Or perhaps he has joined Willibald Pirkheimer at Basle or elsewhere, and they two, crossing the Alps together, have become friends for life? Will they part here ere long, the young burgher prince to proceed to the Universities of Padua and Mantua, the future great painter to trudge back over the Alps, getting a lift now and again in waggon or carriage or on pillion? Let the man of pretentious science say it is bootless to ask such questions; those who ask them know that it is delightful; know that it is the true way to make the past live for them; guess that would historians more generally ask them, their books would be less often dry as dust.

VI

It may be that to this period belongs the meeting with Jacopo de' Barbari to which a passage in his MS. books (now in the British Museum) refers: and that already he began to be exercised on the subject of a canon of proportions for the human figure. In the chapter which I devote to his studies on this subject it will be seen how the determination to work the problem out by experiment, since Jacopo refused to reveal, and Vitruvius only hinted at the secret, led to his discovering something of far more value than it is probable that either could have given him. And yet the belief that there was a hidden secret probably hindered him from fully realising the importance of his discovery, or reaping such benefit from it as he otherwise might have done. How often has not the belief that those of old time knew what is ignored to-day, prevented men from taking full advantage of the conquests over ignorance that they have made themselves! Because what they know is not so much as they suppose might be or has been known, they fail to recognise the most that has yet been known – the best foundation for a new building that has yet been discovered – and search for what they possess, and fail to rival those whose superiority over themselves is a delusion of their own hearts. So early Dürer may have begun this life-long labour which, though not wholly vain, was never really crowned to the degree it merited: while others living in more fertile lands reaped what they had not sown, he could only plough and scatter seed. As Raphael is supposed to have said, all that was lacking to him was knowledge of the antique.

Perhaps many will blame me for writing, unlearned, as I am; in my opinion they are not wrong; they speak truly. For I myself had rather hear and read a learned man and one famous in this art than write of it myself, being unlearned. Howbeit I can find none such who hath written aught about how to form a canon of human proportions, save one man, Jacopo (de' Barbari) by name, born at Venice and a charming painter. He showed me the figures of a man and woman, which he had drawn according to a canon of proportions; and now I would rather be shown what he meant (*i.e.*, upon what principles the proportions were constructed) than behold a new kingdom. If I had it (his canon), I would put it into print in his honour, for the use of all men. Then, however, I was still young and had not heard of such things before. Howbeit I was very fond of art, so I set myself to discover how such a canon might be wrought out. For this aforesaid Jacopo, as I clearly saw, would not explain to me the principles upon which he went. Accordingly I set to work on my own idea and read Vitruvius, who writes somewhat about the human figure. Thus it was from, or out of, these two men aforesaid that I took my start, and thence, from day to day, have I followed up my search according to my own notions.

> When I returned home, Hans Prey treated with my father and gave me
> his daughter, Mistress Agnes by name, and with her he gave me two
> hundred florins, and we were wedded; it was on Monday before
> Margaret's (July 7) in the year 1494.

The general acceptance of the gouty and irascible Pirkheimer's
defamation of Frau Dürer as a miser and a shrew called forth a
display of ingenuity on the part of Professor Thausing to prove
the contrary. And I must confess that if he has not quite done that,
he seems to me to have very thoroughly discredited Pirkheimer's
ungallant abuse. Sir Martin Conway bids us notice that Dürer
speaks of his "dear father" and his "dear mother" and even of his
"dear father-in-law," but that he never couples that adjective with
his wife's name. It is very dangerous to draw conclusions from
such a fact, which may be merely an accident: or may, if it
represents a habit of Dürer's, bear precisely the opposite
significance. For some men are proud to drop such outward marks
of affection, in cases where they know that every day proves to
every witness that they are not needed. He also considers that her
portraits show her, when young, to have been "empty-headed,"
when older, a "frigid shrew." For my own part, if the portrait at
Bremen (see opposite) represents "mein Angnes," as its
resemblance to the sketch at Vienna (see illus.) convinces me it
does, I cannot accept either of these conclusions arrived at by the
redoubtable science of physiognomy. The Bremen portrait shows
us a refined, almost an eccentric type of beauty; one can easily
believe it to have been possessed by a person of difficult
character, but one certainly who must have had compensating
good qualities. The "mein Angnes" on the sketch may well be set
against the absent "dears" in the other mentions her husband
made of her, especially when we consider that he couples this
adjective with the Emperor's name, "my dear Prince Max." Of her
relations to him nothing is known except what Pirkheimer wrote
in his rage, when he was writing things which are demonstrably

false. We know, however, that she was capable, pious, and thrifty; and on several occasions, in the Netherlands, shared in the honours done to her husband. It is natural to suppose that as they were childless, there may have existed a moral equivalent to this infertility; but also, with a man such as we know Dürer to have been, and a woman in every case not bad, have we not reason to expect that this moral barrenness which may have afflicted their union was in some large measure conquered by mutual effort and discipline, and bore from time to time those rarer flowers whose beauty and sweetness repay the conscious culture of the soul? It seems difficult to imagine that a man who succeeded in charming so many different acquaintances, and in remaining life-long friends with the testy and inconsiderate Pirkheimer, should have altogether failed to create a relation kindly and even beautiful with his Agnes, whose portrait we surely have at her best in the drawing at Bremen. Considerations as to the general position of married women in those days need not prevent us of our natural desire to think as well as possible of Dürer and his circumstances. We know that for a great many men the wife was not simply counted among their goods and chattels, or regarded as a kind of superior servant. We are able to take a peep at many a fireside of those days, where the relations that obtained, however different in certain outward characters, might well shame the greater number of the respectable even in the present year of grace. We know what Luther was in these respects; and have rather more than less reason to expect from the refined and gracious Dürer the creation of a worthy and kindly home. Why should we expect him to have been less successful than his parents in these respects?

VIII

Some time after the marriage it happened that my father was so ill
with dysentery that no one could stop it. And when he saw death
before his eyes he gave himself willingly to it, with great patience,
and he commended my mother to me, and exhorted me to live in a
manner pleasing to God. He received the Holy Sacraments and
passed away Christianly (as I have described at length in another
book) in the year 1502, after midnight, before S. Matthew's eve
(September 20). God be gracious and merciful to him.

The only leaf of the "other book" referred to that has survived is
that which I have already quoted at length.

CHAPTER II

THE WORLD
IN WHICH HE LIVED

I

Now let us consider what the world was like in which this virile, accurate and persevering spirit had grown up. Over and over again, the story of the New Birth has been told; how it began in France, and met an untimely fate at the hands of English invaders, then took refuge in Italy, where it grew to be the wonder of the world; and how the corruption of the ruling classes and of the Church, with the indignation and rebellion that this gave rise to, combined to frustrate the promise of earlier days.

When the Roman Empire gradually became an anarchy of hostile fragments, every large monastery, every small town, girded itself with walls and tended to become the germ of a new civilisation. Popes, kings, and great lords, haunted by reminiscence of the vanished empire, made spasmodic attempts to subject such centres to their rule and tax them for their maintenance. In the first times, the Church – the See of Rome – made by far the most successful attempt to get its supremacy acknowledged, and had therefore fewer occasions to resort to violence. It was more respected and more respectable than the other powers which claimed to rule and tax these immured and isolated communities dotted over Europe; but as time went on, the Church became less and less beneficent, more and more tyrannical. Meanwhile kings and emperors, having learned wisdom by experience, found themselves in a position to take advantage of the growing bad odour of the Church; and by favouring the civil communities and creating a stable hierarchy among the class of lords and barons from which they had emerged, were at last able to face the Church, with its *protégés,* the religious communities, on an equal footing.

The religious communities, owing to the vow of celibacy, had become more and more stagnant, while the civil communities increased in power to adapt themselves to the age. All that was virile and creative combined in the towns; all that was inadequate, sterile, useless, coagulated in the monasteries, which thus became cesspools, and ultimately took on the character of festering sores by which the civil bodies which had at first been purged into them were endangered. Luther tells us how there was a Bishop of Würzburg who used to say when he saw a rogue, "'To the cloister with you. Thou art useless to God or man.' He meant that in the cloister were only hogs and gluttons, who did nothing but eat and drink and sleep, and were of no more profit than as many rats." And the loathing that another of these sties created in the young Erasmus, and the difficulty he had to escape from the clutches of its inmates – never feeling safe till the Pope had intervened – show us that by their wealth and by the engine of their malice, the confessional (which they had usurped from the regular clergy), they were as formidable as they were useless. It became necessary that this antiquated system of social drainage should be superseded.

In England and Germany it was swept away. In centres like Nuremberg, the desire for reformation and the horror of false doctrine were grounded in practical experience of intolerable inconveniences, not in a clear understanding of the questions at issue. Intellectually, the leaders of the Reformation had no better foundation than those they opposed: for them, as for their opponents, the question was not to be solved by an appeal to evident truths and experience, but to historical documents and traditions, supposed, to be infallible. For a clear intelligence, there is nothing to choose between the infallibility of oecumenical councils or of Popes, and that of the Bible. Both have been in their time the expression of very worthy and very human sentiments; both are incapable of rational demonstration.

II

Scattered over Europe, wherever the free intelligence was waking and had rubbed her eyes, were men who desired that nuisances should be removed and reforms operated without schism or violence. To these Erasmus spoke. His policy was tentative, and did not proceed, like that of other parties, by declaring that a perfect solution was to hand. Luther's action divided these honest, upright souls, and would-be children of light, into three unequal camps.

As a rule the downright, headstrong, and impatient became reformers. The respectful, cautious and long-suffering, such as More, Warham, and Adrian IV., clung to the Roman establishment, were martyred for it or broke their hearts over it. Erasmus and a handful of others remained true to a tentative policy, and, compared with their contemporaries, were meek and lowly in heart – became children of light. To them we now look back wistfully, and wish that they might have been, if not as numerous as the Churchmen and Beformers, at least a sufficient body to have made their influence an effective force, with the advantage of more light and more patience that was really theirs. But, alas!

they only counted as the first dissolvent which set free more corrosive and detrimental acids. The exhilaration of action and battle was for others; for them the sad conviction that neither side deserved to be trusted with a victory. Yet, beyond the world whose chief interest was the Reformation, we may be sure that such men as Charles V., Michelangelo, Rabelais, Montaigne, and all those whom they may be taken to represent, were in essential agreement with Erasmus. Luther and Machiavelli alone rejected the Papacy as such: the latter's more stringent intellectual development led him also to discard every ideal motive or agent of reform for violent means. He was ready even to regard the passions of men like Caesar Borgia, tyrants in the fullest sense of the word, as the engines by which civilisation, learning, art, and manners, might be maintained. Whereas Luther appealed to the passions of common honest men, the middle classes in fact. It is easy to let either Luther or Machiavelli steal away our entire sympathy. On the one hand, no compromise, not even the slightest, seems possible with criminal ruffians such as a Julius II. and an Alexander Borgia; on the other hand, the power swollen by the tide of minor corruption, which such men ruled by might, did come into the hands of a Leo X., an Adrian IV.; and though that power was obviously tainted through and through, it might have been mastered and wielded in the cause of reform. Erasmus hoped for this. Even Julius II. protected him from the superiors of his convent. Even Julius II. patronised Michelangelo and Raphael and everything that had a definite character in the way of creative power or scholarship; and could appreciate at least the respect which what he patronised commanded. He could appreciate the respect commanded by the austerity and virtue of those who rebelled against him and denounced his cynical abuse of all his powers, whether natural or official. He liked to think he had enemies worth beating. Such a ruler is a sore temptation to a keen intellect. "Everything great is formative," and this Pope was colossal – a colossal bully and robber if you like – but the good he did by his patronage was real good, was practical. Michelangelo and Raphael could work as splendidly as they desired. Erasmus was helped and encouraged. Timid honesty is often petty, does nothing, criticises and finds fault with artists and with learning, runs after them like Sancho Panza after Don Quixote, is helpless and ridiculous and horribly in the way. Leo X. was intelligent and well-meaning; wisdom herself might hope from such a man. Be the throne he is sitting on as monstrous and corrupt a contrivance as it may, yet it is there, it does give him authority; he is on it and dominates the world. It is easy to say, "But the period of the Renascence closed, its glory died away." Suppose Luther had been as subtle as he was whole-hearted, and had added to his force of character a delicacy and charm like that of St. Francis; or suppose that Erasmus instead of his schoolfellow Adrian IV. had become Pope; what a different tale there might have been to tell! Who will presume to point out the necessity by which these things were thus and not otherwise? "Regrets for what 'might have been' are proverbially idle," cries the historian from whom I have chiefly quoted. I do not recollect the proverb, unless he refers to "It is no use crying over spilt milk;" but in any case such regrets are far from being necessarily idle. "What might have been" is even generally "what ought to have been;" and no study has been or is likely to be so pregnant for us as the study of the contrast between "what was" and "what ought to have been," though such studies are inevitably mingled with regrets. We have every reason to regret that the Reformation was so hasty and ill-considered, and that the Papacy was as purblind as it was arrogant. The plant of the Roman Church machinery, which it had taken centuries to lay down, came into the hands of men who grossly ignored its function and the conditions of its working. They used its power partly for the benefit of the human race, by patronising art and scholarship; but chiefly in self-indulgence. If honest intelligence had been given control, a man so partially equipped for his task would not have been goaded into action; but only force, moral or physical, can act at a disadvantage; light and reason must have the advantage of dominant position to effect anything immediate. If they are not on the throne, all they can do is to sow seed, and bewail the present while looking forward to a better future. Now, most educated men are for tolerance, and see as Erasmus saw. We see that Savonarola and Luther were not so right as they thought themselves to be; we see that what they condemned as arrogancy and corruption is partly excusable – is in some measure a condition of efficiency in worldly spheres where one has to employ men already bad. True, the great princes and cardinals of those days not only connived at corruption and ruled by it, but often even professed it. Still in every epoch, under all circumstances, the majority of those who have governed men have more or less cynically employed means that will not bear the light of day. While these magnificoes of the Renascence do stand alone, or almost alone, by the ample generosity of their conception of the objects that power should be exerted in furtherance of; their outlook on life was more commensurate with the variety and competence of human nature than perhaps that of any ruling class has been before or since. As Shakespeare is the amplest of poets, so were theirs the most fruitful of courts. From the great Medicis to our own Elizabeth they all partake of a certain grandiose vitality and variety of intention.

III

Greatness demands self-assertion; self-assertion is a great virtue even in a Julius II. There is a vast deal of humbug in the use we make of the word humility. We talk about Christ's humility, but whose self-assertion has ever been more unmitigated? "I am the Way, the Truth, and the Light." "Learn of Me that I am meek and lowly, and ye shall find rest to your souls." No doubt it is the quality of the self asserted that justifies in our eyes the assertion;

humility then is not opposed to self-assertion. When Michelangelo shows that he thinks himself the greatest artist in the world, he is not necessarily lacking in humility; nor is Luther, asserting the authority of his conscience against the Pope and Emperor; nor Dürer, saying to us in those little finely-dressed portraits with which he signs his pictures, "I am that I am – namely, one of the handsomest of men and the greatest artist north of the Alps." Or when Erasmus lets us see that he thinks himself the most learned man living, – if he is the most learned, so much the better that he should know this also as well as the rest. The artist and the scholar were bound to feel gratitude for the corrupt but splendid Church and courts, which gave them so much both in the way of maintenance and opportunity. It may be asked, has all the honesty and the not always evident purity of Protestantism done so much for the world as those dissolute Popes and Princes? And the artist, judging with a hasty bias perhaps, is likely to answer no.

IV

For us nowadays the pith of history seems no more to be the lives of monarchs, or the fighting of battles, or even the deliberations of councils; these things we have more and more come to regard merely as tools and engines for the creation of societies, homes, and friends. And so, though religion and religious machinery dominated the life of those days, it is not in theological disputes, neither is it in oecumenical councils and Popes, nor in sermons, reformers, and synods, that we find the essence of the soul's life. Rather to us, the pictures, the statues, the books, the furniture, the wardrobes, the letters, and the scandals that have been left behind, speak to us of those days; for these we value them. And we are right, the value of the Renaissance lies in these things, I say "the scandals" of those days; for a part of what comes under that head was perhaps the manifestation of a morality based on a wider experience; though its association with obvious vices and its opposition to the old and stale ideals gave it an illegitimate character; while the re-establishment of the more part of those ideals has perpetuated its reproach. There can be no intellectual charity if the machinery and special sentences of current morality are supposed to be final or truly adequate. Their tentative and inadequate character, which every free intelligence recognises, is what endorses the wisdom of Jesus', saying, "Judge not that ye be not judged." Ordinary honest and good citizens do not realise how much that is in every way superior to the gifts of any single one of themselves is yearly sacrificed and tortured for their preservation as a class. On what agonies of creative and original minds is the safety of their homes based? These respectable Molochs who devour both the poor and the exceptionally gifted, and are so little better for their meal, were during the Renascence for a time gainsaid and abashed; yet even then their engines, the traditional secular and ecclesiastic policies, were a foreign encumbrance with which the human spirit was loaded, and which helped to prevent it from reaping the full result of its mighty upheaval.

To see things as they are, and above all to value them for what is most essential in them with regard to the development of our own characters; – that is, I take it, consciously or unconsciously, the main effort of the modern spirit. On the world, the flesh, and the devil, we have put new values; and it was the first assertion of these new values which caused the Renascence. Fine manners, fine clothes, and varied social interchange make the world admirable in our eyes, not at all a bogey to frighten us. Health, frankness, and abundant exercise make the flesh a pure delight in our eyes; lastly, this new-born spirit has made "a moral of the devil himself," and so for us he has lost his terror.

Rabelais was right when he laughed the old outworn values

down, and declared that women were in the first place female, men in the first place male; that the written word should be a self-expression, a sincerity, not a task or a catalogue or a penance, but, like laughter and speech, essentially human, making all men brothers, doing away with artificial barriers and distinctions, making the scholar shake in time with the toper, and doubling the divine up with the losel; bidding even the lady hold her sides in company with the harlot. Eating and drinking were seen to be good in themselves; the eye and the nose and the palate were not only to be respected but courted; free love was better than married enmity. No rite, no church, no god, could annihilate these facts or restrain their influence any more than the sea could be tamed. Dürer was touched with this spirit; we see it in his fine clothes, in his collector's rapacity, above all in his letters to his friend Pirkheimer – a man more typical of that Rabelaisian age than Dürer and Michelangelo, who were both of them not only modern men but men conservative of the best that had been – men in travail for the future, absorbed by the responsibility of those who create.

Pirkheimer, one year Dürer's senior, was a gross fat man early in life, enjoying the clinking of goblets, the music of fork and knife, and the effrontery of obscene jests. A vain man, a soldier and a scholar, pedantic, irritable, but in earnest; a compli-menter of Emperors, a leader of the reform party, a partisan of Luther's, the friend and correspondent of Erasmus, the elective brother of Dürer. The man was typical; his fellows were in all lands. Dürer was surprised to find how many of them there were at Venice – men who would delight Pirkheimer and delight in him. "My friend, there are so many Italians here who look exactly like you I don't know how it happens! ... men of sense and knowledge, good lute players and pipers, judges of painting, men of much noble sentiment and honest virtue; and they show me much honour and friendship." Something of all this was doubtless in Dürer too; but in him it was refined and harmonised by the sense and serious concern, not only for the things of to-day, but for those of to-morrow and yesterday; the sense of solidarity, the passion for permanent effect, eternal excellence. These things, in men like Pirkheimer, still more in Erasmus, and even in Rabelais and Montaigne, are not absent; but they are less stringent, less religious, than they are in a Dürer or a Michelangelo.

CHAPTER III

DÜRER AT VENICE

I

There are several reasons which may possibly have led Dürer to visit Venice in 1505. The Fondaco dei Tedeschi, or Exchange of the German Merchants at Venice, had been burned down the winter before, and they were in haste to complete a new one. Dürer may have received assurance that the commission to paint the altarpiece for the new chapel would be his did he desire it. At any rate he seems to have set to work on such a picture almost as soon as he arrived there. It is strange to think that Giorgione and Titian probably began to paint the frescoes on the facade while he was still at work in the chapel, or soon after he left. The plague broke out in Nuremberg before he came away; but this is not likely to have been his principal motive for leaving home, as many richer men, such as his friend Pirkheimer, from whom he borrowed money for the journey, stayed where they were. Nor do Dürer's letters reveal any alarm for his friend's, his mother's, his wife's, or his brother's safety. He took with him six small pictures, and probably a great number of prints, for Venice was a first-rate market.

II

The letters which follow are like a glimpse of a distant scene in a *camera obscura*, and, like life itself, they are full of repetitions and over-insistence on what is insignificant or of temporary interest. To-day they call for our patience and forbearance, and it will depend upon our imaginative activity in what degree they repay them; even as it depends upon our power of affectionate assimilation in what degree and kind every common day adds to our real possessions.

I have made my citations as ample as possible, so as to give the reader a just idea of their character while making them centre as far as possible round points of special interest.

To the honourable, wise Master Wilibald Pirkheimer, Burgher of Nürberg, my kind Master. VENICE, *January 6, 1506.*

I wish you and yours many good, happy New Years. My willing service, first of all, to you dear Master Pirkheimer! Know that I am in good health; I pray God far better things than that for you. As to those pearls and precious stones which you gave me commission to buy, you must know that I can find nothing good or even worth its price. Everything is snapped up by the Germans who hang about the Riva. They always want to get four times the value for anything, for they are the falsest knaves alive. No one need look for an honest service from any of them. Some good fellows have warned me to beware of them, they cheat man and beast. You can buy better things at a lower price at Frankfurt than at Venice.

About the books which I was to order for you, the Imhofs have already seen after them; but if there is anything else you want, let me know and I will attend to it for you with all zeal. Would to God I could do you a right good service! gladly would I accomplish it, seeing, as I do, how much you do for me. And I pray you be patient with my debt, for indeed I think much oftener of it than you do. When God helps me home I will honourably repay you with many thanks; for I have a panel to paint for the Germans for which they are to pay me a hundred and ten Rhenish florins – it will not cost me as much as five. I shall have scraped it and laid on the ground and made it ready within eight days; then I shall at once begin to paint and, if God will, it shall be in its place above the altar a month after Easter.

•

VENICE, *February 17*, 1506.

How I wish you were here at Venice! There are so many nice men among the Italians who seek my company more and more every day – which is very pleasing to one – men of sense and knowledge, good lute-players and pipers, judges of painting, men of much noble sentiment and 'honest virtue, and they show me much honour and friendship. On the other hand there are also amongst them some of the most false, lying, thievish rascals; I should never have believed that such were living in the world. If one did not know them, one would think them the nicest men the earth could show. For my own part I cannot help laughing at them whenever they talk to me. They know that their knavery is no secret but they don't mind.

Amongst the Italians I have many good friends who warn me not to eat and drink with their painters. Many of them are my enemies and they copy my work in the churches and wherever they can find it; and then they revile it and say that the style is not *antique* and so not good. But Giovanni Bellini has highly praised me before many nobles. He wanted to have something of mine, and himself came to me and asked me to paint him something and he would pay well for it. And all men tell me what an upright man he is, so that I am really friendly with him. He is very old, but is still the best painter of them all. And that which so well pleased me eleven years ago pleases me no longer, if I had not seen it for myself I should not have believed any one who told me. You must know too that there are many better

✳ 95

painters here than Master Jacob (Jacopo de' Barbari) is abroad (*wider darvsen Meister J.*), yet Anton Kolb would swear an oath that no better painter lives than Jacob. Others sneer at him, saying if he were good he would stay here, and so forth.

I have only to-day begun to sketch in my picture, for my hands were so scabby (*grindig*) that I could do no work with them, but I have got them cured.

Now be lenient with me and don't get in a passion so easily, but be gentle like me. I don't know why you will not learn from me. My friend! I should like to know if any one of your loves is dead – that one close by the water for instance, or the one called... so that you might supply her place by another. ALBRECHT DÜRER.

VENICE, February 28, 1506.

I wish you had occasion to come here, I know you would not find time hang on your hands, for there are so many nice men in this country, right good artists. I have such a throng of Italians about me that at times I have to shut myself up. The nobles all wish me well, but few of the painters.

•

VENICE, *April* 2, 1506.

The painters here, let me tell you, are very unfriendly to me. They have summoned me three times before the magistrates, and I have had to pay four florins to their school. You must also know that I might have gained a great deal of money if I had not undertaken to paint the German picture. There is much work in it and I cannot get it quite finished before Whitsuntide. Yet they only pay me eighty-five ducats for it. Now you know how much it costs to live, and then I have bought some things and sent some money away, so that I have not much before me now. But don't misunderstand me, I am firmly purposed not to go away hence till God enables me to repay you with thanks and to have a hundred florins over besides. I should easily earn this if I had not got the German picture to paint, for all men except the painters wish me well.

Tell my mother to speak to Wolgemut about my brother, and to ask him whether he can make use of him and give him work till I come, or whether he can put him with some one else. I should gladly have brought him with me to Venice, and that would have been useful both to me and him, and he would have learnt the language, but my mother was afraid that the sky would fall on him. Pray keep an eye on him yourself, the women are no use for that. Tell the lad, as you so well can, to be studious and honest till I come, and not to be a trouble to his mother; if I cannot arrange everything I will at all events do all that I can. Alone I certainly should not starve, but to support many is too hard for me, for no one throws his gold away.

Now I commend myself to you. Tell my mother to be ready to sell at the Crown-fair (*Heiligthumsfest*). I am arranging for my wife to have come home by then; I have written to her too about everything. I will not take any steps about buying the diamond ornament till I get your next letter.

I don't think I shall be able to come home before next autumn, when what I earned for the picture, which was to have been ready by Whitsuntide, will be quite used up in living expenses, purchases, and payments; what, however, I gain afterwards I hope to save. If you see fit don't speak of this further, and I will keep putting off my leaving from day to day and writing as though I was just coming. I am indeed very uncertain what to do next. Write to me again soon.

Given on Thursday before Palm Sunday in the year 1506. ALBRECHT DÜRER, Your Servant.

VENICE, *August* 18, 1506.

To the first, greatest man in the world. Your servant and slave

Albrecht Dürer sends salutation to his Magnificent master Wilibald Pirkheimer. My truth! I hear gladly and with great satisfaction of your health and great honours. I wonder how it is possible for a man like you to stand against so many wisest princes, swaggerers and soldiers; it must be by some special grace of God. When I read your letter about this terrible grimace, it gave me a great fright and I thought it was a most important thing,[15] but I warrant that you frightened even Schott's men,[16] you with your fierce look and your holiday hopping step. But it is very improper for such folk to smear themselves with civet. You want to become a real silk-tail and you think that, if only you manage to please the girls, the thing is done. If you were only as taking a fellow as I am, it would not provoke me so. You have so many loves that merely to pay each one a visit you would take a month or more before you got through the list.

For one thing I return you my thanks, namely, for explaining my position in the best way to my wife; but I know that there is no lack of wisdom in you. If only you had my meekness you would have all virtues. Thank you also for all the good you have done me, if only you would not bother me about the rings! If they don't please you, break their heads off and pitch them out on to the dunghill as Peter Weisweber says. What do you mean by setting me to such dirty work? *I* have become a *gentleman* at Venice.

I have also heard that you can make lovely rhymes; you would be a find for our fiddlers here; they fiddle so beautifully that they can't help weeping over it themselves. Would God our Rechenmeister girl could hear them, she would cry too. At your bidding I will again lay aside my anger and bear myself even more bravely than usual.

Now let me commend myself to you; give my willing service to our Prior for me; tell him to pray God for me that I may be protected, and especially from the French sickness; I know of nothing that I now dread more than that, for well nigh every one has got it. Many men are quite eaten up and die of it.

VENICE, *September* 8, 1506.

Most learned, approved, wise, knower of many languages, sharp to detect all encountered lies and quick to recognise plain truth! Honourable much-regarded Herr Wilibald Pirkheimer. Your humble servant Albrecht Dürer wishes you all hail, great and worthy honour *in the devil's name,* so much for the twaddle of which you are so fond. I wager that for this[17] you would think me too an orator of a hundred parts. A chamber must have more than four corners which is to contain the gods of memory. I am not going to cram my head full of them; that I leave to you; for I believe that however many chambers there might be in the head, you would have something in each of them. The Margrave would not grant an audience long enough! – a hundred headings and to each heading, say, a hundred words, that takes 9 days 7 hours 52 minutes, not counting the sighs which I have not yet reckoned in. In fact you could not get through the whole at one go; it would stretch itself out like the speech of some old driveller.

I have taken all manner of trouble about the carpets but cannot find any broad ones; they are all narrow and long. However I still look about every day for them and so does Anton Kolb.

I have given Bernhard Hirschvogel your greeting and he sent you his service. He is full of sorrow for the death of his Son, the nicest lad I ever saw.

I can get none of your foolish featherlets. Oh, if only you were here! how you would like these fine Italian soldiers! How often I think of you! Would to God that you and Kunz Kamerer could see them! They have great scythe-lances with 278 points, if they only touch a man with them he dies, for they are all poisoned. Hey! I can do it well, I'll be an Italian soldier. The Venetians as well as the Pope and the King of France are collecting many men; what will come of it I don't know, but people ridicule our King very much.

Wish Stephan Paumgartner much happiness from me. I don't

wonder at his having taken a wife. Give my greeting to Borsch, Herr Lorenz, and our fair friends, as well as to your Rechenmeister girl, and thank that head-chamber of yours alone for remembering her greeting; tell her she's a nasty one.

I sent you olive-wood from Venice to Augsburg, where I directed it to be left, a full ten hundredweight. She says she would not wait for it; *whence the stink.*

My picture, you must know, says it would give a ducat for you to see it, it is well painted and beautifully coloured. I have earned much praise but little profit by it. In the time it took to paint I could easily have earned 220 ducats, and now I have declined much work, in order that I may come home. I have stopped the mouths of all the painters who used to say that I was good at engraving but, as to painting. I did not know how to handle my colours. Now every one says that better colouring they have never seen.

My French mantle greets you and my Italian coat also. It strikes me that there is an odour of gallantry about you; I can scent it out even at this distance; and they tell me here that when you go a-courting you pretend not to be more than twenty-five years old – oh, yes! double that and I'll believe it. My friend, there are so many Italians here who look exactly like you; I don't know how it happens!

The Doge and the Patriarch have also seen my picture. Herewith let me commend myself to you as your servant. I must really go to sleep as it is striking the seventh hour of the night, and I have already written to the Prior of the Augustines, to my father-in-law, to Mistress Dietrich, and to my wife, and they are all downright whole sheets full. So I have had to hurry over this letter, read it according to the sense. You would doubtless do better if you were writing to a lot of Princes. Many good nights and days too. Given at Venice on our Lady's day in September.

You need not lend my wife and mother anything; they have got money enough,

ALBRECHT DÜRER.

VENICE, *September 23*, 1506.

Your letter telling me of the praise that you get to overflowing from Princes and nobles gave me great delight. You must be altogether altered to have become so gentle; I shall hardly know you when I meet you again.

You must know that my picture is finished as well as another *Quadro*[18] the like of which I have never painted before. And as you are so pleased with yourself, let me tell you that there is no better Madonna picture in the land than mine; for all the painters praise it, as the nobles do you. They say that they have never seen a nobler, more charming painting, and so forth.

·

But in order to come home as soon as possible, I have, since my picture was finished, refused work that would have yielded me more than 2000 ducats. This all men know who live about me here.

Bernhard Holzbeck has told me great things of you, though I think he does so because you have become his brother-in-law. But nothing makes me more angry than when any one says that you are good-looking; if that were so I should become really ugly. That could make me mad. I have found a grey hair on myself, it is the result of so much excitement. And I fear that while I play such pranks with myself there are still bad days before me, &c.

My French mantle, my doublet, and my brown coat send you a hearty greeting, I should be glad to see what great thing your head-piece can produce that you hold yourself so high.

VENICE, about October 13, 1506.

Knowing that you are aware of my devotion to your service there is no need for me to write to you about it; but so much the more necessary is it for me to tell you of the great pleasure it gives me to hear of the high honour and fame which your manly wisdom and learned skill have brought you. This is the more to be wondered at, for seldom or never in a young body can the like be found. It comes to you, however, as to me, by a special grace of God. How pleased we both are when we fancy ourselves worth somewhat – I with my painting, and you with your wisdom. When any one praises us, we hold up our heads and believe him. Yet perhaps he is only some false flatterer who is scorning us all the time. So don't credit any one who praises you, for you've no notion how utterly and entirely unmannerly you are. I can quite see you standing before the Margrave and speaking so pleasantly – behaving exactly as if you were flirting with Mistress Rosentaler, cringing as you do. It did not escape me that, when you wrote your last letter, you were quite full of amorous thoughts. You ought to be ashamed of yourself, an old fellow like you pretending to be so good-looking. Flirting pleases you in the same way that a shaggy old dog likes a game with a kitten. If you were only as fine and gentle a man as I, I could understand it. If I become burgomaster I will serve you with the Luginsland.[19] as you do to pious Zamesser and me. I will have you for once shut up there with the ladies Rechenmeister, Rosentaler, Gärtner, Schutz, and Pör, and many others whom for shortness I will not name; they must deal with you.

People enquire more after me than you, for you yourself write that both girls and honourable wives ask after me – that is a sign of my virtue. When, however, God helps me home I don't know how I shall any longer stand you with your great wisdom; but for your virtue and good temper I am glad, and your dogs will be the better for it, for you will no longer strike them lame. Now however that you are thought so much of at home, you won't dare to talk to a poor painter in the street any more; to be seen with the painter varlet would be a great disgrace for you.

O, dear Herr Pirkheimer, just now while I was writing to you, the alarm of fire was raised and six houses over by Pietro Venier are burnt, and a woollen cloth of mine, for which only yesterday I paid eight ducats, is burnt, so I too am in trouble. There is much excitement here about the fire.

As to your summons to me to come home soon, I shall come as soon as ever I can, but I must first gain money for my expenses. I have paid away about 100 ducats for colours and other things. I have ordered you two carpets for which I shall pay to-morrow, but I could not get them cheap. I will pack them in with my linen.

And as to your threat that, unless I come home soon, you will make love to my wife, don't attempt it – a ponderous fellow like you would be the death of her.

I must tell you that I set to work to learn dancing and went twice to the school, for which I had to pay the master a ducat. No one could get me to go there again. To learn dancing I should have had to pay away all that I have earned, and at the end I should have known nothing about it.

In reply to your question when I shall come home, I tell you, so that my lords may also make their arrangements, that I shall have finished here in ten days; after that I should like to ride to Bologna to learn the secrets of the art of perspective, which a man is willing to teach me. I should stay there eight or ten days and then return to Venice. After that I shall come with the next messenger. How I shall freeze after this sun! Here I am a gentleman, at home only a parasite.

III

Sir Martin Conway writes:

> He (Dürer) enjoyed Venice; he liked the Italians; he was oppressed
> with orders for work; the climate suited him, and the warm sun was
> a pleasant contrast to the snows and frost of a Franconian winter. But
> Dürer's German heart was true; its truth was the secret of his
> success.... The syren voice of Italy charmed to their destruction most
> Germans who listened to it. Brought face to face with the Italian Ideal
> of Grace, they one after another abandoned for it the Ideal of Strength
> peculiarly their own.

We do not resort to these arguments to approve Holbein or
Van Dyck for their long residence in England. I am not sure how
much false sentiment inspired Thausing when he first praised
Dürer in this strain; but I must confess I suspect it was no little. I
incline to think that the best country for an artist is not always the
one he was born in, but often that one where his art finds the best
conditions to foster it. We do not honour Dürer by supposing that
he would have been among that majority of Dutch and German
artists who, weaker than Roger van der Weyden and Burgkmair,
returned from Italy injured and enfeebled; even if he had passed
the greater portion of his life with her syren voice in his ears.

Dürer could not bring himself to undergo for art's sake what
Michelangelo endured; years of exile from a beloved native city,
and, still worse, years of exile from the most congenial spiritual
atmosphere. Nevertheless, we must remember that the difference
of language would have made life in Venice for Dürer a much
more complete exile than life in Verona was for Dante, or life in
Rome for Michelangelo. So he did not share the patronage and
generous recognition which gave Titian such a splendid
opportunity. He ceased for a time at least to be a gentleman to
become a hanger-on, a parasite once more. At Antwerp he once
more was met by the same generosity and recognition only to
refuse again to accept it as a gift for life and return to his beloved
Nuremberg, where it is true his position continually improved,

though it never equalled what had been offered at Venice and Antwerp.

IV

The tone of some of the pleasantries in these letters may rather astonish good people who, having accepted the fact that Dürer was a religious man, have at once given him the tone and address of a meeting of churchwardens, if they have not conjured up a vision of him in a frock coat. "Things are what they are," said Bishop Butler, and so are women; boys will be boys. The distinctive functions of the two sexes were in those days kept more in view if not more in mind than is the case to-day. The fashions in dress and in deportment were particularly frank upon this point, especially for the young. One may allow as much as is desired for the corruption of manners produced by the civil and religious mercenaries, soldiers of fortune, and friars. There will always remain a certain truth and propriety, a certain grace and charm in those costumes and that deportment, as also in the freedom of jest which characterises even the most modest of Shakespeare's heroines; and under the influence of their spell we shall feel that all has not been gain in the change that has gradually been operated. No doubt virtue is a victory over nature, and chastity a refinement; but among conquerors some are easy and good-natured, others tactless, awkward, insulting; and among the chaste some are fearless and enjoy the freedom which courage and clear conscience give, others timid and suffer the oppression of their fears. Even among sinners some make the best of weaknesses and redeem them a great deal more than half, while others magnify smaller faults by lack of self-possession till they are an insupportable nuisance. We may well admit that from the successes of those days, those who succeed to our delight to-day may glean additional attractions.

V

We know that Dürer stopped on at Venice into the year 1507, by a note which he made in a copy of Euclid, now in the library at Wolfenbüttel. "This book have I bought at Venice for a ducat in the year 1507. Albrecht Dürer"; and by another stray note we learn the state of his worldly affairs on his return.

The following is my property, which I have with difficulty acquired by the labour of my hand, for I have had no opportunity of great gain. I have moreover suffered much loss by lending what was not repaid me, and by apprentices who never paid their fees, and one died at Rome whereby I lost my wares.

In the thirteenth year of my wedlock (Le., 1507-8) I have paid great debts with what I earned at Venice. I possess fairly good household furniture, good clothes, chests, some good pewter vessels, good materials for my work, bedding and cupboards, and good colours worth 100 florins Rhenish.

The wares that Dürer lost in Rome were doubtless chiefly woodcuts and engravings which his prentice had taken to sell during his *wanderjahre*, as Dürer himself during his own had very likely sold prints for Wolgemut. One of the reasons which had taken him to Venice may have been to summon Marc Antonio before the Signoria, for having copied not only his engravings, but the monogram with which he signed them; in any case he obtained a decree defending him against such artistic forgery. Dürer's most steady resource seems to have been the sale of prints; it is these that his wife had sold in his absence, and in the diary of his journey to the Netherlands there is constant mention of such sales. Nuremberg was very much behind Antwerp or Venice in the price paid for works of art; and the possibilities of such a market as Rome had very likely tempted Dürer to trust his prentice with an unusual quantity of prints. His worldly affairs were neither brilliant nor secure; yet we shall find him tempted on receiving an important commission to spend so much in time and material as to make it impossible for him to realise a profit. We are accustomed to think that these trials were spared to artists in the past by the munificence of patrons: but apart from the fact that patrons often paid only with promises or by granting credit, at Nuremberg there were few magnificent patrons, and its burghers were in no way so generous or so extravagant as those of Venice or Antwerp. In fact, Dürer's position was very similar to that of the modern artist, who finds little and insufficient patronage, and can make more if he is lucky by the reproduction of his creations for the great public. But Dürer still had one advantage over his fellow-sufferers of to-day – that of being his own publisher. Doubtless portraits were as popular then as nowadays; but if the public taste had not been prostituted by a seductive commercialism to the degree that at present obtains, on the other hand, at Nuremberg at least, the fashion seems to have been very little developed; and most of Dürer's important portraits seem to have been the result of his sojourns away from home.

CHAPTER IV

DÜRER AND HIS PATRONS
AND FRIENDS

I

Dürer had hitherto occasionally enjoyed the patronage of the wise
Elector, Frederick of Saxony, for whom he painted the brilliant
Adoration of the Magi in the Uffizi. He was soon to obtain that of
Maximilian, but this genial and eccentric emperor proved a fussy
patron, as quick to change his mind and to interfere with
impossible demands and criticisms, as he was slow to pay and
deficient in means for being truly generous. There are a certain
number of letters which give a glimpse of Dürer's relations with
his clients; they show him appealing always to the judgment of
artists against the ignorant buyer, and giving more than he
bargained to give, though thereby he eats up his legitimate
profits; lastly, they show him vowing never again to enter upon
work so unprofitable, but to give all his time to the creation of
engravings and woodcuts. The first is written to Michael Behaim,
who died in 1511, and had commissioned him to make a design
for a woodcut of his coat of arms.

DEAR MASTER MICHAEL BEHAIM, – I send you back the coat of arms again. Pray let it stay as it is. No one could improve it for you, for I made it artistically and with care. Those who see it and understand such matters will tell you so. If the leafwork on the helm were tossed up backward, it would hide the fillet. Your humble servant, ALBRECHT DÜRER.

The other letters concern the lost *Coronation of the Virgin*, the centre panel of an altar-piece of which the wings are still at Frankfurt, of which town Jacob Heller, who commissioned it, was a burgher. They were to be studio work, and are supposed to be chiefly due to Dürer's brother Hans. There is, however, one picture extant which gives an idea of the execution of the missing centre panel, the *Holy Trinity and All Saints* at Vienna; which, in spite of his vow never to do such work again, was commenced shortly after the *Coronation*, and for a Nuremberg patron. How much he was paid for it is not known; but it cannot have been a really adequate sum, as towards the end of his life he writes to the Nuremberg Council, "I have not received from people in this town work worth five hundred florins, truly a trifling and ridiculous sum, and not the fifth part of that has been profit." The preceding picture, referred to in the first letters, is the *Martyrdom of the Ten Thousand by Sapor II*. All three pictures were signed, like the *Feast of the Rose Garlands* by little finely-dressed portraits of the painter.

NÜRNBERG, *August* 28, 1507.

I did not want to receive any money in advance on it till I began to paint it, which, if God will, shall be the next thing after the Prince's work;[20] for I prefer not to begin too many things at once and then I do not become wearied. The Prince too will not be kept waiting, as he would be if I were to paint his and your pictures at the same time, as I had intended. At all events have confidence in me, for, so far as God permits, I will yet according to my power make something that not many men can equal.

Now many good nights to you. Given at Nürnberg on Augustine's day, 1507.

ALBRECHT DÜRER.

•

NÜRNBERG, March 19, *1508*.

Dear Herr Jacob Heller. In a fortnight I shall be ready with Duke Friedrich's work; after that I shall begin yours, and, as my custom is, I will not paint any other picture till it is finished. I will be sure carefully to paint the middle panel with my own hand; apart from that, the outer sides of the wings are already sketched in – they will be in stone colour; I have also had the ground laid. So much for news.

I wish you could see my gracious Lord's picture; I think it would please you. I have worked at it straight on for a year and gained very little by it; for I only get 280 Rhenish gulden for it, and I have spent all that in the time.

•

NÜRNBERG, *August 24, 1508*.

Now I commend myself to you. I want you also to know that in all my days I have never begun any work that pleased me better than this picture of yours which I am painting. Till I finish it I will not do any other work; I am only sorry that the winter will so soon come upon me. The days grow so short that one cannot do much.

I have still one thing to ask you; it is about the MADONNA [21] that you saw at my house; if you know of any one near you who wants a picture pray offer it to him. If a proper frame was put to it, it would be a beautiful picture, and you know that it is nicely done. I will let you have it cheap. I would not take less than fifty florins to paint one like it. As it stands finished in the house it might be damaged for me, so I would give you full power to sell it for me cheap for thirty florins – indeed, rather than that it should not be sold I would even let it go for twenty-five florins. I have certainly lost much food over it.

•

Nürnberg, November 4, 1508.

I am justly surprised at what you say in it about my last letter: seeing that you can accuse me of not holding to my promises to you. From such a slander each and everyone exempts me, for I bear myself, I trust, so as to take my stand amongst other straightforward men. Besides I know well what I have written and promised to you, and you know that in my cousin's house I refused to promise you to make a good thing, because I cannot. But to this I did pledge myself, that I would make something for you that not many men can. Now I have given such exceeding pains to your picture, that I was led to send you the aforesaid letter. I know that when the picture is finished all artists will be well pleased with it. It will not be valued at less than 300 florins. I would not paint another like it for three times the price agreed, for I neglect myself for it, suffer loss, and earn anything but thanks from you.

You further reproach me with having promised you that I would paint your picture with the greatest possible care that ever I could. That I certainly never said, or if I did I was out of my senses, for in my whole lifetime I should scarcely finish it. With such extraordinary care I can hardly finish a face in half a year; now your picture contains fully 100 faces, not reckoning the drapery and landscape and other things in it. Besides, who ever heard of making such a work for an altar-piece? no one could see it. But I think it was thus that I wrote to you – that I would paint the picture with great or more than ordinary pains because of the time which you waited for me.

You need not look about for a purchaser for my Madonna, for the Bishop of Breslau has given me seventy-two florins for it, so I have sold it well. I commend myself to you. Given at Nürnberg in the year 1508, on the Sunday after All Saints' Day.

ALBRECHT DÜRER.

•

NÜRNBERG, *March* 21, 1509.

I only care for praise from those who are competent to judge; and if Martin Hess praises it to you, that may give you the more confidence. You might also inquire from some of your friends who have seen it; they will tell you how it is done. And if you do not like the picture when you see it, I will keep it myself, for I have been begged to sell it and make you another. But be that far from me! I will right honourably hold with you to that which I have promised, taking you, as I do, for an upright man.

•

NÜRNBERG, *July* 10, 1509.

As you go on to say that if you had not bargained with me for the picture you would never do so now, and that I may keep it – I return you this answer: to retain your friendship, if I had to suffer loss by the picture, I would have done so, but now since you regret the whole business and provoke me to keep the picture I will do so, and that gladly, for I know how to get 100 florins more for it than you would have given me. In future I would not take 400 florins to paint another such as this.

ALBRECHT DÜRER.

NÜRNBERG, *July* 24, 1509. DEAR HERR HELLER, I have read the letter which you addressed to me. You write that you did not mean to decline taking the picture from me. To that I can only say that I don't understand what you do mean. When you write that if you had not ordered the picture you would not make the bargain again, and that I may keep it as long as I like and so on – I can only think that you have repented of the whole business, so

I gave you my answer in my last letter.

But, at Hans Imhof's persuasion, and having regard to the fact that you ordered the picture of me, and also because I should prefer it to find a place at Frankfurt rather than anywhere else, I have consented to send it to you for 100 florins less than it might well have brought me.

I am reckoning that I shall thus render you a pleasing service; otherwise I know well how I could draw far greater pecuniary advantage from it, but your friendship is dearer to me than any such trifling sum of money. I trust however that you would not wish me to suffer loss over it when you are better off than I. Make therefore your own arrangements and commands. Given at Nürnberg on Wine-Tuesday before James'. ALBRECHT DÜRER.

NÜRNBERG, *August 26*, 1509. First my willing service to you, dear Herr Jacob Heller. In accordance with your last letter I am sending the picture well packed and seen to in all needful points. I have handed it over to Hans Imhof and he has paid me another 100 florins. Yet believe me, on my honour, I am still out of pocket over it besides losing the time which I have bestowed upon it. Here in Nürnberg they were ready to give 300 florins for it, which extra 100 florins would have done very nicely for me had I not preferred to please and serve you by sending you the picture. For I value the keeping of your friendship at more than 100 florins. I would also rather have this painting at Frankfurt than anywhere else in all Germany.

If you think that I have behaved unfairly in not leaving the payment to your own free-will, you must bear in mind that this would not have happened if you had not written by Hans Imhof that I might keep the picture as long as I liked. I should otherwise gladly have left it to you even if thereby I had suffered a greater loss still. My impression of you is that, supposing I had promised to make you something for about ten florins and it cost me twenty, you yourself would not wish me to lose by it. So pray be content with the fact that I took 100 florins less from you than I might have got for the picture – for I tell you that they wanted to take it from me, so to speak, by force.

I have painted it with great care, as you will see, using none but the best colours I could get. It is painted with good ultramarine under, and over, and over that again, some five or six times; and then after it was finished I painted it again twice over so that it may last a long time. If it is kept clean I know it will remain bright and fresh 500 years, for it is not done as men are wont to paint. So have it kept clean and don't let it be touched or sprinkled with holy water. I feel sure it will not be criticised, or only for the purpose of annoying me; and I answer for it it will please you well. No one shall ever compel me to paint a picture again with so much labour. Herr Georg Tausy himself besought me to paint him a Madonna in a landscape with the same care and of the same size as this picture, and he would give me 400 florins for it. That I flatly refused to do, for it would have made a beggar of me. Of ordinary pictures I will in a year paint a pile which no one would believe it possible for one man to do in the time. But very careful nicety does not pay. So henceforth I shall stick to my engraving, and had I done so before I should to-day have been a richer man by 1000 florins.

I may tell you also that, at my own expense, I have had for the middle panel a new frame made which has cost me more than six florins. The old one I have broken off, for the joiner had made it roughly; but I have not had the other fastened on, for you wished it not to be. It would be a very good thing to have the rims screwed on so that the picture may not be shaken.

If anyone wants to see it, let it hang forward two or three finger breadths, for then the light is good to see it by. And when I come over to you, say in one, two, or three years' time, if the picture is properly dry, it must be taken down and I will varnish it over anew with some excellent varnish, which no one else can make; it will then last 100 years longer than it would before. But don't let anybody else varnish it, for all other varnishes are yellow, and the picture would be ruined for you. And if a thing, on which I have spent more than a year's work, were ruined it would be grief to me. When you have it set up be present yourself to see that it gets no harm. Deal carefully with it, for you will hear from your own and from foreign painters how it is done.

Give my greeting to your painter Martin Hess. My wife asks you for a *Trinkgeld*, but that is as you please, I screw you no higher, &c. And now I hold myself commended to you. Read by the sense, for I write in haste. Given at Nürnberg on Sunday after Bartholomew's, 1509. ALBRECHT DÜRER.

NÜRNBERG, *October 12*, 1509.

DEAR HERR JACOB HELLER, I am glad to hear that my picture pleases you, so that my labour has not been bestowed in vain. I am also happy that you are content about the payment – and that rightly, for I could have got 100 florins more for it than you have given me. But I preferred to let you have it, hoping, as I do, thereby to retain you as my friend down in your parts.

My wife thanks you very much for the present you have made her; she will wear it in your honour. My young brother also thanks you for the two florins *Trinkgeld* you sent him. And now I too thank you myself for all the honour &c. In reply to your question how the picture should be adorned I send you a slight design of what I should do if it were mine, but you must do what you like. Now, many happy times to you. Given on Friday before Gall's, 1509. ALBRECHT DÜRER.

Dürer must have commenced the All Saints picture almost immediately after having finished Heller's *Coronation of the Virgin*. Perhaps he had practically accepted the commission from Matthsus Landauer before he wrote to Heller that he would never again undertake a picture with so much work and labour in it, for he afterwards was as good as his word. This new work was for the chapel of an almshouse founded by Landauer and Erasmus Schiltkrot for twelve old men citizens of Nuremberg. The original frame designed by Dürer is now in the Germanic Museum, though a copy has replaced the picture. After the completion of the *Trinity and All Saints*, Dürer apparently carried out his threat and gave up painting for a dozen years, devoting his energies more especially to a magnificent series of engravings on copper. He also completed his series of wood engravings and published them with text, and produced a number of single cuts, many of them among his very best, like the *Assumption of the Magdalen*, and the *St. Christopher*, here reproduced.

II

In 1514 his mother died. He has recounted her death twice over, as he did that of his father already cited; for the single surviving leaf of the "other book" happens to contain this also. In the briefer chronicle he says:

Two years after my Father's death (i.e., 1504) I took my Mother into my house, for she had nothing more to live upon. So she dwelt with me till the year 1513, as they reckon it; when, early one Tuesday morning, she was taken suddenly and deadly ill, and thus she lay a whole year long. And a whole year after the day she was first taken ill, she received the holy sacraments and christianly passed away two hours before nightfall – it was on a Tuesday, the 17th day of May in the year 1514. I said the prayers for her myself. God Almighty be gracious to her.

The account in the "other book" is more circumstantial:

Now you must know that, in the year 1513, on a Tuesday before Rogation week, my poor afflicted Mother, whom two years after my Father's death, as she was quite poor, I took into my house, and after she had lived nine years with me, was one morning suddenly taken so deadly ill that we broke into her chamber; otherwise, as she could not open, we had not been able to come to her. So we carried her into a room downstairs and she received both sacraments, for every one thought she would die, because ever since my Father's death she had never been in good health.

Her most frequent habit was to go much to the church. She always upbraided me well if I did not do right, and she was ever in great anxiety about my sins and those of my brother. And if I went out or in her saying was always, "Go in the name of Christ." She constantly gave us holy admonitions with deep earnestness and she always had great thought for our souls' health. I cannot enough praise her good works and the compassion she showed to all, as well as her high character.

This my pious Mother bare and brought up eighteen children; she often had the plague and many other severe and strange illnesses, and she suffered great poverty, scorn, contempt, mocking words, terrors, and great adversities. Yet she bore no malice.

In 1514 (as they reckon it), on a Tuesday – it was the 17th day of May – two hours before nightfall and more than a year after the above-mentioned day in which she was taken ill, my Mother, Barbara Dürer, christianly passed away, with all the sacraments, absolved by papal power from pain and sin. But she first – gave me her blessing and wished me the peace of God, exhorting me very beautifully to keep myself from sin. She asked also to drink S. John's blessing, which she then did.

She feared Death much, but she said that to come before God she feared not. Also she died hard, and I marked that she saw something dreadful, for she asked for the holy-water, although, for a long time, she had not spoken. Immediately afterwards her eyes closed over. I saw also how Death smote her two great strokes to the heart, and how she closed mouth and eyes and departed with pain. I repeated to her the prayers. I felt so grieved for her that I cannot express it. God be merciful to her.

To speak of God was ever her greatest delight, and gladly she beheld the honour of God. She was in her sixty-third year when she died and I have buried her honourably according to my means.

God, the Lord, grant me that I too may attain a happy end, and that God with his heavenly host, my Father, Mother, relations, and friends may come to my death. And may God Almighty give unto us eternal life. Amen.

And in her death she looked much sweeter than when she was still alive.

III

Such was the home life of this great artist; and from homes presenting variations on this type proceeded probably all the giants of the Renaissance, whose work we think so surpasses in effort, in scope, and in efficiency, all that has been achieved since. This Christianity was unreformed; it existed side by side with dissolute monasteries and worldly cynical prelates, surrounded by sordid hucksters and brutal soldiery. Turn to Erasmus' portrait of Dean Colet, and we see that it existed in London, among the burghers, even in the household of a Lord Mayor. We are almost forced on the reflection that nothing that has succeeded to it has produced men equal to those who sprang immediately out of it.

However much and however justly the assurance of Christian assertion in the realm of theory may be condemned, the success of the Christian life, wherever it has approached a conscientious realisation, stands out among the multitudinous forms of its corruption; and those who catch sight of it are almost bound to exclaim in the spirit of Shakespeare's:

"How far that little candle throws his beams!
So shines a good deed in a naughty world."

I have heard a Royal Academician remark how even the poorest copies and reproductions of the masterpieces of Greek sculpture retain something of the charm and dignity of the original: whereas the quality of modern work is quickly lost in a reduction or even in a cast. I believe this may be best explained by the fact that the chief research of the Greek artist was to establish a beautiful proportion between the parts and the whole; and that fidelity to nature, dexterity of execution, the symbolism of the given subject, and even the finish of the surfaces, were always when necessary sacrificed to this. Whereas in modern work, even when the proportions of the whole are considered, which is rarely the case, they are almost without exception treated as secondary to one or more of these other qualities. Is it not possible that Jesus in his life laid down a proportion, similar to that of Greek masterpieces for the body, between the efforts and intentions which create the soul and pour forth its influence? – a proportion which, when it has been once thoroughly apprehended, may be subtly varied to suit new circumstances, and produce a similar harmony in spheres of activity with which Jesus himself had not even a distant connection? We often find that the rudest copies from copies of his actual life are like the biscuit china Venus of Milo sold by the Italian pedlar, which still dimly reflects the main beauties of the marble in the Louvre.

IV

In 1512 Kaiser Maximilian came to Nuremberg, and soon
afterward Dürer began working for him. The employment he
found for the greatest artist north of the Alps was sufficiently
ludicrous; and perhaps Dürer showed that he felt this, by treating
the major portion as studio work; though, no doubt, the
impatience of his imperial patron in a measure necessitated the
employment of many aids.

It is difficult to do justice to the fine qualities of Maximilian.
Perhaps he was not really so eccentric as he seems. The oddity of
his doings and sayings may be perhaps more properly attributed
to his having been a thorough German. The genial men of that
nation, even to-day and since it has come more into line in point
of culture with France and England, are apt to have a something
ludicrous or fantastic clinging to them; even Goethe did not
wholly escape. Maximilian was strong in body and in mind, and
brimming over with life and interest. We are told that when a
young man he climbed the tower of Ulm Cathedral by the help of
the iron rings that served to hold the torches by which it was
illuminated on high days and holidays. Again we read: "A
secretary had embezzled 3000 gulden. Maximilian sent for him
and asked what should be done to a confidential servant who had
robbed his master. The secretary recommended the gallows.
'Nay, nay,' the Emperor said, and tapped him on the shoulder, 'I
cannot spare you yet'"; an anecdote which reveals more good
sense and a larger humanity than either monarchs or others are
apt to have at hand on such vexing occasions. Thausing says
admirably, "A happy imagination and a great idea of his exalted
position made up to him for any want of success in his many wars
and political negotiations," and elsewhere calls him the last of the
"nomadic emperors," who spent their lives travelling from palace
to palace and from city to city, beseeching, cajoling, or threatening
their subjects into obedience. He himself said, "I am a king of
kings. If I give an order to the princes of the empire, they obey if

they please, if they do not please they disobey." He was even then called "the last of the knights," because he had an amateurish passion for a chivalry that was already gone, and was constantly attempting to revive its costumes and ordinances. Then, like certain of the Pharaohs of Egypt, he was pleased to read of, and see illustrated by brush and graver, victories he had never won, and events in which he had not shone. He himself dictated or planned out those wonderful lives or allegories of a life which might have been his. It was on such a work of futile self-glorification that he now wished to employ Dürer.

The novelty of the art of printing, and the convenience to a nomadic emperor of a monument that could be rolled up, suggested the form of this last absurdity – a monster woodcut in 92 blocks which, when joined together, produced a picture 9 feet by 10, representing what had at first been intended as an imitation of a Roman triumphal arch; but so much information about so many more or less dubious ancestors, &c., had to be conveyed by quaint and conceited inventions, that in the end it was rather comparable to the confusion of a Juggernaut car, which never-the-less imposes by a barbarous wealth and magnificence of fantastic detail. And to this was to be joined another monster, representing on several yards of paper a triumphal procession of the emperor, escorted by his family, and the virtues of himself and ancestors, &c. Such is fortune's malice that Dürer, who alone or almost alone had conceived of the simplicity of true dignity and the beauty of choice proportions and propriety, should have been called upon by his only royal patron to superintend a production wherein the rank and flaccid taste of the time ran riot. The absurdity, barbarism, and grotesque quaintness of this monument to vanity cannot be laid exclusively at Maximilian's door; for the architecture, particularly of the fountains, in Altdorfer's or Manuel's designs, and in those of many others, reveals a like wantonness in delighted elaboration of the impossible and unstructural. The scholars and pedantic posturers who surrounded the emperor no doubt improved and abetted. Probably it was this

Juggernaut element, inherited from the Gothic gargoyle, which Goethe censured when he said that "Dürer was retarded by a gloomy fantasy devoid of form or foundation." Perhaps this was written at a period when the great critic was touched with that resentment against the Middle Ages begotten by the feeling that his own art was still encumbered by its irrational and confused fantasy. We who certainly are able to take a more ample view of Dürer's situation in the art of his times, see that he is rather characterised by an effort which lay in exactly the same direction as that of Goethe's own; and while sympathising with the irritation expressed, can also admire the great engraver for having freed himself in so large a degree from the influence of fantasy "devoid of form and foundation," even as the justest Shakespearean criticism admires the degree in which the author of Othello freed himself from Elizabethan conceits. It is difficult to appreciate the difference for a great artist in having the general taste with rather than against the purer tendencies of his art. Probably the Greeks and certain Italians owe their freedom from eccentricity, in a very large measure, to this cause. But I intend to treat these questions more at length in dealing with Dürer's character as an artist and creator. It was necessary to touch on the subject here, because Maximilian embodies the peculiar and fantastic aftergrowth, which sprouted up in some northern minds from the old stumps remaining from the great mediaeval forest of thoughts and sentiments which had gradually fallen into decay. All around, even in the same minds, waved the saplings of the New Birth when these old stumps put forth their so fantastic second youth, seeming for a time to share in the new vigour, though they were never to attain expansion and maturity.

V

Thausing shrewdly remarks, "This love of fame and naïve delight in the glorification of his own person are further proofs that the Emperor Max was the true child of his age. No one was so akin to him in this respect as the painter of his choice, Albert Dürer." This last is a reference to those strutting, finely-dressed portraits of the artist which stand beside the entablatures bearing his name, that of his birthplace, the date, &c., in four out of the five most elaborate pictures which Dürer painted. But I would like to suggest that probably this apparent resemblance to his royal patron is not thus altogether well accounted for. May there not have been something of Homer's invocation of his Muse, or of that sincerity which makes Dante play such a large part in the "Divine Comedy"? – something resembling the ninth verse of the Apocalypse: "I John, who also am your brother and companion in tribulation ... was in the isle that is called Patmos ... and heard behind me a great voice as of a trumpet, saying...." Those little strutting portraits of himself sprung, perhaps, out of this relation to those about him of the man by native gift very superior, who is not made contemptuous or inclined to emphasise his isolation, but who is ever ready to say, "It is I, be not afraid." The man who painted and conceived this is the man you know, whom you have admired because he carried his fine clothes so well in your streets. Here I am even in the midst of this massacre of saints, I have conceived it all and taken a whole year to elaborate it; and since you see me looking so cool and well-dressed in the midst of it, you need not be offended or overwhelmed. Such is ever the naïvety of great souls among those whose culture is primitive. It is like the boasted bravery of the eldest among little children, wholly an act of kindness and consideration, not a selfish vaunt. That they should be admired and trusted is for them a foregone conclusion; and when they call on that admiration and trust, they do it merely for the sake of those whom they would encourage and console, for whose sakes they will even hide whatever in them is really unworthy of such admiration and such trust.

We do not easily realise the corporate character of life in those days. Very much that seems to us quaint and absurd drew proper significance from the practical solidarity that then obtained; what appears to us a strange vanity or parade may have appeared to them respect for the guild, the town, the country to which they belonged. Dürer signed "Noricus," – of Nuremberg; – and preferred its little lucrative citizenship to those more remunerative offered by Venice and Antwerp. "Let all the world behold how fine the artist of Nuremberg is." Just as he says, "God gave me diligence," so it seems natural to him to attribute a large half of his fame and glory to his native town. In many respects the great man of those days felt less individual than an ordinary man does now; for classes did not so merge one into the other, and their character was more distinct and authoritative. The little portrait of himself added to those wonderful *tours-de-force* made them something that belonged to Nuremberg and to Germans. Even so it would be with some treasure cup, all gold and jewels, belonging to a village schoolmaster, which none of his neighbours dared look at save in his presence; for he was the son of a great baron whom his elder brothers robbed of everything except this, and his presence among them alone made them able to feel that it really belonged to their village, was theirs in a fashion. These suggestions will not, I think, appear fantastic to those who ponder on the apparently vainglorious address of much of Dürer's work, and keep in mind such a passage from his writings as this:

> "I would gladly give everything I know to the light, for the good of cunning students who prize such art more highly than silver and gold. I further admonish all who have any knowledge in these matters that they write it down. Do it truly and plainly, not toilsomely and at great length, for the sake of those who seek and are glad to learn, to the great honour of God and your own praise. If I then set something burning, and ye all add to it skilful furthering, a blaze may in time arise therefrom which shall shine throughout the whole world."[22]

But still, even if such considerations may bring many to accept my explanation of this contrast, I do not want to over-insist on it. I think that wherever men have been superior in character, as well as in gift or rank, to those about them, something of this spirit of the good eldest child in a family is bound to be manifested. But just as such a child may be veritably boastful and vain at other times, – however purely now and then, in crises of apparent difficulty or danger, its vaunt and strut may spring from real kindness and a considerate wish to inspire courage in the younger and weaker; – so doubtless there was a haughtiness, sometimes a fault, in Dürer as in Milton.

VI

But we have been led a long way from Kaiser Max and his portable monument. The reader will re-picture how the court arrived at Nuremberg like a troop of actors, whose performance was really their life, and was taken quite seriously and admired heartily by the good and solid burghers. This old comedy, often farce, entitled "The Importance of Authority," is no longer played with such a telling make-up, or with such showy properties as formerly, but is still as popular as ever; as we Londoners know, since the last few years have given us perhaps an over-dose of processions, illuminations, &c. &c. In this case the chief actors in the show piece were men of mark of an exceptionally entertaining character; with many of them Dürer and Pirkheimer were soon on the best of terms.

Foremost, Johann Stabius, the companion of the Emperor for sixteen years without intermission in war and in peace, who was associated with Dürer to provide the written accompaniment for the monument; a literary jack-of-all-trades of ready wit and lively presence. A contemporary records: "The emperor took constant pleasure in the strange things which Stabius devised, and esteemed him so highly that he instituted a new chair of Astronomy and Mathematics for him at Vienna," in the Collegium Poetarum et Mathematicorum founded in the year 1501, under the presidency of Conrad Celtes.

In all probability there would have been besides the learned protonotary of the supreme court, Ulrich Varenbuler, often mentioned as a friend in the letters of Erasmus and Pirkheimer, and the subject of the largest of Dürer's portrait woodcuts, which shows him to us some ten years later, still a handsome trenchant personality, with a liking for fine clothes, and the self-reliant expression of a man who is conscious that the thought he takes for the morrow is not likely to be in vain.

It may be that Dürer then met for the first time too the Imperial architect, Johannes Tscherte, for whom he afterwards drew two armillary spheres, to take the place of those on which he had cast ridicule; for Pirkheimer wrote to Tscherte: "I wish you could have heard how Albert Dürer spoke to me about your plate, in which there is not one good stroke, and laughed at me. What honour it will do us when it makes its appearance in Italy, and the clever painters there see it!" To which Tscherte replied: "Albert Dürer knows me well, he is also well aware that I love art, though I am no expert at it; let him if he likes despise my plate, I never pretended it was a work of art." And in a later letter he speaks "of the armillary spheres drawn by our common friend Albert Dürer." He was one of those who helped Dürer in his mathematical and geometrical studies; and he, like Pirkheimer, dedicated books to him. Although the mathematics of those times are hardly considered seriously nowadays, they then ranked with verse-making as a polite accomplishment, and had all the charm of novelty. Dürer, no doubt, had some gift that way, as he seems to have made a hobby of them during many years. Besides those who came in the Imperial troop, Dürer had many opportunities of meeting men of this kind, for such were constantly passing through Nuremberg. Dürer has left us what are evidently portraits of some whose names are lost: of others we have both name and likeness, among them the English ambassador, Lord Morley.

In 1515 "Rafahel de' Urbin, who is held in such high esteem by the Pope, he made these naked figures and sent them to Albrecht Dürer at Nuremberg to show him his hand." This shows us that travellers through Nuremberg sometimes brought with them something of the breath of the great Renaissance in Italy. The drawing, which bears the above inscription in Dürer's own handwriting on the back, is a fine one in red sanguine, representing the same male model in two different poses, in the Albertina. Raphael had, we are told by Lodovico Dolce, drawings, engravings, and woodcuts of Dürer's hanging in his studio; and Vasari tells us he said: "If Dürer had been acquainted with the antique he would have surpassed us all." The Nuremberg master, in return for the drawing, sent a portrait of himself to Raphael, which has unfortunately been lost. There appears to have been quite a rage for Dürer's work in Italy, and above all at Rome: we know that it provoked Michelangelo to remonstrate; probably on many lips it was merely a vaunt of superior knowledge or taste, as rapture over the conjectural friends or aids of a great quatrocentist is to-day. The tokens of esteem which he won from distinguished travellers, and this drawing which reached him testifying to the interest and friendship felt for him by the Italian whose fame was most widespread, must have been full of encouragement, and have compensated in some measure for the feeling he had that he was only a hanger-on at Nuremberg, though he might still have been "a gentleman" in Venice. Yet Nuremberg itself furnished many desirable or notable acquaintances. There was Dürer's neighbour, the jurist, Lazarus Spengler; later the most prominent reformer in Nuremberg, who in 1520 dedicated to him his "Exhortation and Instruction towards the leading of a virtuous life," addressing him as "his particular and confidential friend and brother," whom he considers, "without any flattery, to be a man of understanding, inclined to honesty and every virtue, who has often in our daily familiar intercourse been to me in no common degree a pattern and an example to a more circumspect way of life;" whom, finally, he asks to improve his little book to the best of his ability. Dürer had before this rendered him service in designing his coat of arms for a woodcut and furnishing a frontispiece to his translation of Eusebius' "Life of St. Jerome." He was, moreover, a poet, author of "an often-translated song"; he wrote verses to discourage Dürer from spending his time in producing the doggerel rhymes which at one time he was moved to attempt, – framing poems of didactic import, and publishing one or two on separate sheets with a woodcut at the top, in spite of the inappreciative reception given to them by Spengler and Pirkheimer. Besides Spengler, there were "Christopher Kress, a soldier, a traveller, and a town councillor;" and Caspar Nützel, of one of the oldest families, and Captain-general of the town bands. Both of these went with Dürer to the Diet at Augsburg in 1518. The martial Paumgartners were two brothers for whom Dürer painted the early triptych at Munich (see page 204). One of them is supposed to figure as St. George in the All Saints picture. Lastly, there were the Imhoffs, the merchant princes of Nuremberg, as the Fuggers were at Augsburg. A son of the family married Felicitas, Pirkheimer's favourite daughter, in 1515, and Dürer stood godfather to their little Hieronymus in 1518. It is easy to imagine that there was many a supper and dinner, when a thousand strange subjects were even more strangely discussed; when Pirkheimer now made them roar with a hazardous joke, or again dumbfounded them with Greek quotations pompously done into German, or made their flesh creep and the superstitions of their race stir in them by mysteriously enlarging on his astrological lore, – for to his many weaknesses he added this, which was then scarcely recognised as one.

VII

In spite of all his wealthy and influential friends, Dürer found it difficult to get the emperor to indemnify him for his labours, though the Town Council had received a royal mandate as early as 1512 from Landau. The following is an extract:

> Whereas our and the Empire's trusty Albrecht Dürer has devoted much zeal to the drawings he has made for us at our command, and has promised henceforth ever to do the like, whereat we have received particular pleasure; and whereas we are informed on all hands that the said Dürer is famous in the art of painting before all other Masters: we have therefore felt ourself moved, to further him with our especial grace, and we accordingly desire you with earnest solicitude, for the affection you bear us, to make the said Dürer free of all town imposts, having regard to our grace and to his famous art, which should fairly turn to his profit with you, &c.

The town councillors sent some of their principal members to treat with Dürer, and he resigned his claim "in order to honour the said councillors and to maintain their privileges, usages, and rights." In 1515 the drawings for the "Gate of Honour" were finished, and Dürer began to press again for pay. Stabius had promised to speak for him, but nothing had come of it. Albrecht thought Christoph Kress could be of more avail; so he wrote to him:

(No date, but certainly 1515). DEAR HERR KRESS, The first thing I have to ask you is to find out from Herr Stabius whether he has done anything in my business with his Imperial Majesty, and how it stands. Let me know this in the next letter you write to my Lords. Should it happen that Herr Stabius has made no move in the matter, ... Point out in particular to his Imperial Majesty that I have served his Majesty for three years, spending my own money in so doing, and if I had not been diligent the ornamental work would have been nowise so successfully finished. I therefore pray his Imperial Majesty to recompense me with the 100 florins – all which you know well how to do. You must know also that I made many other drawings for his Majesty besides the "Triumph."

Not long after this, Maximilian, by a *Privilegium* (dated Innsbruck, September 6, 1515), settled an annual pension of 100 florins on the artist.

> We Maximilian, by God's grace, &c., make openly known by this letter for ourself and our successors in the Empire, and to each and every one to wit, that we have regarded and considered the art, skill, and intelligence for which our and the Empire's trusty and well-beloved Albrecht Dürer has been praised before us, and likewise the pleasing, honest and useful services which he has often and willingly done for us and the Holy Empire and also for our own person in many ways, and which he still daily does and henceforward may and shall do: and that we therefore, of set purpose, after mature deliberation, and with the full knowledge of ourself and the Princes and Estates of the Empire, have graciously promised and granted to this same Dürer what we herewith and by virtue of this letter make known:
>
> *That is to say*, that one hundred florins Rhenish shall be yielded, given, and paid by the honourable, our and the Empire's trusty and well-beloved Burgomaster and Council of the town of Nürnberg and their successors unto the said Albrecht Dürer, against his quittance, all his life long and no longer, yearly and in every year, on our behalf, out of the customary town contributions which the said Burgomaster and Council of the town of Nürnberg are bound to yield and pay, yearly and in every year, into our Treasury. And whatever the said Burgomaster and Council of the town of Nürnberg and their successors shall yield, give, and pay to the said Albrecht Dürer, as stands written above, against his quittance, the same sum shall be accepted and reckoned to them as paid and yielded for the customary town contributions which they, as stands written above, are bound to pay into our Treasury, as if they had paid the same into our own hands and received our quittance therefor, and no harm or detriment shall in anywise be done therefor unto them or their successors by us or our successors in the Empire. Whereof this letter, sealed with our affixed seal, is witness.
>
> Given, &c.

Thus Dürer became Court painter: in return for his salary he had to work. As soon as the "Gate of Honour" was finished, there was the "Car of Triumph" to be taken in hand, the first sketch for it (now in the Albertina) having already been made about 1514-15. In December 1514 Schönsperger, the Augsburg printer, printed a splendid "Book of Hours" for Maximilian. The type was specially made for the book, and only a few copies were printed, some on fine vellum with large margins. One copy which Maximilian intended for his own use was sent to Dürer that he might decorate the margins with pen-drawings in various coloured inks. Of this work there exist forty-three pages by Dürer himself and eight by Cranach at Munich, and at Besançon thirty-five pages by Burgkmair, Altdorfer, Baldung Grien, and Hans Dürer. Marvellously deft and light-handed as are Dürer's free-hand arabesques, embellished by racy sketches of which these borders consist, they are nevertheless touched with a like unsatisfactory character with the other works undertaken for Maximilian, and are almost as far removed from the spirit and performance of the best period for this kind of work, as is the *Triumphal Arch* from that of Titus.

Dürer was also employed on another woodcut representing a long row of saintly ancestors of this eccentric sovereign. He accompanied Caspar Nützel and Lazarus Spengler, the representatives of Nuremberg, to the Diet of Augsburg, and there made some drawings of his royal patron, on one of which is written, "This is my dear Prince Max, whom I, Albrecht Dürer, drew at Augsburg in his little room upstairs in the palace, in the year 1518, on the Monday after St. John the Baptist's day." And Melanchthon narrates that "once Max himself took the charcoal in hand to make his mind clear to his trusty Albert, and was vexed to find that the charcoal kept breaking short in his hand when Dürer said; 'Most gracious emperor, I would not that your Majesty should draw so well as I do!' by which he meant, 'I am practised in this, and it is my province; thou, Emperor, hast harder tasks and another calling.'"

VIII

A charming letter from Charitas Pirkheimer gives us a little sunlit glimpse of the tone of Dürer's lighter hours.

The prudent and wise Masters Caspar Nützel, Lazarus Spengler, and Albrecht Dürer, for the time being at Augsburg, our gracious Masters and good friends.

Jesus.

As a friendly greeting, prudent, wise, gracious Masters and especially good friends, cousins, and wellwishers, I desire every good thing for you, from the Highest Good. I received with great pleasure your friendly letter and its news of a kind suited to my order, or rather my trade; and I read it with such great devotion that more than once tears ran down my eyes over it – truly rather tears of laughter than of sorrow. I consider it a subject for great thankfulness that, with such important business and so much gaiety on hand, your Wisdoms do not forget me, but find time to instruct me, poor little nun, about the monastic life whereof you now have a clear reflection before your eyes. I conclude from this that doubtless some good spirit drove you, my gracious and dear Masters, to Augsburg, so that you might learn from the example of the free Swabian spirits how to instruct and govern the poor imprisoned sand-bares.[23]

For since our trusty Master Warden (Caspar Nützel), as a lover of the Church, likes to help in a thorough reformation, he should first behold a pattern of holy observance in the Swabian League. Let Master Lazarus Spengler, too, inform himself well about the apostolic mode of common life, so that at the annual audit he may be able to give us and others counsel and guidance, how we may run through everything, that nought remain over. And Master Albrecht Dürer, also, who is such a genius and master at drawing, he may very carefully inspect the stately buildings, and then if some day we want to alter our choir he will know how to give us advice and help in making ample slide-windows (? blinds), so that our eyes may not be quite blinded.

I shall not further trouble you, however, to bring us music to learn to sing by notes, for our beer is now so very sour that I fear the dregs might stick fast among the four reeds or voices, and produce such strange sounds that the dogs would fly out of the church. But I must humbly pray you not quite to wear out your eyes over the black and white magpies, so as no longer to know the little grey wolves at Nürnberg. I have heard much of the sharp-witted Swabians all my life, but it would be well if we learnt more from them, now that they are so wisely labouring with his Imperial Majesty to save the Apostolic life from being done away with. It is easy to see what very different lovers of the Church they are from our Masters here.

Pardon me, my dear and gracious Masters, this my playful letter. It is all done *in caritate – summa summarum*; and the end of it is that I should rejoice at your speedy return in health and happiness with the glad accomplishment of the business committed to you. For this I and my sisters heartily pray God day and night; still we cannot carry it through alone, so I counsel you to entreat the pious and pure hearts (of Augsburg) to sing in high quavers that thereby things may speed well. And now many happy times to you!

Given at Nürnberg on September 3, 1518.

SISTER CHARITAS, unprofitable Abbess of S. Clara's at Nürnberg.

Dürer returned with a letter to the Town Council of Nürnberg, from which the following extract is taken:

Honourable, trusty, and well-beloved, Whereas you are bound to pay us on next St. Martin's day year a remainder, to wit 200 florins Rhenish, out of the accustomed town contribution which you are wont to render into our and the Empire's treasury....We earnestly charge you to deliver and pay the said 200 florins, accepting our quittance therefor, unto our and the

Empire's trusty and well-beloved Albrecht Dürer, our painter, on account of his honest services, willingly rendered to us at our command for our "Car of Triumph" and in other ways; and, at the said time, these 200 florins shall be deducted for you from the accustomed town contribution. Thus you will perform our earnest desire.

Given, &c.

Dürer procured a receipt for the 200 florins, signed by the emperor himself. But before "next St. Martin's day year," Maximilian was dead, and the 200 florins no longer his to dispose of, being due to the new Emperor Charles V. The municipal authorities of Nürnberg refused to pay until his Privilegium had been confirmed by Maximilian's successor.

Dürer wrote the following letter to the Council:

NÜRNBERG, April 27, 1519.

Prudent, honourable and wise, gracious, dear Lords. Your Honours are aware that, at the Diet lately holden by his Imperial Roman Majesty, our most gracious lord of very praiseworthy memory, I obtained a gracious assignment from his Imperial Majesty of 200 florins from the yearly payable town contributions of Nürnberg. This assignment was granted to me, after many applications and much trouble, in return for the zealous work and labour, which, for a long time previously, I had devoted to his Majesty. And he sent you order and command to that effect, signed with his accustomed signature, and quittance in all form, which quittance, duly sealed, is in my hands.

Now I rest humbly confident that your Honours will graciously remember me as your obedient burgher, who has employed much time in the service and work of his Imperial Majesty, our most rightful Lord, with but small recompense, and has thereby lost both profit and advantage in other ways. And

* 134

therefore I trust that you will now deliver me these 200 florins to his Imperial Majesty's order and quittance, that so I may receive a fitting reward and satisfaction for my care, pains, and work – as, no doubt, was his Imperial Majesty's intention.

But seeing that some Emperor or King might in the future claim these 200 florins from your Honours, or might not be willing to spare them, but might some day demand them back again from me, I am, therefore, willing to relieve your Honours and the town of this chance, by appointing and mortgaging, as security and pledge therefor, my tenement situated at the corner under the Veste, and which belonged to my late father, that so your Honours may suffer neither prejudice nor loss thereby. Thus am I ready to serve your Honours, my gracious rulers and Lords.

Your Wisdoms' willing burgher, ALBRECHT DÜRER.

Dürer next wrote "to the honourable, most learned Master Georg Spalatin, Chaplain to my most gracious lord, Duke Friedrich, the Elector" of Saxony.

The letter is undated, but clearly belongs to the early part of the year 1520.

Most worthy and dear Master, I have already sent you my thanks in the short letter, for then I had only read your brief note. It was not till afterwards, when the bag in which the little book was wrapped was turned inside out, that I for the first time found the real letter in it, and learnt that it was my most gracious Lord himself who sent me Luther's little book. So I pray your worthiness to convey most emphatically my humble thanks to his Electoral Grace, and in all humility to beseech his Electoral Grace to take the praiseworthy Dr. Martin Luther under his protection for the sake of Christian truth. For that is of more importance to us than all the power and riches of this world; because all things pass away with time, Truth alone endures for ever.

God helping me, if ever I meet Dr. Martin Luther, I intend to draw a careful portrait of him from the life and to engrave it on copper, for a lasting remembrance of a Christian man who helped me out of great distress. And I beg your worthiness to send me for my money anything new that Dr. Martin may write.

As to Spengler's "Apology for Luther," about which you write, I must tell you that no more copies are in stock; but it is being reprinted at Augsburg, and I will send you some copies as soon as they are ready. But you must know that, though the book was printed here, it is condemned in the pulpit as heretical and meet to be burnt, and the man who published it anonymously is abused and defamed. It is reported that Dr. Eck wanted to burn it in public at Ingolstadt, as was done to Dr. Reuchlin's book.

With this letter I send for my most gracious lord three impressions of a copper-plate of my most gracious lord of Mainz, which I engraved at his request. I sent the copper-plate with 200 impressions as a present to his Electoral Grace, and he graciously sent me in return 200 florins in gold and 20 ells of damask for a coat. I joyfully and thankfully accepted them, especially as I was in want of them at that time.

His Imperial Majesty also, of praiseworthy memory, who died too soon for me, had graciously made provision for me, because of the great and long-continued labour, pains, and care, which I spent in his service. But now the Council will no longer pay me the 100 florins, which I was to have received every year of my life from the town taxes, and which was yearly paid to me during his Majesty's lifetime. So I am to be deprived of it in my old age and to see the long time, trouble, and labour all lost which I spent for his Imperial Majesty. As I am losing my sight and freedom of hand my affairs do not look well. I don't care to withhold this from you, kind and trusted Sir.

If my gracious lord remembers his debt to me of the staghorns, may I ask your Worship to keep him in mind of them, so that I may get a fine pair. I shall make two candlesticks of them.

I send you here two little prints of the Cross from a plate

engraved in gold. One is for your Worship. Give my service to Hirschfeld and Albrecht Waldner. Now, your Worship, commend me faithfully to my most gracious lord, the Elector.

Your willing ALBRECHT DÜRER at Nürnberg.

CHAPTER V

DÜRER, LUTHER
AND THE HUMANISTS

I

But while Dürer was thus busily at work or dunning his great debtors, Luther had appeared. In 1517 he nailed his ninety-five theses to the door of Wittenberg church, and Cardinal Caietan by the unlucky Leo X. was poured like oil upon the fire which they had lighted. Luther had been summoned to meet the Cardinal at the Diet of Augsburg, where Dürer went to see Maximilian, though he only arrived there after our friends from Nuremberg had departed. However, Luther passed through Nuremberg on foot, and borrowed a coat of a friend there in order to figure with decency before the Diet. Yet Dürer probably did not meet him, although the words in the letter to George Spalatin, quoted above, "If ever I meet Dr. Martin Luther, I intend to draw a careful portrait of him and engrave it on copper," do not forbid the possibility of this early meeting before the Reformer had become so famous. Next the Pope tried to soothe by sending Miltitz with flatteries and promises – a man that could smile and weep to order, but who succeeded neither with the Elector Frederic, nor with Luther, nor with Germany. At Nuremberg the preacher Wenzel Link soon formed a little reformed congregation, to which Dürer, Pirkheimer, Spengler, Nützel, Scheurl, Ebner, Holz-schurher, and others belonged. We have already seen how, soon after this, Dürer was anxious for Luther's safety, by the letter to the wise Elector, quoted above; and in 1518 he sent Luther a number of his prints, and soon after joined with others of Link's hearers to send a greeting of encouragement. And before long we find him jotting down a list of sixteen of Luther's tracts, either because he intended to get and read them, or because they were already his; and on the back of a drawing we find the following outline of the faith such as he then apprehended it, in which we see clearly that Christ has become the voice of conscience – the power in a man by which he recognises and creates good.

Seeing that through disobedience of sin we have fallen into everlasting Death, no help could have reached us save through the incarnation of the Son of God, whereby He through His innocent suffering might abundantly pay the Father all our guilt, so that the Justice of God might be satisfied. For He has repented, of and made atonement for the sins of the whole world, and has obtained of the Father Everlasting Life. Therefore Christ Jesus is the Son of God, the highest power, who can do all things, and He is the Eternal life. Into whomsoever Christ comes he lives, and himself lives in Christ. Therefore all things are in Christ good things. There is nothing good in us except it becomes good in Christ. Whosoever, therefore, will altogether justify himself is unjust. *If we will what is good, Christ wills it in us.* No human repentance is enough to equalise deadly sin and be fruitful.

In this the old mythological language is retained, but it has received a new interpretation or significance, and this quite without the writer's perceiving what he is doing. Christ is affirmed to have repented of the sins of the whole world. Among the early heresiarchs there were, I believe, some who went so far as to hold that he had committed the sins before he repented of them, and triumphed over their effects by his sufferings and death. In any case, a similar feeling is expressed by our odd mystic Blake in his "Everlasting Gospel":

> "If He (Jesus) intended to take on sin,
> His mother should an harlot have bin."

The actual records of Christ are too meagre the moment he is regarded as an allegory of human life; and such additions to the creed spring naturally out of the ardent seeker's desire to realise the universality implied in the dogma of his Godhead, which is accepted even by Blake as a historical fact beyond question. It was not the character of so much as can be perceived of the universe which daunted Luther and Dürer, as it daunts the serious man to-day. They accepted what appears to us a cheap and easy subterfuge, because they believed it to have been prescribed by God; the ambiguous inferences which such a prescription must logically cast on the Divine character did not arrest their attention. What they gained was a free conscience, a conscience in which Christ was, to use their language, and which was in Christ; and for practical piety this was sufficient. They themselves had not made up their minds on theoretical points; it was only in the face of their opponents that they thought of arming themselves with like weapons, and sought a mechanical agreement upon questions about which no one ever has known, or probably ever can know, anything at all. This was where Luther's pugnacity betrayed him; so that little by little he seems to lose spiritual beauty, as the monk, all fire and intensity, is transformed into the "plump doctor," and again into the bird of ill omen who croaked.

> "The arts are growing as if there was to be a new start and the world was to become young again. I hope God will finish with it. We have come already to the White Horse. Another hundred years and all will be over."

Compare this with Dürer's:

"Sure am I that many notable men will arise, all of whom will write both well and better about this art than I."

"Would to God that it were possible for me to see the work and art of the mighty masters to come, who are yet unborn, for I know that I might be improved."

I do not want to judge Luther harshly; he had done splendidly, and it is difficult to meddle with worldly things without soiling one's fingers and depressing one's heart; but I ask which of these two quotations expresses man's most central character best – the desire for nobler life – which reveals the more admirable temper? (Dürer had been touched by the spirit of the Renaissance as well as by that of the Reformation; we can distinguish easily when he is speaking under the one influence, when under the other, and the contrast often impresses one as the contrast between the above quotations. And it gives us great reason to deplore that the two spirits could not work side by side as they did in Dürer and a few rare souls, but that in the world there was war between them.) It seems inevitable that the things men fight about should always be spoiled. The best part of written thought is something that cannot be analysed, cannot therefore be defended or used for offence; it is a spirit, an emanation, something that influences us more subtly than we know how to describe.

We see by the passage quoted that Dürer was not only influenced by Luther's heroism, but by his doctrinal theorising. Unfortunately we do not know whether he outgrew this second and less admirable influence. Did he feel like his friend Pirkheimer in the end, that "the new evangelical knaves made the old popish knaves seem pious by contrast?" Milton under similar circumstances came to think that "New Presbyter is but old Priest writ large." Probably not; for just as we know he did not abandon what seemed to him beautiful and helpful in old Catholic ceremonies, usages, and conceptions, so probably he would not confuse what had been real gain in the Reformation with the excesses of Anabaptists or Socialists, or even of Luther himself or his followers. There is no reason to suppose he would have judged so hastily as the gouty irascible Pirkheimer, however much he may have deplored the course of events. It must have been evident to thoughtful men, then, that it was impossible for so large an area to be furnished with properly trained pastors in so short a time, and that therefore more or less deplorable material was bound to be mingled in the official *personnel* of the new sect. It is impossible, when we consider how he solved the precisely parallel difficulty in aesthetics, not to feel that if he had had time given him, he would have arrived in point of doctrine at a moderation similar to that of Erasmus.

Men deliberate and hold numberless differing opinions about beauty.... Being then, as we are, in such a state of error, I know not certainly what the ultimate measure of true beauty is.... Because now we cannot altogether attain unto perfection shall we, therefore, wholly cease from learning? By no means ... for it behoveth the rational man to choose the good.

Luther imagined that the faith that saved was entire confidence in the fact that a bargain had been struck between the Persons of the Trinity, according to which Christ's sacrifice should be accepted as satisfying the justice of his Father, outraged by Adam's fault. To-day this appears to the majority of educated men a fantastic conception. For them the faith that saves is love of goodness, as love of beauty saves the artist from mistakes into which his intelligence would often plunge him. Jesus has no claim upon us superior to his goodness and his beauty; nor can we conceive of the possibility of such a claim. But we recognise with Dürer that we do not know what the true measure of goodness and beauty is, and all that we can do is to choose always the good and the beautiful according to the measure of our reason – to the fulness of the light at present granted to us.

II

The curiosity of the modern man of science no doubt is descended from that of men like Leonardo and the early Humanists, but it differs from almost more than it resembles it. The motive power behind both is no doubt the confidence of the healthy mind that the human intelligence will ultimately prove adequate to comprehend the spectacle of the universe. But for the Humanists, for Dürer and his friends, the consciousness of the irreconcilableness of that spectacle with the necessary ideals of human nature had not produced, as in our contemporaries and our immediate forerunners it has produced, either the atrophy of expectation which afflicts some, or the extravagance of ingenuity that cannot rest till it has rationalised hope, which torments others. They were saddled with neither the indifference nor the restlessness of the modern intellect. They escaped like boys on a holiday. They felt conscious of doing what their schoolmaster meant them to do, though they were actually doing just what they liked. It was all for the glory of God in Dürer's mind; but how or why God should be pleased with what he did, did not trouble him. He engraved and sold impressions of a plate representing a sow with eight legs; he made a drawing, which is at Oxford, of an infant girl with two heads and four arms, and calmly wrote beneath it: –

Item, in the year reckoned 1512, after the birth of Christ, such a creature (*Frucht*) as is represented above, was born in Bavaria, on the Lord of Werdenberg's land, in a village named Ertingen over against Riedlingen. It was on the 20th of the hay month (July), and they were baptized, the one head Elspett, the other Margrett.

Just so, Luther is no more than St. Paul abashed to say that God had need of some men intended for dishonour, as a potter makes some vessels for honourable, some for dishonourable uses. The modern mind at once reflects: "If that is the case, so much the worse for God; by so much is it impossible that I should ever worship Him;" and it will prefer any prolongation of "that most wholesome frame of mind, a suspended judgment," to accepting a solution so cheap as that offered by the Apostle and Reformer, which has come to seem simply injurious.

The spirit of the enlarged schoolboy was, I think, really the attitude of the best minds then and onwards to Descartes and Spinoza. They gave themselves up to the study of nature without ceasing to belong to their school, yet freed, as on a holiday, from the constraint of being actually in it. Yet, in regard to their personal and social life, at least north of the Alps, the majority of such men were very consciously and dutifully under "their great taskmaster's eye"; and in that also they differ in a measure from the more part of modern scientists.

Dürer made up a rhinoceros from a sketch and description sent to him from Portugal, whither the uncouth creature had been brought in a ship from Goa. Dürer's drawing was engraved and became the parent of innumerable rhinoceroses in lesson-books, doing service right down well into the late century, as Thausing assures us. The unfortunate original was sent as a present to Leo X., who wanted to see him fight with an elephant which had made him laugh by squirting water and kneeling down to be blessed as sensibly as a Christian. So the poor beast was shipped again, only to be shipwrecked near Porto Venere, where he was last seen swimming valiantly, but hopelessly impeded by his chain, and baffled by the rocky shore. In the Netherlands, Dürer's curiosity to see a whale nearly resulted in his own shipwreck, and indirectly produced the malady which finally killed him. But Dürer's curiosity was really most scientific where it was most artistic; in his portraits, in his studies of plants and birds and the noses of stags, or the slumber of lions.

Doubtless it was not a very dissimilar motive which gained him entrance into the women's bath at Nuremberg, for we see he must have been there by the beautiful pen drawing at Bremen and the slighter one of the same subject at Chatsworth. These drawings may also illustrate what in his book on the Proportion he calls the words of difference – stout, lean, short, tall, &c. (see p. 285), as he would seem to have chosen types as various as possible, ranging from the human sow to the slim and dignified beauty. In the same spirit he studied perspective and the art of measuring; he felt the importance to art of inquiry in these directions; nevertheless, to seize the beautiful elements in nature was ever the object of his efforts, however, roundabout they may sometimes appear to us. "The sight of a fine human figure is above all things the most pleasing to us, wherefore I will first construct the right proportions of a man." His aesthetic curiosity had nothing in common with that which considers all objects and appearances as equally interesting. What he meant by Nature, when he bid the artist have continual recourse to her, was far from being the momentary and accidental appearance of any thing or things anywhere, – which the modern "student of Nature" admires because he has neither sufficient force of character to prefer, nor sufficient right feeling to defer to the preferences of those who have more.

Leonardo's natural history is delightful reading, because it combines such fantastic and inventive fables as surpass even the happiest efforts of our nonsense writers with a beautiful openness of mind which we see oftener in children than in sages, – which is, in fact, the seriousness of those who are truly learning, and are not too conscious of what has already been learnt.

As a boy adds to the pleasure he has in adventuring further and further into a cave the delight of awesome supposition – for what may not the next turn reveal? – and is pleased to feel all his young machinery ready instantly to enact a panic if his torch should blow out, and laughs at each furtive rehearsal of his own terror in which he indulges; – so the Humanists turned from astronomy to astrology, and used their skill in mathematics to play with horoscopes which they more than half believed might bite. There was just enough doubt as to whether any given wonder was a miracle to make it interesting; and at any moment the pall of superstition might stifle the flickering light of inquiry, as we feel was the case when Dürer writes:

The most wonderful thing I ever saw occurred in the year 1503, when crosses fell upon many persons, and especially on children rather than on elder people. Amongst others, I saw one of the form which I have represented below. It had fallen into Eyrer's maid's shift, as she was sitting in the house at the back of Pirkheimer's (i.e., in the house where Dürer was born). She was so troubled about it that she wept and cried aloud, for she feared that she must die because of it.

I have also seen a comet in the sky.

And again, the terror caused by a very bad and strange dream passes the bounds of play; and one feels that the belief that a vision of the night might produce or prefigure dreadful change was for him something a great deal more serious than for the dilettante spiritualist and wonder-tickler of to-day. He writes:

In the night between Wednesday and Thursday after Whit Sunday (May 30-31, 1525), I saw this appearance in my sleep – how many great waters fell from heaven. The first struck the earth about four miles away from me with terrific force and tremendous noise, and it broke up and drowned the whole land. I was so sore afraid that I awoke from it. Then the other waters fell, and as they fell they were very powerful, and there were many of them, some further away, some nearer. And they came down from so great a height that they all seemed to fall with an equal slowness. But when the first water that touched the earth had very nearly reached it, it fell with such swiftness, with wind and roaring, and I was so sore afraid that when I awoke my whole body trembled, and for a long while I could not recover myself. So when I arose in the morning, I painted it above here as I saw it God turn all these things to the best. ALBRECHT DÜRER.

The instinct for recording which dictates such a note as this is characteristic of Dürer, and called into being many of his drawings. Many such naïve and explicit records as that on the drawing which Raphael sent him are to be found in the flyleaves of books and on the margins of prints and drawings, his possessions. In such notes we may see not only an effect of the curiosity, and desire to arrange and co-ordinate information, which resulted in modern science; but something that is akin to that worship and respect for the deeds and productions of those long dead or in distant countries, in which the human spirit relieved itself from the oppressive expectation of judgment and vengeance which had paralysed it, as the beauty of the supernatural world was lost sight of behind its terrors, and witches and wizards engrossed the popular mind, in which for a time saints and angels had held the ascendancy. The future now became the return of a golden age; not a garish and horrible novelty called heaven and hell, but a human society beautiful as that of the Greeks, grand as that of republican Rome, sweet and hospitable as the household of Jesus and Mary. The Reformation is in part a return of the old fears; but Dürer has recorded only one bad dream, whereas he tells that he was often visited by dreams worthy of the glorious Renascence. "Would to God it were possible for me to see the work and art of the mighty masters to come, who are yet unborn, for I know that I might be improved. Ah! *how often in my* sleep do I behold great works of art and beautiful things, the like whereof never appear to me awake, but so soon as I awake even the remembrance of them leaveth me!" Why was he not sent to Rome to see the ceiling of the Sistina and Raphael's Stanze? Perchance it was these that he saw in his dreams?

CHAPTER VI

DÜRER'S JOURNEY
TO THE NETHERLANDS

I

It is even more the case with Dürer's journal written in the Netherlands than with the letters from Venice that, like life itself, it is full of repetitions and over-insistence on what is insignificant. I quote the most interesting passages, and as there is never a good reason for doing again what has already been well done; I am happy to quote Sir Martin Conway's excellent notes, having found occasion to add only one. Dürer set out on July 12, 1520, with his wife and her maid Susanna. It was probably this Susanna who three years later married Georg Penz, one of "the three godless painters." Dürer took a great many prints and woodcuts, books both to sell and to give as presents; and besides he took a sketch book in which he made silver-point sketches and portraits. A good number of its pages have come down to us, and a great many of the portraits he mentions having taken were done in it, and then cut out to give to the sitter. All these drawings are on the same sized paper. We reproduce one of them here (see page 156). Besides this sketch-book he evidently had a memorandum-book in which he recorded what he did, what he spent, whom he saw, and occasionally what he felt or what he wished. The original is lost, but an old copy of it is in the Bamberg Library.

July 12. – On Thursday after Kilian's, I, Albrecht Dürer, at my own charges and costs, took myself and my wife (and maid Susanna) away to the Netherlands. And the same day, after passing through Erlangen, we put up for the night at Baiersdorf and spent there 3 pounds less 6 pfennigs.

July 13. – Next day, Friday, we came to Forchheim, and there I paid 22 pf. for the convoy.

Thence I journeyed to Bamberg, where I presented the Bishop (Georg III. Schenk von Limburg[24]) with a Madonna painting, a Life of our Lady, an Apocalypse, and a Horin's worth of engravings. He invited me as his guest, gave me a Toll-pass[25] and three letters of introduction, and paid my bill at the inn, where I had spent about a florin.

I paid six florins in gold to the boatman who took me from Bamberg to Frankfurt.

Master Lukas Benedict and Hans,[26] the painter, sent me wine.

•

ANTWERP, *August* 2-26, 1520.

At Antwerp I went to Jobst Plankfelt's[27] inn, and the same evening at Fuggers' Factor,[28] Bernhard Stecher invite and gave us a costly meal. My wife, however, dined at the inn. I paid the driver three gold florins for bringing us three, and one st. I paid for carrying the goods.

August 4. – On Saturday after the feast of St. Peter in Chains my host took me to see the Burgomaster's (Arnold van Liere) house at Antwerp. It is newly built and beyond measure large, and very well ordered, with spacious and exceedingly beautiful chambers, a tower splendidly ornamented, a very large garden – altogether a noble house, the like of which I have nowhere seen in all Germany. The house also is reached from both sides by a very long street, which has been quite newly built according to the Burgomaster's liking and at his charges.

I paid three st. to the messenger, two pf. for bread, two pf. for ink.

August 5. – On Sunday, it was St. Oswald's Day, the painters invited me to the hall of their guild, with my wife and maid. All their service was of silver, and they had other splendid ornaments and very costly meats. All their wives also were there. And as I was being led to the table the company stood on both sides as if they were leading some great lord. And there were amongst them men of very high position, who all behaved most respectfully towards me with deep courtesy, and promised to do everything in their power agreeable to me that they knew of. And as I was sitting there in such honour the Syndic (Adrian Horebouts) of Antwerp came, with two servants, and presented me with four cans of wine in the name of the Town Councillors of Antwerp, and they had bidden him say that they wished thereby to show their respect for me and to assure me of their good will. Wherefore I returned them my humble thanks and offered my humble service. After that came Master Peeter (Frans), the town-carpenter, and presented me with two cans of wine, with the offer of his willing services. So when we had spent a long and merry time together till late in the night, they accompanied us home with lanterns in great honour. And they begged me to be ever assured and confident of their good will, and promised that in whatever I did they would be all-helpful to me. So I thanked them and laid me down to sleep.

The Treasurer (Lorenz Sterk) also gave me a child's head (painted) on linen, and a wooden weapon from Calicut, and one of the light wood reeds. Tomasin, too, has given me a plaited hat of alder bark. I dined once with the Portuguese, and have given a brother of Tomasin's three fl. worth of engravings.

Herr Erasmus[29] has given me a small Spanish *mantilla* and three men's portraits.

I took the portrait of Herr Niklas Kratzer,[30] an astronomer. He lives with the King of England, and has been very helpful and useful to me in many matters. He is a German, a native of Munich. I also made the portrait of Tomasin's daughter, Mistress Zutta by name. Hans Pfaffroth[31] gave me one Philips fl. for taking his portrait in charcoal. I have dined once more with Tomasin. My host's brother-in-law entertained me and my wife once. I changed two light florins for twenty-four st. for living expenses, and I gave one st. *t&k&d* to a man who let me see an altar-piece.

August 19. – On the Sunday after our dear Lady's Assumption I saw the great Procession from the Church of our Lady at Antwerp, when the whole town of every craft and rank was assembled, each dressed in his best according to his rank. And all ranks and guilds had their signs, by which they might be known. In the intervals great costly pole-candles were borne, and their long old Frankish trumpets of silver. There were also in the German fashion many pipers and drummers. All the instruments were loudly and noisily blown and beaten.

I saw the procession pass along the street, the people being arranged in rows, each man some distance from his neighbour, but the rows close one behind another. There were the Goldsmiths, the Painters, the Masons, the Broderers, the Sculptors, the Joiners, the Carpenters, the Sailors, the Fishermen, the Butchers, the Leatherers, the Clothmakers, the Bakers, the Tailors, the Cordwainers – indeed, workmen of all kinds, and many craftsmen and dealers who work for their livelihood. Likewise the shopkeepers and merchants and their assistants of all kinds were there. After these came the shooters with guns, bows, and cross-bows, and the horsemen and foot-soldiers also. Then followed the watch of the Lords Magistrates. Then came a fine troop all in red, nobly and splendidly clad. Before them, however, went all the religious Orders and the members of some Foundations very devoutly, all in their different robes.

A very large company of widows also took part in this procession. They support themselves with their own hands and observe a special rule. They were all dressed from head to foot in white linen garments, made expressly for the occasion, very sorrowful to see. Among them I saw some very stately persons. Last of all came the Chapter of our Lady's Church, with all their clergy, scholars, and treasurers. Twenty persons bore the image of the Virgin Mary with the Lord Jesus, adorned in the costliest manner, to the honour of the Lord God.

In this procession very many delightful things were shown, most splendidly got up. Waggons were drawn along with masques upon ships and other structures. Behind them came the company of the Prophets in their order, and scenes from the New Testament, such as the Annunciation, the Three Holy Kings riding on great camels and on other rare beasts, very well arranged; also how our Lady fled to Egypt – very devout – and many other things, which for shortness I omit. At the end came a great Dragon which St. Margaret and her maidens led by a girdle; she was especially beautiful. Behind her came St. George with his squire, a very goodly knight in armour. In this host also rode boys and maidens most finely and splendidly dressed in the costumes of many lands, representing various Saints. From beginning to end the procession lasted more than two hours before it was gone past our house. And so many things were there that I could never write them all in a book, so I let it well alone.

•

BRUSSELS *August* 26-*September* 3, 1520.

In the golden chamber in the Townhall at Brussels I saw the four paintings which the great Master Roger van der Weyden[32] made. And I saw out behind the King's house at Brussels the fountains, labyrinth, and Beast-garden[33]; anything more beautiful and pleasing to me and more like a Paradise I have never seen. Erasmus is the name of the little man who wrote out my supplication at Herr Jacob de Bannisis' house. At Brussels is a very splendid Townhall, large, and covered with beautiful carved stonework, and it has a noble open tower. I took a portrait at night by candlelight of Master Konrad of Brussels, who was my host; I drew at the same time Doctor Lamparter's son in charcoal, also the hostess.

I saw the things which have been brought to the King from the new land of gold (Mexico), a sun all of gold a whole fathom broad, and a moon all of silver of the same size, also two rooms full of the armour of the people there, and all manner of wondrous weapons of theirs, harness and darts, very strange clothing, beds, and all kinds of wonderful objects of human use, much better worth seeing than prodigies. These things were all so precious that they are valued at 100,000 florins. All the days of my life I have seen nothing that rejoiced my heart so much as these things, for I saw amongst them wonderful works of art, and I marvelled at the subtle *Ingenia* of men in foreign lands. Indeed, I cannot express all that I thought there.

At Brussels I saw many other beautiful things besides, and especially I saw a fish bone there, as vast as if it had been built up of squared stones. It was a fathom long and very thick, it weighs up to 15 cwt., and its form resembles that drawn here. It stood up behind on the fish's head. I was also in the Count of Nassau's house,[34] which is very splendidly built and as beautifully adorned. I have again dined with my Lords (of Nürnberg).

When I was in the Nassau house in the chapel there, I saw the good picture[35] that Master Hugo van der Goes painted, and I saw the two fine large halls and the treasures everywhere in the house, also the great bed wherein fifty men can lie. And I *saw* the great stone which the storm cast down in the field near the Lord of Nassau. The house stands high, and from it there is a most beautiful view, at which one cannot but wonder: and I do not believe that in all the German lands the like of it exists.

Master Bernard van Orley, the painter, invited me and prepared so costly a meal that I do not think ten fl. will pay for it. Lady Margaret's Treasurer (Jan de Marnix), whom I drew, and the King's Steward, Jehan de Metenye by name, and the Town-Treasurer named Van Busleyden invited themselves to it, to get me good company. I gave Master Bernard a *Passion* engraved in copper, and he gave me in return a black Spanish bag worth three fl. I have also given Erasmus of Rotterdam a *Passion* engraved in copper.

I have once more taken Erasmus of Rotterdam's portrait[36] I gave Lorenz Sterk a sitting *Jerome* and the *Melancholy*, and took a portrait of my hostess' godmother. Six people whose portraits I drew at Brussels have given me nothing. I paid three st. for two buffalo horns, and one st. for two Eulenspiegels.[37]

ANTWERP, *September 6-October 4*, 1520.

I have paid one st for the printed "Entry into Antwerp," telling how the King was received with a splendid triumph – the gates very costly adorned – and with plays, great joy, and graceful maidens whose like I have seldom seen.[38] I changed one fl. for expenses. I saw at Antwerp the bones of the giant. His leg above the knee is 5-1/2 ft. long and beyond measure heavy and very thick; so with his shoulder blades – a single one is broader than a strong man's back – and his other limbs. The man was 18 ft. high, had ruled at Antwerp and done wondrous great feats, as is more fully written about him in an old book,[39] which the Lords of the Town possess.

The studio (school) of Raphael of Urbino has quite broken up since his death,[40] but one of his scholars, Tommaso Vincidor of Bologna[41] by name, a good painter, desired to see me. So he came to me and has given me an antique gold ring with a very

✳ 154

well cut stone. It is worth five fl., but already I have been offered the double for it. I gave him six fl. worth of my best prints for it. I bought a piece of calico for three st.; I paid the messenger one st.; three st. I spent in company.

I have presented a whole set of all my works to Lady Margaret, the Emperor's daughter, and have drawn her two pictures on parchment with the greatest pains and care. All this I set at as much as thirty fl. And I have had to draw the design of a house for her physician the doctor, according to which he intends to build one; and for drawing that I would not care to take less than ten fl. I have given the servant one st., and paid one st. for brick-colour.

•

October 1. – On Monday after Michaelmas, 1520, I gave Thomas of Bologna a whole set of prints to send for me to Rome to another painter who should send me Raphael's work[42] in return. I dined once with my wife. I paid three st. for the little tracts. The Bolognese has made my portrait;[43] he means to take it with him to Rome.

•

AACHEN, *October 7-26, 1520.*

October 7. – At Aachen I saw the well-proportioned pillars,[44] with their good capitals of green and red porphyry (*Gassenstein*) which Charles the Great had brought from Rome thither and there set up. They are correctly made according to Vitruvius' writings.

October 23. – On October 23 King Karl was crowned at Aachen. There I saw all manner of lordly splendour, more magnificent than anything that those who live in our parts have seen – all, as it has been described.

•

KÖLN, *October 26 – November 14, 1520.*

I bought a tract of Luther's for five white pf., and the "Condemnation of Luther," the pious man, for one white pf.; also a rosary for one white pf. and a girdle for two white pf., a pound of candles for one white pf.

November 12. – I have made the nun's portrait. I gave the nun seven white pf. and three half-sheet engravings. My confirmation[45] from the Emperor came to my Lords of Nürnberg for me on Monday after Martin's, in the year 1520, after great trouble and labour.

ANTWERP, *November* % – *December* 3, 1520.

At Zierikzee, in Zeeland, a whale has been stranded by a high tide and a gale of wind. It is much more than 100 fathoms long, and no man living in Zeeland has seen one even a third as long as this is. The fish cannot get off the land; the people would gladly see it gone, as they fear the great stink, for it is so large that they say it could not be cut in pieces and the blubber boiled down in half a year.

ZEELAND, *December* 3-14, 1520.

December 8. – I went to Middelburg. There, in the Abbey, is a great picture painted by Jan de Mabuse – not so good in the modelling (*Hauptstreichen*) as in the colouring. I went next to the Veere, where lie ships from all lands; it is a very fine little town.

At Arnemuiden, where I landed before, a great misfortune befel me. As we were pushing ashore and getting out our rope, a great ship bumped hard against us, as we were in the act of landing, and in the crush I had let every one get out before me, so that only I, Georg Kotzler,[46] two old wives, and the skipper with a small boy were left in the ship. When now the other ship bumped against us, and I with those named was still in the ship and could not get out, the strong rope broke; and thereupon, in the same moment, a storm of wind arose, which drove our ship back with force. Then we all cried for help, but no one would risk himself for us. And the wind carried us away out to sea. Thereupon the skipper tore his hair and cried aloud, for all his men had landed and the ship was unmanned. Then were we in fear and danger, for the wind was strong and only six persons in the ship. So I spoke to the skipper that he should take courage (*er sollt ein Herz fahen*) and have hope in God, and that he should consider what was to be done. So he said that if he could haul up the small sail he would try if we could come again to land. So we toiled all together and got it feebly about half-way up, and went on again towards the land. And when the people on shore, who had already given us up, saw how we helped ourselves, they came to our aid and we got to land.

Middelburg is a good town; it has a very beautiful Townhall with a fine tower. There is much art shown in all things here. In the Abbey the stalls are very costly and beautiful, and there is a splendid gallery of stone; and there is a fine Parish Church. The town was besides excellent for sketching (*köstlich au konterfeyen*). Zeeland is fine and wonderful to see because of the water, for it stands higher than the land. I made a portrait of my host at Arnemuiden. Master Hugo and Alexander Imhof and Friedrich the Hirschvogels' servant gave me, each of them, an Indian cocoa-nut which they had won at play, and the host gave me a sprouting bulb.

December 9 – Early on Monday we started again by ship and went by the Veere and Zierikzee and tried to get sight of the great fish,[47] but the tide had carried him off again.

ANTWERP, *December* 14 – *April* 6, 1521

I have eaten alone thus often.

I took portraits of Gerhard Bombelli and the daughter of Sebastian the Procurator.

February 10. – On Carnival Sunday the goldsmiths invited me to dinner early with my wife. Amongst their assembled guests were many notable men. They had prepared a most splendid meal, and did me exceeding great honour. And in the evening the old Bailiff of the town[48] invited me and gave a splendid meal, and did me great honour. Many strange masquers came there. I have drawn the portrait in charcoal of Florent Nepotis, Lady Margaret's organist. On Monday night Herr Lopez invited me to the great banquet on Shrove-Tuesday, which lasted till two o'clock, and was very costly. Herr Lorenz Sterk gave me a Spanish fur. To the above-mentioned feast very many came in costly masks, and especially Tomasin and Brandan. I won two fl. at play.

I dined once with the Frenchman, twice with the Hirschvogels' Fritz, and once with Master Peter Aegidius[49] the Secretary, when Erasmus of Rotterdam also dined with us.

I have twice more drawn with the metal-point the portrait of the beautiful maiden for Gerhard.

I made Tomasin a design, drawn and tinted in half colours, after which he intends to have his house painted.

I bought the five silk girdles, which I mean to give away, for three fl. sixteen st.; also a border (*Borte*) for twenty st. These six borders I sent to the wives of Caspar Nützel, Hans Imhof, Sträub, the two Spenglers, and Löffelholz,[50] and to each a good pair of gloves. To Pirkheimer I sent a large cap, a costly inkstand of buffalo horn, a silver Emperor, one pound of pistachios, and three sugar canes. To Caspar Nützel I sent a great elk's foot, ten large fir cones, and cones of the stone-pine. To Jacob Muffel I sent a scarlet breastcloth of one ell; to Hans Imhof's child an embroidered scarlet cap and stone-pine nuts; to Kramer's wife four ells of silk worth four fl.; to Lochinger's wife one ell of silk worth one fl.; to the two Spenglers a bag and three fine horns each; to Herr Hieronymus Holzschuher a very large horn.

BRUGES AND GHENT, *April* 6-11, 1521.

I saw the chapel[51] there which Roger painted, and some pictures by a great old master. I gave one st. to the man who showed us them. Then I bought three ivory combs for thirty st. They took me next to St. Jacob's and showed me the precious pictures by Roger and Hugo,[52] who were both great masters. Then I saw in our Lady's Church the alabaster[53] Madonna, sculptured by Michelangelo of Rome. After that they took me to many more churches and showed me all the good pictures, of which there is an abundance there; and when I had seen the Jan van Eyck[54] and all the other works, we came at last to the painters' chapel, in which there are good things. Then they prepared a banquet for me, and I went with them from it to their guild-hall, where many honourable men were gathered together, both goldsmiths, painters and merchants, and they made me sup with them. They gave me presents, sought to make my acquaintance, and did me great honour. The two brothers, Jacob and Peter Mostaert, the councillors, gave me twelve cans of wine; and the whole assembly, more than sixty persons, accompanied me home with many torches. I also saw at their shooting court the great fish-tub on which they eat; it is 19 feet long, 7 feet high, and 7 feet wide. So early on Tuesday we went away, but before that I drew with the metal-point the portrait of Jan Prost, and gave his wife ten st. at parting.

•

On my arrival at Ghent the Dean of the Painters came to me and brought with him the first masters in painting; they showed me great honour, received me most courteously, offered me their goodwill and service, and supped with me. On Wednesday they took me early to the Belfry of St. John, whence I looked over the great wonderful town, yet in which even I had just been taken for something great. Then I saw Jan van Eycks picture;[55] it is a most precious painting, full of thought (*ein überköstlich hochverständig Gemühl*), and the Eve, Mary, and God the Father are specially good. Next I saw the lions and drew one with the metal-point.[56] And I saw at the place where men are beheaded on the bridge, the two statues erected (in 1371) as a sign that there a son beheaded his father.[57] Ghent is a fine and remarkable town; four great waters flow through it. I gave the sacristan (at St. Bavon's) and the lions' keepers three st. *trinkgeld*. I saw many wonderful things in Ghent besides, and the painters with their Dean did not leave me alone, but they ate with me morning and evening and paid for everything, and were very friendly to me. I gave away five st. at the inn at leaving. ANTWERP, *April 11-May 17*, 1521.

In the third week after Easter (April 21-27) a violent fever seized me, with great weakness, nausea, and headache. And before, when I was in Zeeland, a wondrous sickness overcame me, such as I never heard of from any man, and this sickness remains with me. I paid six st. for cases. The monk has bound two books for me in return for the art-wares which I gave him. I bought a piece of arras to make two mantles for my mother-in-law and my wife, for ten fl. eight st. I paid the doctor eight st., and three st. to the apothecary. I also changed one fl. for expenses, and spent three st. in company. Paid the doctor ten st. I again paid the doctor six st. During my illness Rodrigo has sent me many sweetmeats. I gave the lad four st. *trinkgeld*.

On Friday (May 17) before Whit Sunday in the year 1521, came tidings to me at Antwerp, that Martin Luther had been so treacherously taken prisoner; for he trusted the Emperor Karl, who had granted him his herald and imperial safe conduct. But as soon as the herald had conveyed him to an unfriendly place near Eisenach he rode away, saying that he no longer needed him. Straightway there appeared ten knights, and they treacherously carried off the pious man, betrayed into their hands, a man enlightened by the Holy Ghost, a follower of the true Christian faith. And whether he yet lives I know not, or whether they have put him to death; if so, he has suffered for the truth of Christ and because he rebuked the unchristian Papacy, which strives with its heavy load of human laws against the redemption of Christ. And if he has suffered it is that we may again be robbed and stripped of the truth of our blood and sweat, that the same may be shamefully and scandalously squandered by idle-going folk, while the poor and the sick therefore die of hunger. But this is above all most grievous to me, that, may be, God will suffer us to remain still longer under their false, blind doctrine, invented and drawn up by the men alone whom they call Fathers, by whom also the precious Word of God is in many places wrongly expounded or utterly ignored.

Oh God of heaven, pity us! Oh Lord Jesus Christ, pray for Thy people! Deliver us at the fit time. Call together Thy far-scattered sheep by Thy voice in the Scripture, called Thy godly Word. Help us to know this Thy voice and to follow no other deceiving cry of human error, so that we, Lord Jesus Christ, may not fall away from Thee. Call together again the sheep of Thy pasture, who are still in part found in the Roman Church, and with them also the Indians, Muscovites, Russians, and Greeks, who have been scattered by the oppression and avarice of the Pope and by false appearance of holiness. Oh God, redeem Thy poor people constrained by heavy ban and edict, which it nowise willingly obeys, continually to sin against its conscience if it disobeys them. Never, oh God, hast Thou so horribly burdened a people with human laws as us poor folk under the Roman Chair, who daily long to be free Christians, ransomed by Thy blood. Oh highest, heavenly Father, pour into our hearts, through Thy Son, Jesus Christ, such a light, that by it we may know what messenger we are bound to obey, so that with good conscience we may lay aside the burdens of others and serve Thee, eternal, heavenly Father, with happy and joyful hearts.

And if we have lost this man, who has written more clearly than any that has lived for 140 years, and to whom Thou hast given such a spirit of the Gospel, we pray Thee, oh heavenly Father, that Thou wouldst again give Thy Holy Spirit to one, that he may gather anew everywhere together Thy Holy Christian Church, that we may again live free and in Christian manner, and so, by our good works, all unbelievers, as Turks, Heathen, and Calicuts, may of themselves turn to us and embrace the Christian faith. But, ere Thou judgest, oh Lord, Thou wiliest that, as Thy Son, Jesus Christ, was fain to die by the hands of the priests, and to rise from the dead and after to ascend up to heaven, so too in like manner it should be with Thy follower Martin Luther, whose life the Pope compasseth with his money, treacherously towards God. Him wilt thou quicken again. And as Thou, oh my Lord, ordainedst thereafter that Jerusalem should for that sin be destroyed, so wilt thou also destroy this self-assumed authority of the Roman Chair. Oh Lord, give us then the new beautified Jerusalem, which descendeth out of heaven, whereof the Apocalypse writes, the holy, pure Gospel, which is not obscured by human doctrine.

Every man who reads Martin Luther's books may see how clear and transparent is his doctrine, because he sets forth the holy Gospel. Wherefore his books are to be held in great honour, and not to be burnt; unless indeed his adversaries, who ever strive against the truth and would make gods out of men, were also cast into the fire, they and all their opinions with them, and afterwards a new edition of Luther's works were prepared. Oh God, if Luther be dead, who will henceforth expound to us the holy Gospel with such clearness? What, oh God, might he not still have written for us in ten or twenty years!

Oh all ye pious Christian men, help me deeply to bewail this man, inspired of God, and to pray Him yet again to send us an enlightened man. Oh Erasmus of Rotterdam, where wilt thou stop? Behold how the wicked tyranny of worldly power, the might of darkness, prevails. Hear, thou knight of Christ! Ride on by the side of the Lord Jesus. Guard the truth. Attain the martyr's crown. Already indeed art thou an aged little man (*ein altes*

Männiken), and myself have heard thee say that thou givest thyself but two years more wherein thou mayest still be fit to accomplish somewhat. Lay out the same well for the good of the Gospel and of the true Christian faith, and make thyself heard. So, as Christ says, shall the Gates of Hell (the Roman Chair) in no wise prevail against thee. And if here below thou wert to be like thy master Christ and sufferedst infamy at the hands of the liars of this time, and didst die a little the sooner, then wouldst thou the sooner pass from death unto life and be glorified in Christ. For if thou drinkest of the cup which He drank of, with Him shalt thou reign and judge with justice those who have dealt unrighteously. Oh Erasmus, cleave to this that God Himself may be thy praise, even as it is written of David. For thou mayest, yea verily thou mayest overthrow Goliath. Because God stands by the Holy Christian Church, even as He only upholds the Roman Church, according to His godly will. May He help us to everlasting salvation, who is God, the Father, the Son, and Holy Ghost, one eternal God. Amen.

Oh ye Christian men, pray God for help, for His judgment draweth nigh and His justice shall appear. Then shall we behold the innocent blood which the Pope, Priests, Bishops, and Monks have shed, judged and condemned (*Apocal.*). These are the slain who lie beneath the Altar of God and cry for vengeance, to whom the voice of God answereth: Await the full number of the innocent slain, then will I judge.

•

ANTWERP, *May* 17 – *June* 7, 1521.

Master Gerhard,[58] the illuminator, has a daughter about eighteen years old named Susanna. She has illuminated a *Salvator* on a little sheet, for which I gave her one fl. It is very wonderful that a woman can do so much. I lost six st. at play. I saw the great Procession at Antwerp on Holy Trinity day. Master Konrad gave me a fine pair of knives, so I gave his little old man a *Life of our Lady* in return. I have made a portrait in charcoal of Master

Jan,[59] goldsmith of Brussels, also one of his wife. I have been paid two fl. for prints. Master Jan, the Brussels goldsmith, paid me three Philips fl. for what I did for him, the drawing for the seal and the two portraits. I gave the Veronica, which I painted in oils, and the *Adam and Eve* which Franz did, to Jan, the goldsmith, in exchange for a jacinth and an agate, on which a Lucretia is engraved. Each of us valued his portion at fourteen fl. Further, I gave him a whole set of engravings for a ring and six stones. Each valued his portion at seven fl. I bought two pairs of shoes for fourteen st., and two small boxes for two st. I changed two Philips fl. for expenses. I drew three *Leadings-forth*[60] and two Mounts of Olives on five half-sheets. I took three portraits in black and white on grey paper. I also sketched in black and white on grey paper two Netherland costumes. I painted for the Englishman his coat of arms, and he gave me one fl. I have also at one time and another done many drawings and other things to serve different people, and for the more part of my work have received nothing. Andreas of Krakau paid me one Philips fl. for a shield and a child's head. Changed one il. for expenses. I paid two fl. for sweeping-brushes. I saw the great procession at Antwerp on Corpus Christi day; it was very splendid. I gave four st. as trinkgeld. I paid the doctor six st. and one st. for a box. I have dined five times with Tomasin. I paid ten st. at the apothecary's, and gave his wife fourteen st. for the clyster and himself.... To the monk who confessed my wife I gave eight st.

•

MECHLIN, June 7 and 8, 1521.

At Mechlin I lodged with Master Heinrich, the painter, at the sign of the Golden Head.[61] And the painters and sculptors bade me as guest at my inn and did me great honour in their gathering. I went also to Poppenreuter[62] the gunmaker's house, and found wonderful things there. And I went to Lady Margaret's and showed her my *Emperor*,[63] and would have presented it to her, but she so disliked it that I took it away with me.

And on Friday Lady Margaret showed me all her beautiful things. Amongst them I saw about forty small oil pictures, the like of which for precision and excellence I have never beheld. There also I saw more good works by Jan (de Mabuse), and Jacob Walch.[64] I asked my Lady for Jacob's little book, but she said she had already promised it to her painter.[65] Then I saw many other costly things and a precious library.[66]

ANTWERP, *June* 8 – *July* 3, 1521.

Master Lukas, who engraves in copper, asked me as his guest. He is a little man, born at Leyden in Holland; he was at Antwerp.

I have drawn with the metal-point the portrait of Master Lukas van Leyden.[67]

The man with the three rings has overreached me by half. I did not understand the matter. I bought a red cap for my god-child[68]for eighteen st. Lost twelve st. at play. Drank two st.

Cornelius Grapheus, the Secretary, gave me Luther's "Babylonian Captivity,"[69] in return for which I gave him my three Large Books.

I reckoned up with Jobst and found myself thirty-one fl. in his debt, which I paid him; therein were charged and deducted the two portrait heads which I painted in oils, for which he gave five pounds of borax Netherlands weight. In all my doings, spendings, sales, and other dealings, in all my connections with high and low, I have suffered loss in the Netherlands; and Lady Margaret in particular gave me nothing for what I made and presented to her. And this settlement with Jobst was made on St. Peter and Paul's day.

On our Lady's Visitation, as I was just about to leave Antwerp, the King of Denmark sent to me to come to him at once, and take his portrait, which I did in charcoal. I also did that of his servant Anton, and I was made to dine with the King, and he behaved graciously towards me. I have entrusted my bale to

Leonhard Tucher and given over my white cloth to him. The carrier with whom I bargained did not take me; I fell out with him. Gerhard gave me some Italian seeds. I gave the new carrier (*Vicarius*) the great turtle shell, the fish-shield, the long pipe, the long weapon, the fish-fins, and the two little casks of lemons and capers to take home for me, on the day of our Lady's Visitation, 1521.

BRUSSELS, *July* 3-12, 1521.

I noticed how the people of Antwerp marvelled greatly when they saw the King of Denmark, to find him such a manly, handsome man and come hither through his enemy's land with only two attendants. I saw, too, how the Emperor rode forth from Brussels to meet him, and received him honourably with great pomp. Then I saw the noble, costly banquet, which the Emperor and Lady Margaret held next day in his honour.

Thomas Bologna has given me an Italian work of art; I have also bought a work for one st.

A few days later when the Dürers arrived at Cologne the journal breaks off abruptly, as the last few leaves are missing: but there is every reason to suppose that they got back safely to Nuremberg two or three weeks later.

II

This journal shows us how the influence of a greater centre of civilisation strengthened the spirit of the Renascence in Dürer: it is marked by his having again taken up the paint brushes to do the best sort of work, by a new out-break of the collector's acquisitiveness, lastly by the tone of such a passage as that wherein the procession on the Sunday after our Lady's Assumption (p. 145) is spoken of with admiration. "Twenty persons bore the image of the Virgin Mary with the Lord Jesus, adorned in the costliest manner, to the honour of the Lord God." Such a spectacle has a very different significance to his mind from that of another procession in honour of the Virgin, depicted in a woodcut by Michael Ostendorfer, which presents a large space in front of a temporary church; in the midst is a gaudy statue of the Virgin set upon a pillar, around whose base seven or eight persons of both sexes, whom one might suppose from their attitudes to be drunk, are seen writhing, while a procession headed by huge cierges and a cardinal's hat on a pole encircles the whole building; those in the procession carrying offerings or else candles, two men being naked save for scanty hair shirts. On the margin of the copy now at Coburg Dürer has written: "1523, this Spectre, contrary to Holy Scripture, has set itself up at Regensburg and has been dressed out by the Bishop. God help us that we should not so dishonour His precious mother but (honour her?) in Christ Jesus. Amen." Indeed, it would be difficult to distinguish between the kind of honour done the Virgin in many of Dürer's pictures and etchings and that done her in the Antwerp procession; but both are infinitely removed from the degradation of emotion produced by an orgy of superstition such as that depicted in Ostendorfer's print, which is truly nearer akin to the scenes that occasionally occur in Salvation Army or Methodist revivals, and is even more repugnant to the spirit of the Renascence than to that of the Reformation as Luther and Dürer conceived of it. It is well to remind ourselves, by reading such a passage and by gazing at Dürer's Virgins enthroned and crowned with stars, that the attitude of later Protestants in regard to the worship of the Virgin was in no sense shared by Dürer. And we touch the very pulse of the Renaissance in the phrase, "Being a painter, I looked about me a little more boldly," – by which Dürer explains that the beautiful maidens, almost naked, who figured in the mythological groups along the route of Charles V.'s

* 167

triumphal entry into Antwerp received a very different reward, in his attentive gaze, to that which was meted to them by the young, austere, and unreformed Charles. One might almost be listening to Vasari when Dürer says: "I saw out behind the King's house at Brussels the fountains, labyrinth and Beast-garden; anything more beautiful and pleasing to me and more like Paradise I have never seen." Dürer's admiration for Luther was like Michelangelo's for Savonarola, and he never doubted that fiery indignation was directed against the abuse of wealth, force, and beauty, not against their use; though perhaps both the Italian and the German reformer occasionally confused the two.

III

Dürer's journey was successful in that he obtained from Charles V. what he sought – the confirmation of his privilegium.

CHARLES, by God's grace, Roman Emperor Elect, etc.

Honourable, trusty, and well-beloved,

Whereas the most illustrious Prince, Emperor Maximilian, our dear lord and grandfather of praiseworthy memory, appointed and assigned unto our and the Empire's trusty and well-beloved Albrecht Dürer the sum of 100 florins Rhenish every year of his life to be paid from and out of our and the Empire's customary town contributions, which you are bound to render yearly into our Imperial Treasury; and whereas we, as Roman Emperor, have graciously agreed thereto, and have granted anew this life pension unto him according to the terms of the above letter; we therefore earnestly command you, and it is our will, that you render and give unto the said Albrecht Dürer henceforward every year of his life, from and out of the said town contributions and in return for his proper quittance, the said life pension of 100 florins Rhenish, together with whatever part of it stands over unpaid since the Emperor Maximilian's grant; etc.

Given at our and the Holy Empire's town Köln on the fourth day of the month November (1520), etc.

(Signed) KARL.

(Signed) ALBRECHT, Cardinal, Archbishop of Mainz, Chancellor.

Besides, he got back to Nuremberg without falling in with highwaymen, though the following little letter shows us that in this he was fortunate.

Dear Master Wolf Stromer, – My most gracious lord of Salzburg has sent me a letter by the hand of his glass-painter. I shall be glad to do anything I can to help him. He is to buy glass and materials here. He tells me that near Freistadtlein he was robbed and had twenty florins taken from him. He has asked me to send him to you, for his gracious lord told him if he wanted anything to let you know. I send him, therefore, to your Wisdom with my apprentice. Your Wisdom's,

ALBRECHT DÜRER.

No doubt he had enriched his mind and cheered his heart in the company of prosperous, go-ahead, and earnest men; but as he says, "when I was in Zeeland, a wondrous sickness overcame me, such as I never heard of from any man, and this sickness remains with me" (see p. 156). And, alas! it was to remain with him till he died of it. So that his journey cannot be considered as altogether fortunate.

CHAPTER VII

DÜRER'S LAST YEARS

I

Dürer came back home with health broken: yet it is to this period that the magnificent portraits at Berlin of Nuremberg Councillors belong, and certainly his hand and eye had never been more sure than when he produced them. The hall of the Rathhaus was decorated under his direction and from his designs, the actual painting being, it is supposed, chiefly the work of George Penz, who with his fellow prentices became famous in 1524 as one of "the three godless painters."

We now come to a letter dated

NÜRNBERG, *December* 5, 1523, Sunday after Andrew's

My dear and gracious Master Frey – I have received the little book you sent to Master (Ulrich) Varnbüler and me; when he has finished reading it I will read it too. As to the monkey-dance you want me to draw for you, I have drawn this one here, unskilfully enough, for it is a long time since I saw any monkeys; so pray put up with it. Convey my willing service to Herr Zwingli (the reformer), Hans Leu (a Protestant painter), Hans Urich, and my other good masters. ALBRECHT DÜRER. Divide these five little prints amongst you: I have nothing else new.

This Master Felix Frey was a reformer at Zurich: he was probably not closely related to Hans Frey, Dürer's father-in-law, whose death is thus recorded in Dürer's book:

In the year 1523 (as they reckon it), on our dear Lady's Day, when she was offered in the Temple, early, before the morning chimes, Hans Frey, my dear father-in-law, passed away. He had lain ill for almost six years and suffered quite incredible adversities in this world. He received the Sacraments before he died. God Almighty be gracious to him.

Next we have letters from and to Niklas Kratzer, Astronomer to Henry VIII. He had been present when Dürer drew Erasmus' portrait at Antwerp. Dürer had also made a drawing of Kratzer, and later on Holbein was to paint his masterpiece in the Louvre from the Oxford professor.

To the honourable and accomplished Albrecht Dürer, burgher of Nürnberg, my dear Master and Friend. LONDON, *October* 24, 1524. Honourable, dear Sir,

I am very glad to hear of your good health and that of your wife. I have had Hans Pomer staying with me in England. Now that you are all evangelical in Nürnberg I must write to you. God grant you grace to persevere; the adversaries, indeed, are strong, but God is stronger, and is wont to help the sick who call upon Him and acknowledge Him. I want you, dear Herr Albrecht Dürer, to make a drawing for me of the instrument you saw at Herr Pirkheimer's, wherewith they measure distances both far and wide. You told me about it at Antwerp. Or perhaps Herr Pirkheimer would send me the design of it – he would be doing me a great favour. I want also to know how much a set of impressions of all your prints costs, and whether anything new has come out at Nürnberg relating to my art. I hear that our friend Hans, the astronomer, is dead. Would you write and tell me what instruments and the like he has left, and also where our Stabius' prints and wood-blocks are to be found? Greet Herr Pirkheimer for me. I hope to make him a map of England, which is a great country, and was unknown to Ptolemy. He would like to see it. All those who have written about England have seen no more than a small part of it. You cannot write to me any longer through Hans Pomer. Pray send me the woodcut which represents Stabius as S. Koloman.[70]I have nothing more to say that would interest you, so God bless you. Given at London, October 24. Your servant, NIKLAS KRATZEH. Greet your wife heartily for me.

To the honourable and venerable Herr Niklas Kratzer, servant to his Royal Majesty in England, my gracious Master and Friend.

NÜRNBERG, Monday after Barbara's (*December* 5), 1524.

First my most willing service to you, dear Herr Niklas. I have received and read your letter with pleasure, and am glad to hear that things are going well with you. I have spoken for you to Herr Wilibald Pirkheimer about the instrument you wanted to have. He is having one made for you, and is going to send it to you with a letter. The things Herr Hans left when he died have all been scattered; as I was away at the time of his death I cannot find out where they are gone to. The same has happened to Stabius' things; they were all taken to Austria, and I can tell you no more about them. I should like to know whether you have yet begun to translate Euclid into German, as you told me, if you had time, you would do.

We have to stand in disgrace and danger for the sake of the Christian faith, for they abuse us as heretics; but may God grant us His grace and strengthen us in His word, for we must obey Him rather than men. It is better to lose life and goods than that

God should cast us, body and soul, into hell-fire. Therefore, may He confirm us in that which is good, and enlighten our adversaries, poor, miserable, blind creatures, that they may not perish in their errors.

Now God bless you! I send you two likenesses, printed from copper, which you will know well. At present I have no good news to write you, but much evil. However, only God's will cometh to pass. Your Wisdom's,

ALBRECHT DÜRER.

Another letter to Dürer from Cornelius Grapheus at Antwerp gives us some help towards understanding how the Reformation affected Dürer and his friends.

To Master Albrecht Dürer, unrivalled chief in the art of painting, my friend and most beloved brother in Christ, at Nürnberg; or in his absence to Wilibald Pirkheimer.

I wrote a good long letter to you, some time ago, in the name of our common friend Thomas Bombelli, but we have received no answer from you. We are, therefore, the more anxious to hear even three words from you, that we may know how you are and what is going on in your parts, for there is no doubt that great events are happening. Thomas Bombelli sends you his heartiest greeting. I beg you, as I did in my last letter, to greet Wilibald Pirkheimer a score of times for me. Of my own condition I will tell you nothing. The bearers of this letter will be able to acquaint you with everything. They are very good men and most sincere Christians. I commend, them to you and my friend Pirkheimer as if they were myself; for they, themselves the best of men, merit the highest recommendation to the best of men. Farewell, dearest Albrecht. Amongst us there is a great and daily increasing persecution on account of the Gospel. Our brethren, the bearers, will tell you all about it more openly. Again farewell.

Wholly yours,

CORNELIUS GRAPHEUS.

ANTWERP, *February* 23, 1524.

II

The events which made Dürer an ardent Evangelical and
Reformer in a coarser paste proved a leaven of anarchy and
subversion. Young, hot-headed nobles like Ulrich Von Hutten
became iconoclastic, were foremost at the dispersion of convents
and nunneries, often playing a part on such occasions that was
anything but a credit to the cause they were championing.
Among the prentice lads and among the peasants, the unrest,
discontent, and appetite for change took forms if not more
offensive at least more alarming. The Peasants' War gave rulers a
foretaste of the panic they were to undergo at the time of the
French Revolution. And in the towns men like "the three godless
painters" made the burghers shake in their shoes for the social
order which kept them rich and respected and others poor and
servile. It is strange that all three should have come from Dürer's
workshop. Probably they were the most talented prentices of the
craft, since the great master chose them: besides, painting was an
occupation which allowed of a certain intellectual development.
They may have often listened with hungry ears to disputes
between Pirkheimer and Dürer, and envied the good luck, grace
and gift which had enabled the latter to bridge over a gulf as
great as that which separated them from him, between him and
Pirkheimer or Vambüler. All this and much more we can by
taking thought imagine to our satisfaction; but the point which we

would most desire to satisfactorily conjecture we are utterly in the dark about. Though his prentices were tried, Dürer appeared neither for nor against them; nor can we help ourselves to understand a fact so strange by any other mention of his attitude. He had a year or two previously married his servant, (perhaps the girl that his wife took with her to the Netherlands), to Georg Penz, who went the farthest in his scepticism, recanted soonest, and possessed least talent of the three. But this fact, which is not quite assured, narrows the grounds of conjecture but little; we still face an almost boundless blank. It is difficult to imagine that Dürer was quite as shocked as the Town Council by a man who said "he had some idea that there was a God, but did not know rightly what conception to form of him," who was so unfortunate as to think "nothing" of Christ, and could not believe in the Holy Gospel or in the word of God; and who failed to recognise "a master of himself, his goods and everything belonging to him" in the Council of Nuremberg. Now-a-days, when we think of the licence of assertion that has obtained on these questions, we are inclined to admire the honesty and intellectual clarity of such a confession. And Dürer, who resolved the similar question of authority as to "things beautiful" in a manner much the same as this, may, we can at least hope, have viewed his prentices with more of pity than of anger. All the three "godless painters" were banished from reformed Nuremberg; but Georg, whose confession had been most godless, recanted and was allowed to return. The others, Sebald and Barthel Beham, managed to perpetuate their names as "little masters" without the approbation of the Town Councillors, and are to-day less forgotten than those who condemned them. Hieronymus Andreae, the most skilful and famous of Dürer's wood engravers, caused the Council the same kind of alarm and concern. He took part with the peasants in their rebellion; but rebellion against a known authority was more pardonable than that against the unknown, or else his services were of greater value. At any rate he was pardoned not once but many times, being apparently an obstreperous character.

If we can form no conjecture as to Dürer's relations with his heretical aids, we have evidence as to his relations with their judges; for in 1524 he wrote to the Town Council thus:

Prudent, honourable and wise, most gracious Masters, – During long years, by hardworking pains and labour under Gods blessing, I have saved out of my earnings as much as 1000 florins Rhenish, which I should now be glad to invest for my support.

I know, indeed, that your Honours are not often wont at the present time to grant interest at the rate of one florin for twenty; and I have been told that before now other applications of a like kind have been refused. It is not, therefore, without scruple that I address your Honours in this matter. Yet my necessities impel me to prefer this request to your Honours, and I am encouraged to do so above all by the particularly gracious favour which I have always received from your Honourable Wisdoms, as well as by the following considerations.

Your Wisdoms know how I have always hitherto shown myself dutiful, willing, and zealous in all matters that concerned your Wisdoms and the common weal of the town. You know, moreover, how, before now, I have served many individual members of the Council, as well as of the community here, gratuitously rather than for pay, when they stood in need of my help, art, and labour. I can also write with truth that, during the thirty years I have stayed at home, I have not received from people in this town work worth 500 florins – truly a trifling and ridiculous sum – and not a fifth part of that has been profit. I have, on the contrary, earned and attained all my property (which, God knows, has grown irksome to me) from Princes, Lords, and other foreign persons, so that I only spend in this town what I have earned from foreigners.

Doubtless, also, your Honours remember that at one time Emperor Maximilian, of most praiseworthy memory, in return for the manifold services which I had performed for him, year after year, of his own impulse and imperial charity wanted to make me free of taxes in this town. At the instance, however, of some of the elder Councillors, who treated with me in the matter in the name of the Council, I willingly resigned that privilege, in order to honour the said Councillors and to maintain their privileges, usages, and rights.

Again, nineteen years ago, the government of Venice offered to appoint me to an office and to give me a salary of 200 ducats a year. So, too, only a short time ago when I was in the Netherlands, the Council of Antwerp would have given me 300 Philipsgulden a year, kept me there free of taxes, and honoured me with a well-built house; and besides I should have been paid in addition at both places for all the work I might have done for the gentry. But I declined all this, because of the particular love and affection which I bear to your honourable Wisdoms and to my fatherland, this honourable town, preferring, as I did, to live under your Wisdoms in a moderate way rather than to be rich and held in honour in other places.

It is, therefore, my most submissive prayer to your Honours, that you will be pleased graciously to take these facts into consideration, and to receive from me on my account these 1000 florins, paying me 50 florins a year as interest. I could, indeed, place them well with other respectable parties here and elsewhere, but I should prefer to see them in the hands of your Wisdoms. I and my wife will then, now that we are both growing daily older, feebler, and more helpless, possess the certainty of a fitting household for our needs; and we shall experience thereby, as formerly, your honourable Wisdoms' favour and goodwill. To merit this from your Honours with all my powers I shall ever be found willing.

Your Wisdoms' willing, obedient burgher,

ALBRECHT DÜRER.

Dürer obtained the desired five per cent. on his savings annually until his death, and afterwards his widow received four per cent. until her death.

In 1526 the grateful artist finished and dedicated to his fellow-townsmen his most important picture, representing the four temperaments in the persons of St. John, St. Peter, St. Paul, and St. Mark; he wrote thus to the Council:

Prudent, honourable, wise, dear Masters, – I have been intending, for a long time past, to show my respect for your Wisdoms by the presentation of some humble picture of mine as a remembrance; but I have been prevented from so doing by the imperfection and insignificance of my works, for I felt that with such I could not well stand before your Wisdoms. Now, however, that I have just painted a panel upon which I have bestowed more trouble than on any other painting, I considered none more worthy to keep it as a remembrance than your Wisdoms.

Therefore, I present it to your Wisdoms with the humble and urgent prayer that you will favourably and graciously receive it, and will be and continue, as I have ever found you, my kind and dear Masters.

Thus shall I be diligent to serve your Wisdoms in all humility.

Your Wisdoms' humble

ALBRECHT DÜRER.

The gift was accepted, and the Council voted Dürer 100 florins, his wife 10, and his apprentice 2. Underneath the two panels which form the picture, the following was inscribed; the texts being from Luther's Bible:

All worldly rulers in these dangerous times should give good heed that they receive not human misguidance for the Word of God, for God will have nothing added to His Word nor taken away from it. Hear, therefore, these four excellent men, Peter, John, Paul, and Mark, their warning.

Peter says in his Second Epistle in the second chapter: There were false prophets also among the people, even as there shall be false teachers among you, who privily shall bring in damnable heresies, even denying the Lord that bought them, and bring upon themselves swift destruction. And many shall follow their pernicious ways; by reason of whom the way of truth shall be evil spoken of. And through covetousness shall they with feigned words make merchandise of you: whose judgment now of a long time lingereth not, and their damnation slumbereth not.

John in his First Epistle in the fourth chapter writes thus: Beloved, believe not every spirit, but try the spirits whether they are of God: because many false prophets are gone out into the world. Hereby know ye the Spirit of God: Every spirit that confesseth that Jesus Christ is come in the flesh, is of God: and every spirit that confesseth not that Jesus Christ is come in the flesh, is not of God: and this is that spirit of antichrist, whereof ye have heard that it should come; and even now already is it in the world.

In the Second Epistle to Timothy in the third chapter St. Paul writes: This know, also, that in the last days perilous times shall come. For men shall be lovers of their own selves, covetous, boasters, proud, blasphemers, disobedient to parents, unthankful, unholy, without natural affection, truce-breakers, false accusers, incontinent, fierce, despisers of those that are good, traitors, heady, high-minded, lovers of pleasures more than lovers of God; having a form of godliness, but denying the power thereof: from such turn away. For of this sort are they which creep into houses, and lead captive silly women laden with sins, led away with divers lusts, ever learning, and never able to come to the knowledge of the truth.

St. Mark writes in his Gospel in the twelfth chapter: He said unto them in His doctrine, Beware of the scribes, which love to go in long clothing, and love salutations in the market-places, and the chief seats in the synagogues, and the uppermost rooms at feasts; which devour widows' houses, and for a pretense make long prayers: these shall receive greater damnation.

These rather tremendous texts may make one fear that the "three godless painters" had found little pity in their master; but most sincere Christians are better than their creeds, and more charitable than the old-world imprecations, admonitions, and denunciations, with which they soothe their Cerberus of an old Adam, who is not allowed to use his teeth to the full extent that their formidable nature would seem to warrant. For have they not been told above all things to love their enemies, and do good to those whom they would naturally hate, by a master whom they really love and strive to imitate?

IV

Dürer's last years were given more and more to writing down his ideas for the sake of those who, coming after him, would, he was persuaded, go on far before him in the race for perfection. In 1525 he published his first book – "Instruction in the Measurement with the Compass, and Rules of Lines, Surfaces, and Solid Bodies, drawn up by Albert Dürer, and printed, for the use of all lovers of art, with appropriate diagrams." It contains a course of applied geometry in connection with Euclid's Elements. Dürer states from the very commencement that "his book will be of no use to any one who understands the geometry of the 'very acute' Euclid; for it has been written only for the young, and for those who have had no one to instruct them accurately." Thausing tells us his work shows certain resemblances to that of Luca Pacioli, a companion of Leonardo's, who may have been the "man who is willing to teach me the secrets of the art of perspective," and whom Dürer in 1506 travelled from Venice to Bologna to see; it is even possible that he saw Leonardo himself in the latter town. In 1527 he issued an essay on the "Art of Fortification," which the development of artillery was then transforming; and authorities on this very special science tell us that Dürer is the true author of the ideas on which the "new Prussian system" was founded. It was dread of the unchristian Turk who was then besieging Vienna which called forth from Dürer this excursion. He dedicated it in the following terms:

To the most illustrious, mighty prince and lord, Lord Ferdinand, King of Hungary and Bohemia, Infant of Spain, Archduke of Austria, Duke of Burgundy and Brabant, Count of Hapsburg, Flanders, and Tirol, his Roman Imperial Majesty, our most gracious Lord, Regent in the Holy Empire, my most gracious Sire.

Most illustrious mighty King, most gracious Sire, – During the lifetime of the most illustrious and mighty Emperor Maximilian of praiseworthy memory, your Majesty's Lord and Grandsire, I experienced grace and favour from his Imperial Majesty; wherefore I consider myself no less bound to serve your Majesty according to my small powers. As it happeneth that your Majesty has commanded some towns and places to be fortified, I am induced to make known what little I know about these matters, if perchance it may please your Majesty to gather somewhat therefrom. For though my theory may not be accepted in every point, still I believe something will arise from it, here and there, useful not to your Majesty only, but to all other Princes, Lords, and Towns, that would gladly protect themselves against violence and unjust oppression. I therefore humbly pray your Majesty graciously to accept from me this evidence of my gratitude, and to be my most gracious lord,

Your Royal Majesty's most humble
ALBRECHT DÜRER.

✳ 181

It seems that at any rate the Kronenburg Gate and Roseneck bastion of Strasburg were actually constructed in accordance with Dürer's method.

When, on April 6, 1528, Dürer died suddenly, two volumes of his great work on "Human Proportions" were ready for the press, and enough raw material, notes, drawings,&c., to enable his friend Pirkheimer to prepare and issue the remaining two with them. Of the misunderstanding of this the most important of Dürer's writings I shall say nothing here, as I have devoted a separate chapter to it.

V

It seems probable that the "wondrous sickness which overcame me in Zeeland, such as I never heard of from any man, and which sickness remains with me" of the Netherlands Journal (p. 156) was an intermittent fever. There exists at Bremen a sketch of Dürer, nude down to the waist, and pointing with his finger to a spot between the pit of the stomach and the groin, which spot he has coloured yellow; and from its size, with the other descriptions of his malady, the skilful have arrived at the above diagnosis. The words on the sketch, "The yellow spot to which my finger points is where it pains me," seem to indicate that he had made it to send to some skilled physician. Thausing suggests either Master Jacob or Master Braun, whom he had met at Antwerp, and deduces from the length of his hair and the apparent vigour of his body, that the drawing was made soon after the disease was contracted. All doubt as to its nature would be removed, could it be made certain that by the words, "I have sent to your Grace early this year before I became ill," in a letter to the Elector Albert dated September 4, 1523, Dürer meant to imply that at a certain period he became ill every year; but of course it is impossible to be sure of this.

VI

If not rich, Dürer died comfortably off. Thausing tells us that his "widow entered into possession of his whole fortune;" a fourth part belonged, according to Nuremberg law, to his brothers, but she was not bound to render it to them before her death. On June 9, 1530, however, she "of her own desire, and on account of the friendly feeling which she entertained for them for her husband's sake, and as her dear brothers-in-law," made over both to Andreas Dürer, goldsmith, and to Caspar Altmulsteiner, on behalf of Hans Dürer, then in the service of the King of Poland, a sum of 553 florins, three pounds, eleven pfennigs, and gave them a mortgage for the remaining sum of 608 florins, two pounds, twenty-four pfennigs on the corner house in the Zistelgasse, now called the Dürer House; for the property had been valued at 6848 florins, seven pounds, twenty-four pfennigs. Johann Neudörffer, who lived opposite the Dürers, has recorded the fact that Dürer's brother Endres inherited all his expensive colours, his copper plates and wood blocks, as well as any impressions there were, and all his drawings beside. And a year before her death, Agnes Dürer gave the interest on the 1000 florins invested in the town to found a scholarship for theological students at the University of Wittenberg; about which Melanchthon wrote to von Dietrich that he thanked God for this aid to study, and that he had praised this good deed of the widow Dürer before Luther and others. And yet Pirkheimer, in his spleen at having lost the chance of procuring some stags' antlers which had belonged to his friend, and which he coveted, could write of Agues Dürer: "She watched him day and night and drove him to work ... that he might earn money and leave it her when he died. For she always thought she was on the borders of ruin – as for the matter of that she does still – though Albrecht left her property worth as much as six thousand florins. But there! nothing was enough; and, in fact, she alone is the cause of his death!" We know that what with the four Apostles and his books Dürer's last years were not spent on remunerative labours; nor does the Netherlands Journal contain any hint that his wife tried to restrict the employment either of his time or money. His journey into Zeeland was a pure extravagance; for the sale of a copper engraving or woodcut of a whale would have taken some time to make up for such an expense, and, as it turned out, no whale was seen or drawn; and there is no hint that Frau Dürer made reproach or complaint. On the other hand, Pirkheimer's words probably had some slight basis; and as Dürer's sickness increased upon him, while at the same time he applied himself less and less to making money, the anxious Frau may have become fretful or even nagging at times; and Pirkheimer, whose companionship was probably a cause of extravagances to Dürer, may have been scolded by Agnes, or heard his friend excuse himself from taking part in some convivial meeting, on the plea that his wife found he was spending out of proportion to his takings at the moment.

VII

We have the testimony of a good number of Dürer's friends as to the value of his character; and first let us quote from Pirkheimer – writing immediately after Dürer's death and before' the loss of the coveted antlers had vexed him – to a common friend Ulrich, probably Ulrich Varnbüler.

What can be more grievous for a man than to have continually to mourn, not only children and relations whom death steals from him, but friends also, and among them those whom he loved best? And though I have often had to mourn the loss of relations, still I do not know that any death ever caused me such grief as fills me now at the sudden departure of our good and dear Albrecht Dürer. Nor is this without reason, for of all men not united to me by ties of blood, I have never loved or esteemed any like him for his countless virtues and rare uprightness. And because I know, my dear Ulrich, that this blow has struck both you and me alike, I have not been afraid to give vent to my grief before you of all others, so that together we may pay the fitting tribute of tears to such a friend. He is gone, good Ulrich; our Albrecht is gone! Oh, inexorable decree of fate! Oh, miserable lot of man! Oh, pitiless severity of death! Such a man, yea, such a man, is torn from us, while so many useless and worthless men enjoy lasting happiness, and live only too long!

Thausing insists on the fact that in this letter there is no mention of Dürer's death having been caused by his wife's behaviour; but as the relation of Ulrich to the deceased seems to have been well-nigh as intimate as his own, there may have been no need to mention a fact painfully present to both their minds. On the other hand, it is at least as probable that the idea was not present even to the mind of the writer, who, in a style less studiously commonplace, inscribed on Dürer's tomb:

Me. AL. DU.

QVICQVID ALBERTI DVRERI MORTALE FVIT, SVB HOC CONDITVR TVMVLO. EMIGRAVIT VIII IDVS APRILIS MDXXVIII.

(To the memory of Albrecht Dürer. All that was mortal of Albrecht Dürer is laid beneath this mound. He departed on April 6, 1528.)

Luther wrote to Eoban Hesse:

As to Dürer, it is natural and right to weep for so excellent a man; still you should rather think him blessed, as one whom Christ has taken in the fulness of His wisdom, and by a happy death, from these most troublous times, and perhaps from times even more troublous which

✳ 185

are to come, lest one who was worthy to look upon nothing but excellence should be forced to behold things most vile. May he rest in peace. Amen.

Erasmus had some months before written and printed in a treatise on the right pronunciation of Latin and Greek an eulogy of Dürer. It is not known whether a copy had reached him before his death; in any case to most people it came like a funeral oration from the greatest scholar on the greatest artist north of the Alps. Thausing quotes the following passage from it:

I have known Dürer's name for a long time as that of the first celebrity in the art of painting. Some call him the Apelles of our time. But I think that did Apelles live now, he, as an honourable man, would give the palm to Dürer. Apelles, it is true, made use of few and unobtrusive colours, but still he used colours; while Dürer, – admirable as he is, too, in other respects, – what can he not express with a single colour – that is to say, with black lines? He can give the effect of light and shade, brightness, foreground and background. Moreover, he reproduces *not merely the natural aspect of a thing, but also observes the laws of perfect symmetry and harmony with regard to the position of it*. He can also transfer by enchantment, so to say, upon the canvas, things which it seems not possible to represent, such as fire, sunbeams, storms, lightning, and mist; he can portray every passion, show us the whole soul of a man shining through his outward form; nay, even make us hear his very speech. All this he brings so happily before the eye with those black lines, that the picture would lose by being clothed in colour. Is it not more worthy of admiration to achieve without the winning charm of colour what Apelles only realised with its assistance?

Melanchthon wrote in a letter to Camerarius:

"It grieves me to see Germany deprived of such an artist and such a man."

And we learn from his son-in-law, Caspar Penker, that he often spoke of Dürer with affection and respect; he writes:

Melanchthon was often, and many hours together, in Pirkheimer's company, at the time when they were advising together about the churches and schools at Nürnberg; and Dürer, the painter, used *also* to be invited to dinner with them. Dürer was a man of great shrewdness, and Melanchthon used to say of him that though he excelled in the art of painting, it was the least of his accomplishments. Disputes often arose between Pirkheimer and Dürer on these occasions about the matters recently discussed, and Pirkheimer used vehemently to oppose Dürer. Dürer was an excessively subtle disputant, and refuted his adversary's arguments, just as if he had come fully prepared for the discussion. Thereupon Pirkheimer, who was rather a choleric man and liable to very severe attacks of the gout, fired up and burst forth again and again into such words as these, "What you say cannot be painted." "Nay!" rejoined Dürer, "but what you advance cannot be put into words or even figured to the mind." I remember hearing Melanchthon often tell this story, and in relating it he confessed his astonishment at the ingenuity and power manifested by a painter in arguing with a man of Pirkheimer's renown.

Such scenes no doubt took place during the years after Dürer's return from the Netherlands. Melanchthon also wrote in a letter to George von Anhalt:

> I remember how that great man, distinguished alike by his intellect and his virtue, Albrecht Dürer the painter, said that as a youth he had loved bright pictures full of figures, and when considering his own productions had always admired those with the greatest variety in them. But as an older man, he had begun to observe nature and reproduce it in its native forms, and had learned that this simplicity was the greatest ornament of art. Being unable completely to attain to this ideal, he said that he was no longer an admirer of his works as heretofore, but often sighed when he looked at his pictures and thought over his want of power.

And in another letter he remembers that Dürer would say that in his youth he had found great pleasure in representing monstrous and unusual figures, but that in his later years he endeavoured to observe nature, and to imitate her as closely as possible; experience, however, had taught him how difficult it was not to err. And Thausing continues: "Melanchthon speaks even more frequently of how Dürer was pleased with pictures he had just finished, but when he saw them after a time, was ashamed of them; and those he had painted with the greatest care displeased him so much at the end of three years that he could scarcely look at them without great pain."

And this on his appreciation of Luther's writings:

> Albrecht Dürer, painter of Nürnberg, a shrewd man, once said that there was this difference between the writings of Luther and other theologians. After reading three or four paragraphs of the first page of one of Luther's works he could grasp the problem to be worked out in the whole. This clearness and order of arrangement was, he observed, the glory of Luther's writings. He used, on the contrary, to say of other writers that, after reading a whole book through, he had to consider attentively what idea it was that the author intended to convey.

Lastly, Camerarius, the professor of Greek and Latin in the new school of Nuremberg, in his Latin translation of Dürer's book on "Human Proportions," writes thus:

> It is not my present purpose to talk about art. My purpose was to speak somewhat, as needs must be, of the artificer, the author of this book. He, I trust, has become known by his virtue and his deserts, not only to his own country, but to foreign nations also. Full well I know that his praises need not our trumpetings to the world, since by his excellent works he is exalted and honoured with undying glory. Yet, as we were publishing his writings, and an opportunity arose of committing to print the life and habits of a remarkable man and a very dear friend of ours, we have judged it expedient to put together some few scraps of information, learnt partly from the conversations of others and partly from our own intercourse with him. This will give some indication of his singular skill and genius as artist and man, and cannot fail of affording pleasure to the reader. We have heard that our Albrecht was of Hungarian extraction, but that his forefathers emigrated to Germany. We can, therefore, have but little to say of his origin and birth. Though they were honourable, there can be no question but that they gained more glory from him than he from them.

Nature bestowed on him a body remarkable in build and stature, and not unworthy of the noble mind it contained; that in this, too, Nature's Justice, extolled by Hippocrates, might not be forgotten – that Justice, which, while it assigns a grotesque form to the ape's grotesque soul, is wont also to clothe noble minds in bodies worthy of them. His head was intelligent,[71] his eyes flashing, his nose nobly formed, and, as the Greeks say, tetrágônon. His neck was rather long, his chest broad, his body not too stout, his thighs muscular, his legs firm and steady. But his fingers – you would vow you had never seen anything more elegant.

His conversation was marked by so much sweetness and wit, that nothing displeased his hearers so much as the end of it. Letters, it is true, he had not cultivated, but the great sciences of Physics and Mathematics, which are perpetuated by letters, he had almost entirely mastered. He not only understood principles and knew how to apply them in practice, but he was able to set them forth in words. This is proved by his geometrical treatises, wherein I see nothing omitted, except what he judged to be beyond the scope of his work. An ardent zeal impelled him towards the attainment of all virtue in conduct and life, the display of which caused him to be deservedly held a most excellent man. Yet he was not of a melancholy severity nor of a repulsive gravity; nay, whatever conduced to pleasantness and cheerfulness, and was not inconsistent with honour and rectitude, he cultivated all his life and approved even in his old age. The works he has left on Gymnastic and Music are of such character.

But Nature had specially designed him for a painter, and therefore he embraced the study of that art with all his energies, and was ever desirous of observing the works and principles of the famous painters of every land, and of imitating whatever he approved in them. Moreover, with respect to those studies, he experienced the generosity and won the favour of the greatest kings and princes, and even of Maximilian himself and his grandson the Emperor Charles; and he was rewarded by them with no contemptible salary. But after his hand had, so to speak, attained its maturity, his sublime and virtue-loving genius became best discoverable in his works, for his subjects were fine and his treatment of them noble. You may judge the truth of these statements from his extant prints in honour of Maximilian, and his memorable astronomical diagrams, not to mention other works, not one of which but a painter of any nation or day would be proud to call his own. The nature of a man is never more certainly and definitely shown than in the works he produces as the fruit of his art.... What single painter has there ever been who did not reveal his character in his works? Instead of instances from ancient history, I shall content myself with examples from our own time. No one can fail to see that many painters have sought a vulgar celebrity by immodest pictures. It is not credible that those artists can be virtuous, whose minds and fingers composed such works. We have also seen pictures minutely finished and fairly well coloured, wherein, it is true, the master showed a certain talent and industry; but art was wanting. Albrecht, therefore, shall we most justly admire as an earnest guardian of piety and modesty, and as one who showed, by the magnitude of his pictures, that he was conscious of his own powers, although none even of his lesser works is to be despised. You will not find in them a single line carelessly or wrongly drawn, not a single superfluous dot.

What shall I say of the steadiness and exactitude of his hand? You might swear that rule, square, or compasses had been employed to draw lines, which he, in fact, drew with the brush, or very often with pencil or pen, unaided by artificial means, to the great marvel of those who watched him. Why should I tell how his hand so closely followed the ideas of his mind that, in a moment, he often dashed upon paper, or, as painters say, composed, sketches of every kind of thing with pencil or pen? I see I shall not be believed by my readers when I relate, that sometimes he would draw separately, not only the different parts of a composition, but even the different parts of bodies, which, when joined together, agreed with one another so well that nothing could have fitted better. In fact this consummate artist's mind endowed with all knowledge and understanding of the truth and of the agreement of the parts one with another, governed and guided his hand and bade it trust to itself without any other aids. With like accuracy he held the brush, wherewith he drew the smallest things on canvas or wood without sketching them in beforehand, so that, far from giving ground for blame, they always won the highest praise. And this was a subject of greatest wonder to most distinguished painters, who, from their own great experience, could understand the difficulty of the thing.

I cannot forbear to tell, in this place, the story of what happened between him and Giovanni Bellini. Bellini had the highest reputation as a painter at Venice, and indeed throughout all Italy. When Albrecht was there he easily became intimate with him, and both artists naturally began to show one another specimens of their skill. Albrecht frankly admired and made much of all Bellini's works. Bellini also candidly expressed his admiration of various features of Albrecht's skill, and particularly the fineness and delicacy with which he drew hairs. It chanced one day that they were talking about art, and when their conversation was done Bellini said: "Will you be so kind, Albrecht, as to gratify a friend in a small matter?" "You shall soon see," says Albrecht, "if you will ask of me anything I can do for you." Then says Bellini: "I want you to make me a present of one of the brushes with which you draw hairs." Dürer at once produced several, just like other brushes, and, in fact, of the kind Bellini himself used, and told him to choose those he liked best, or to take them all if he would. But Bellini, thinking he was misunderstood, said: "No, I don't mean these, but the ones with which you draw several hairs with one stroke; they must be rather spread out and more divided, otherwise in a long sweep such regularity of curvature and distance could not be preserved." "I use no other than these," says Albrecht, "and to prove it, you may watch me." Then, taking up one of the same brushes, he drew some very long wavy tresses, such as women generally wear, in the most regular order and symmetry. Bellini looked on wondering, and afterwards confessed to many that no human being could have convinced him by report of the truth of that which he had seen with his own eyes.

A similar tribute was given him, with conspicuous candour, by Andrea Mantegna, who became famous at Mantua by reducing painting to some severity of law – a fame which he was the first to merit, by digging up broken and scattered statues, and setting them up as examples of art. It is true all his work is hard and stiff, inasmuch as his hand was not trained to follow the perception and nimbleness of his mind; still it is held that there is nothing better or more perfect in art. While Andrea was lying ill at Mantua he heard that Albrecht was in Italy, and had him summoned to his side at once, in order that he might fortify his (Albrecht's) facility and certainty of hand with scientific knowledge and principles. For Andrea often lamented in conversation with his friends that Albrecht's facility in drawing had not been granted to him nor his learning to Albrecht. On receiving the message Albrecht, leaving all other engagements, prepared for the journey without delay. But before he could reach Mantua Andrea was dead, and Dürer used to say that this was the saddest event in all his life; for, high as Albrecht stood, his great and lofty mind was ever striving after something yet above him.

Almost with awe have we gazed upon the bearded face of the man, drawn by himself, in the manner we have described, with the brush on the canvas and without any previous sketch. The locks of the beard are almost a cubit long, and so exquisitely and cleverly drawn, at such regular distances and in so exact a manner, that the better any one understands art, the more he would admire it, and the more certain would he deem it that in fashioning these locks the hand had employed artificial aid.

Further, there is nothing foul, nothing disgraceful in his work. The thoughts of his most pure mind shunned all such things. Artist worthy of success! How like, too, are his portraits! How unerring! How true!

All these perfections he attained by reducing mere practice to art and method, in a way new at least to German painters. With

Albrecht all was ready, certain, and at hand, because he had brought painting into the fixed track of rule and recalled it to scientific principles; without which, as Cicero said, though some things may be well done by help of nature, yet they cannot always be ready to hand, because they are done by chance. He first worked his principles out for his own use; afterwards with his generous and open nature he attempted to explain them in books, written to the illustrious and most learned Wilibald Pirkheimer. And he dedicated them to him in a most elegant letter which we have not translated, because we felt it to be beyond our power to render it into Latin without, so to speak, disfiguring its natural countenance. But before he could complete and publish the books, as he had hoped, he was carried off by death – a death, calm indeed and enviable, but in our view premature. If there was anything at all in that man which could seem like a fault, it was his excessive industry, which often made unfair demands upon him.

Death, as we have said, removed him from the publication of the work which he had begun, but his friends completed the task from his own manuscript. About this, in the next place, and about our own version, we shall say a few words. The work, being founded on a sort of geometrical system, is unpolished and devoid of literary style; so it seems rather rugged. But that is easily forgiven in consideration of the excellence of the matter. He requested me himself, only a few days before his death, to translate it into Latin while he should correct it; and I willingly turned my attention and studies to the work. But death, which takes everything, took from him his power of supervision and correction. His friends subsequently, after publishing the work, prevailed on me, by their claims rather than their requests, to undertake the Latin translation, and to complete after his death the task Dürer had laid upon me in his life.

If I find that my industry and devotion in this matter meet with my readers' approval, I shall be encouraged to translate into Latin the rest of Albrecht's treatise on painting, a work at once more finished and more laborious than the present. Moreover, his writings on other subjects will also be looked for, his Geometries and Tichismatics, in which he explained the fortification of towns according to the system of the present day. These, however, appear to be all the subjects on which he wrote books. As to the promise, which I hear certain persons are making in conversation or in writing, to publish a book by Dürer on the symmetry of the parts of the horse, I cannot but wonder from what source they will obtain after his death what he never completed during his life. Although I am well aware that Albrecht had begun to investigate the law of truth in this matter too, and had made a certain number of measurements, I also know that he lost all he had done through the treachery of certain persons, by whose means it came about that the author's notes were stolen, so that he never cared to begin the work afresh. He had a suspicion, or rather a certainty, as to the source whence came the drones who had invaded his store; but the great man preferred to hide his knowledge, to his own loss and pain, rather than to lose sight of generosity and kindness in the pursuit of his enemies. We shall not, therefore, suffer anything that may appear to be attributed to Albrecht's authorship, unworthy as it must evidently be of so great an artist.

A few years ago some tracts also appeared in German, containing rules, in general faulty and inappropriate, about the same matter. On these I do not care now to waste words, though the author, unless I am much mistaken, has not once repented of his publication. But these rules above-mentioned, which are easily proved to be Albrecht's, not only because he prepared them himself for publication, but also because of their own excellence, you will, I think, obtain considerably better here than from other sources. Not that they are more finished in point of erudition and learning in the present book than elsewhere, but because those who interpret them in the author's own workshop, among the expansions and corrections of his autograph manuscripts and the variations of his different copies, stand in the light about many points, which must of necessity seem obscure to others, however learned they may be.

This will be seen in the case of the book on Geometry, which a learned man has in hand and will shortly publish in a more elaborate form, and with more explanation of certain points than it possesses at present. For it will be increased by no less than twenty-six [Greek: schêmata] (figures) and countless corrections or improvements of earlier editions. The author himself on rereading had thus improved and amplified what had already been issued. As though he foresaw that he would publish no more, he had directed his future editors as to what was to be done about the letterpress and figures; and we shall take care that it is published at the earliest possible date in the German language, in which the author wrote it. It is only to be expected that this will be welcome to the public, who will thus return thanks for the author's burning desire to do something by his discoveries for the public good, and for our own labour and eagerness in publishing to all nations what appears to be written only for one.

Though these testimonies may often seem either trifling, or obscured by the pedantic affectation of the writers, they, like the signatures of well-respected men, endorse the impression produced by Dürer's works and writings. As we study the character of Dürer's creative gift in relation to his works, several of the phrases used by Erasmus, Camerarius, and Melanchthon should take added significance, being probably remembered from conversations with the great artist himself.[72] Dürer, like Luther, was depressed and distressed at the course the Reformation had run; but, like Erasmus, though regretting and disparaging the present, he looked forward to the future, and knew "that he would be surpassed," and had no morbid inclination to see the end and final failure of human effort in his own exhaustion.

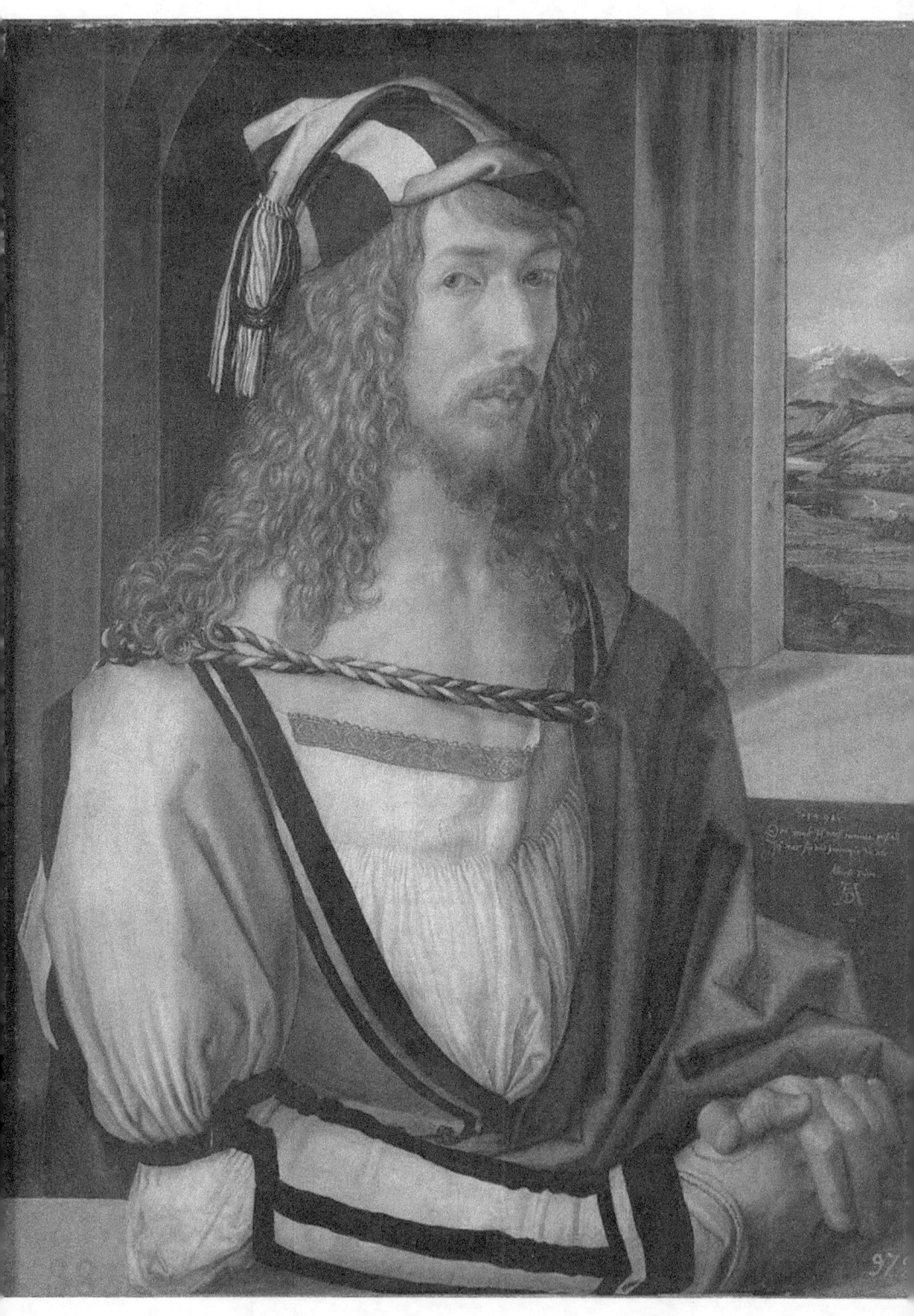

Albrecht Dürer, Self-Portrait, 1498, Prado, Madrid

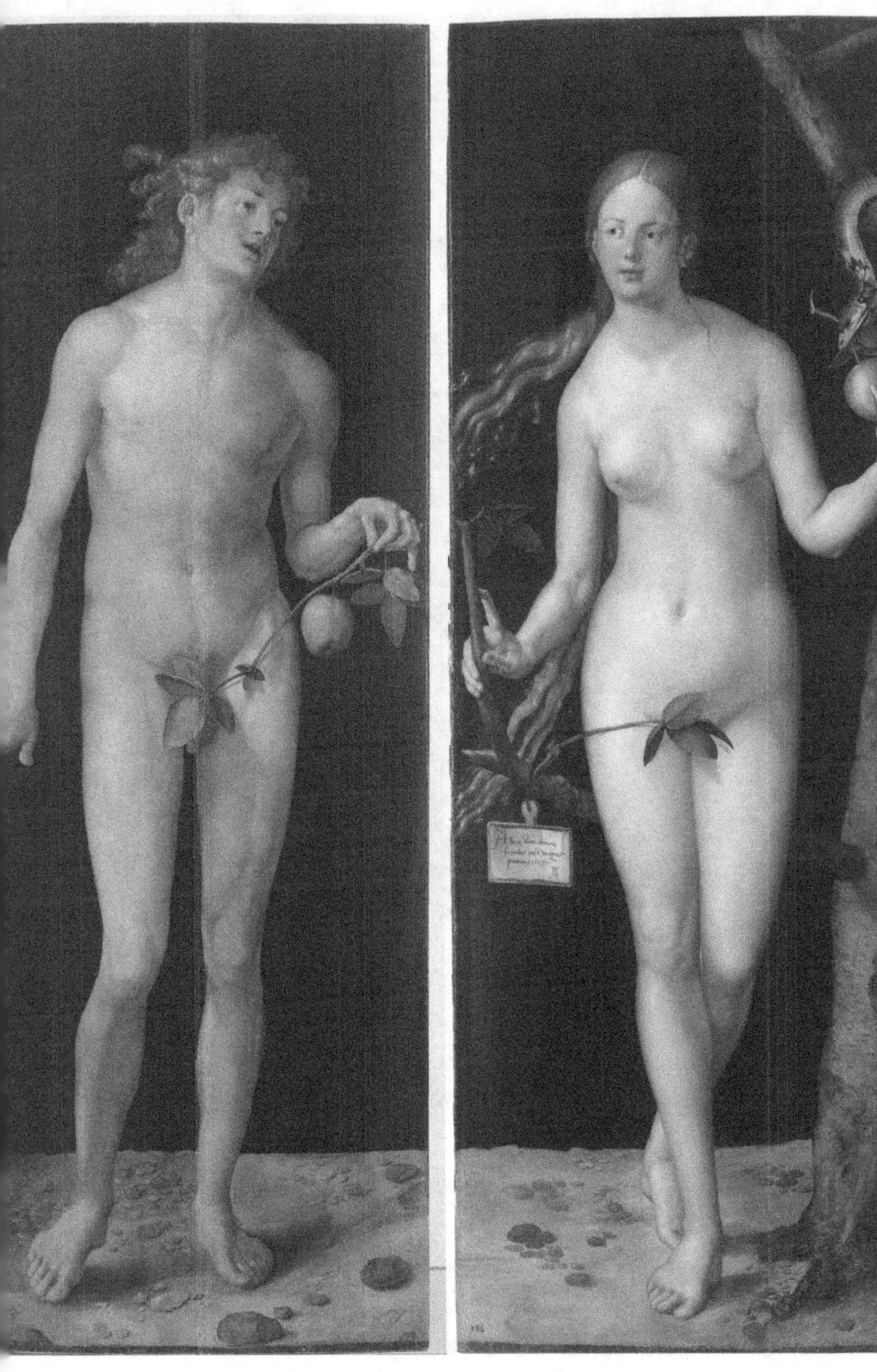

Albrecht Dürer, Adam and Eve, 1507, Prado, Madrid

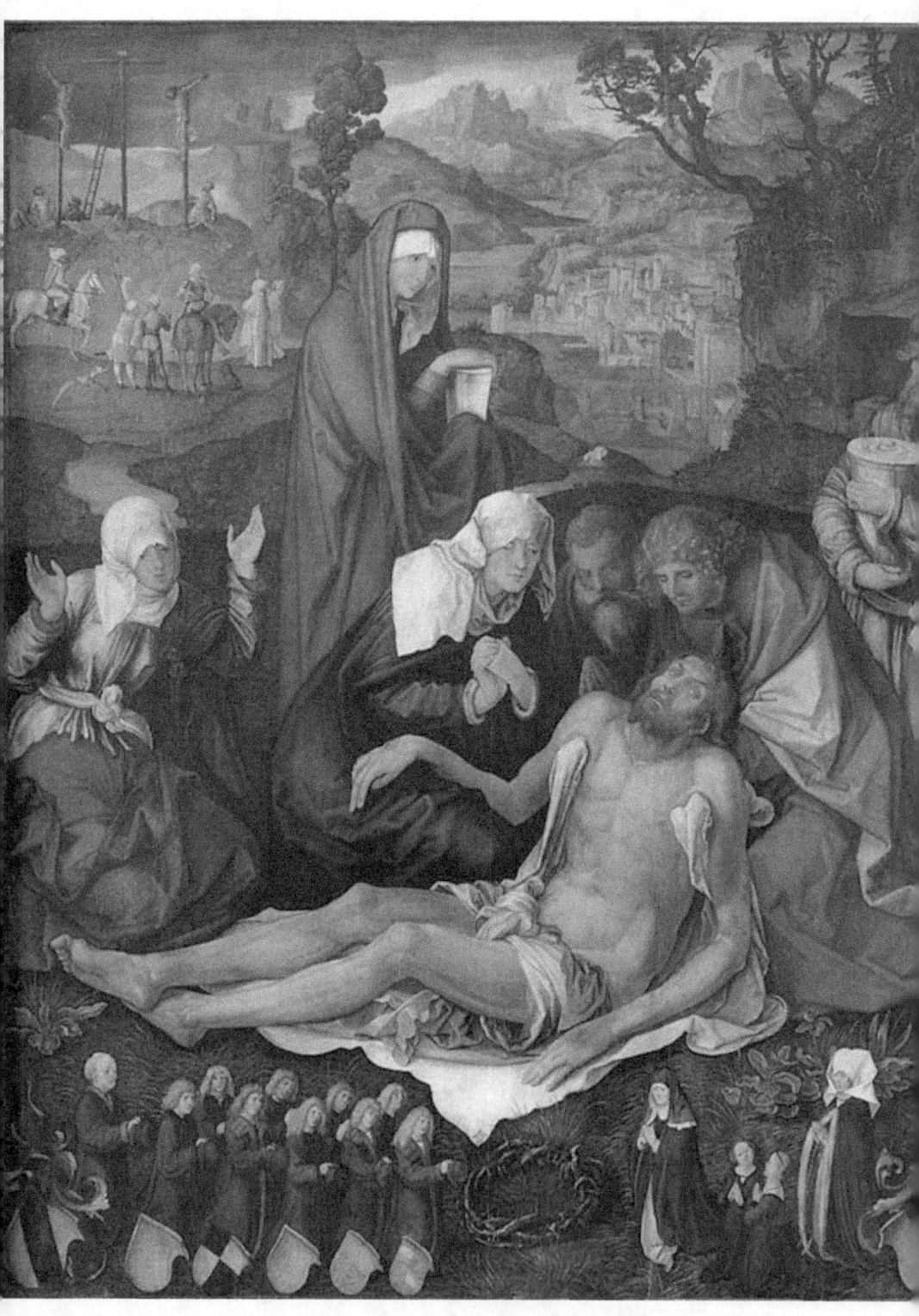

Albrecht Dürer, Lamentation, 1500, Nuremberg

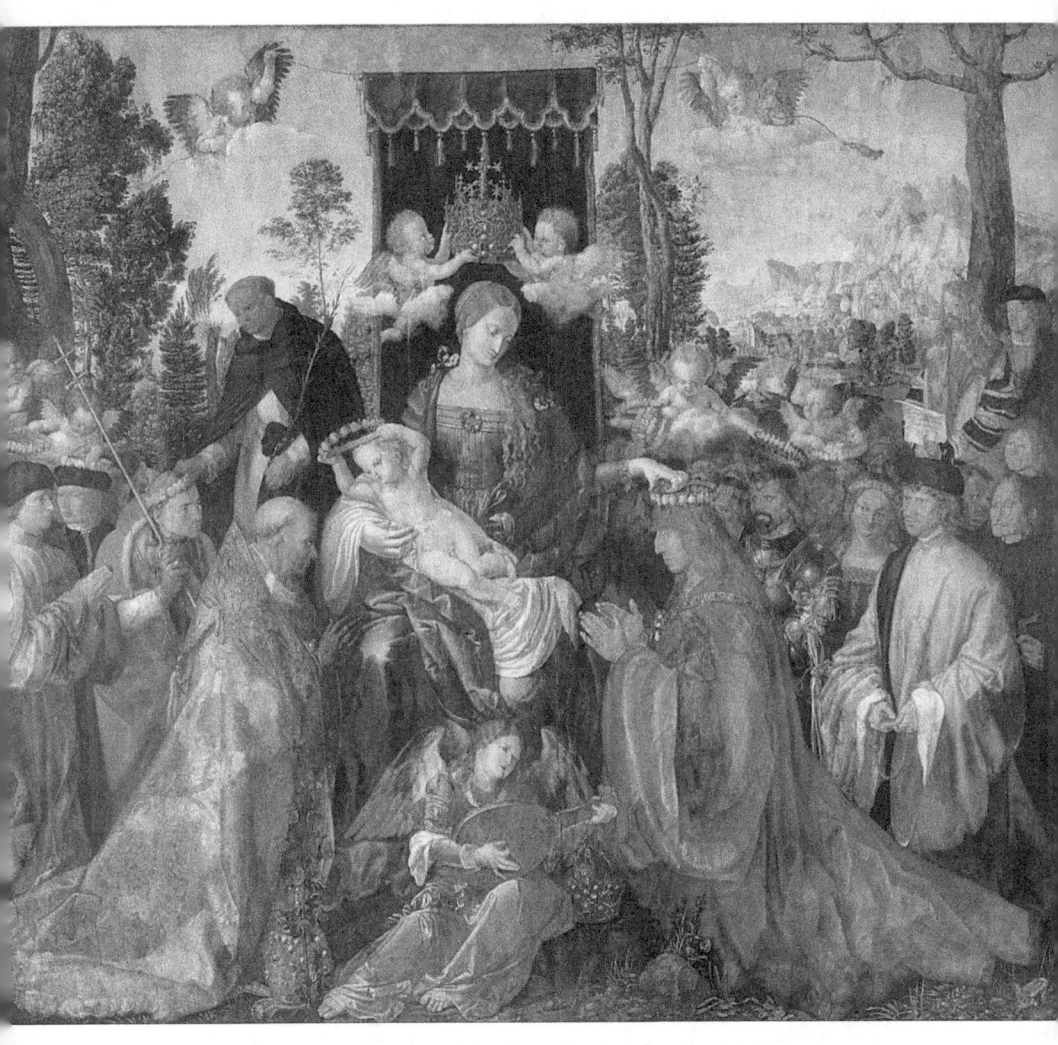

Albrecht Dürer, The Feast of Rose Garlands, 1506, Prague

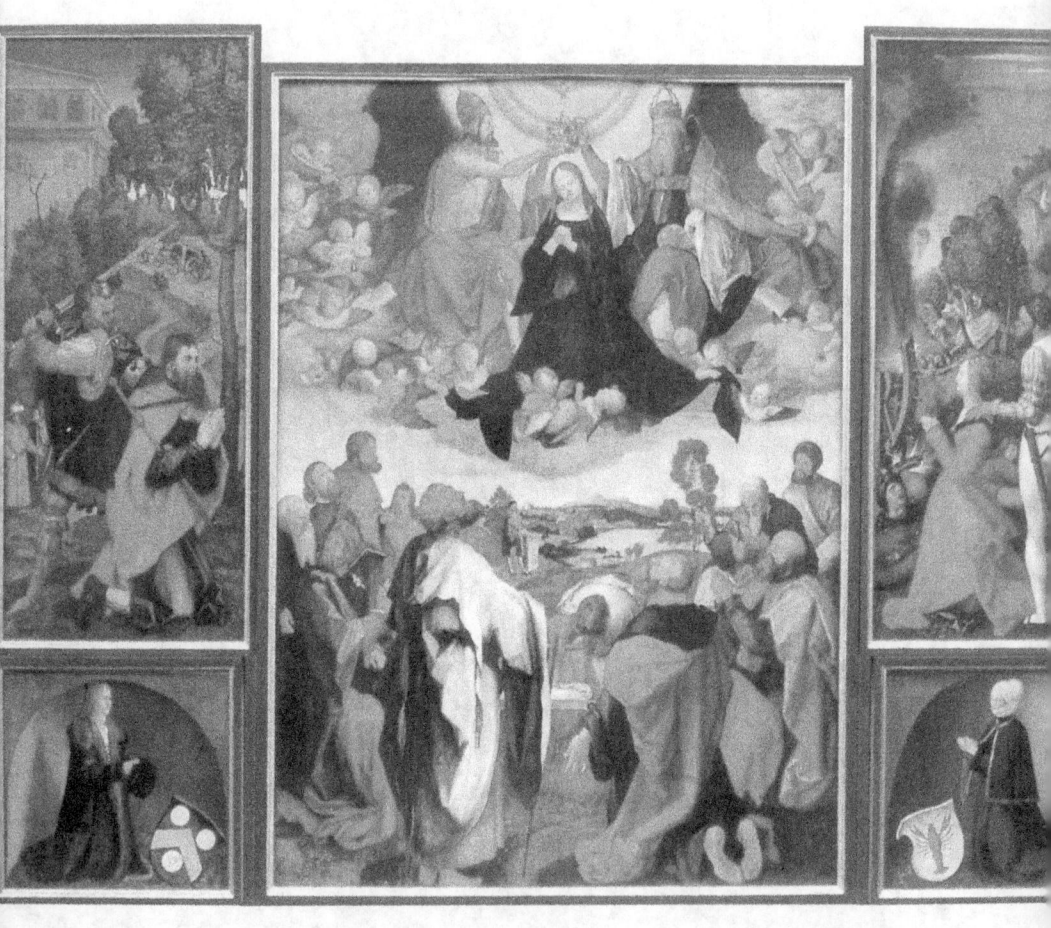

Albrecht Dürer, Heller Altarpiece, 1506-08, Frankfurt

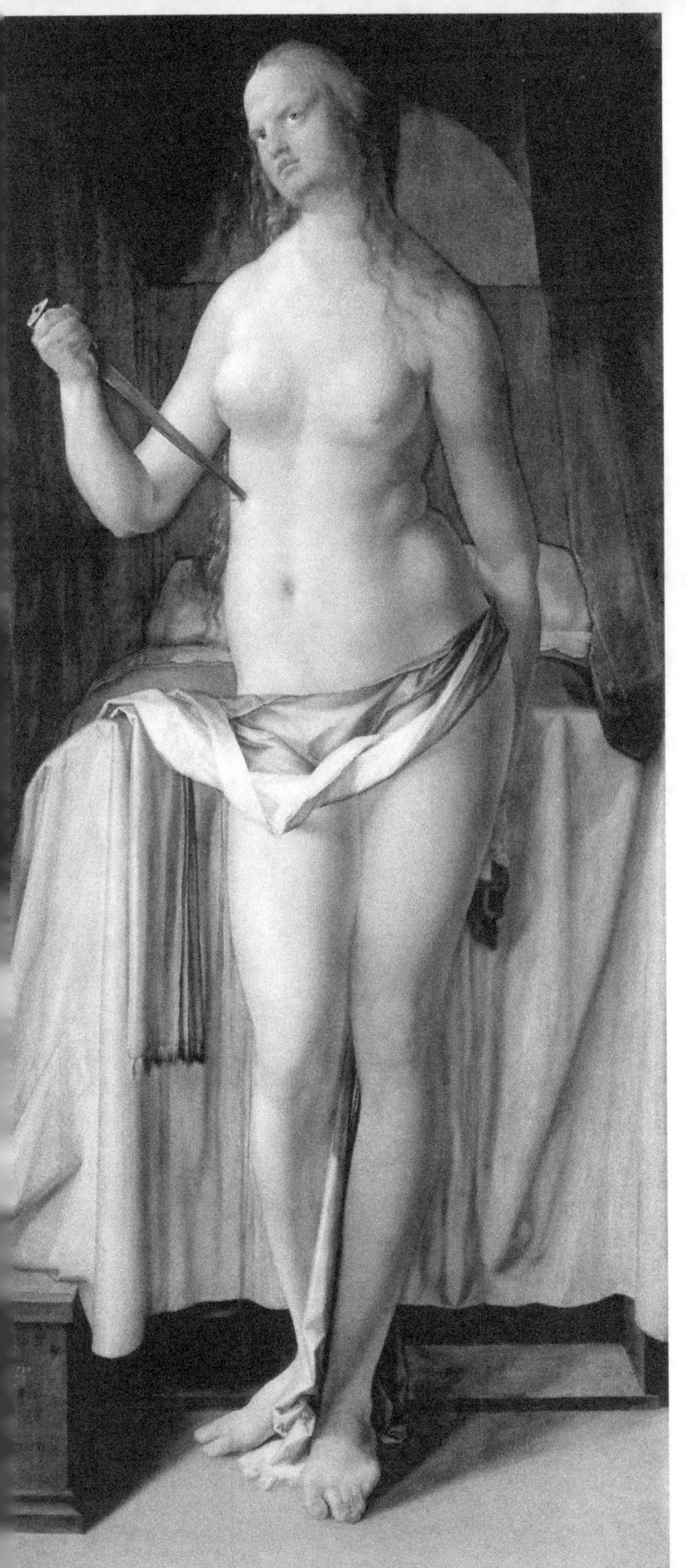

Albrecht Dürer,
Lucrezia, 1518,
Munich

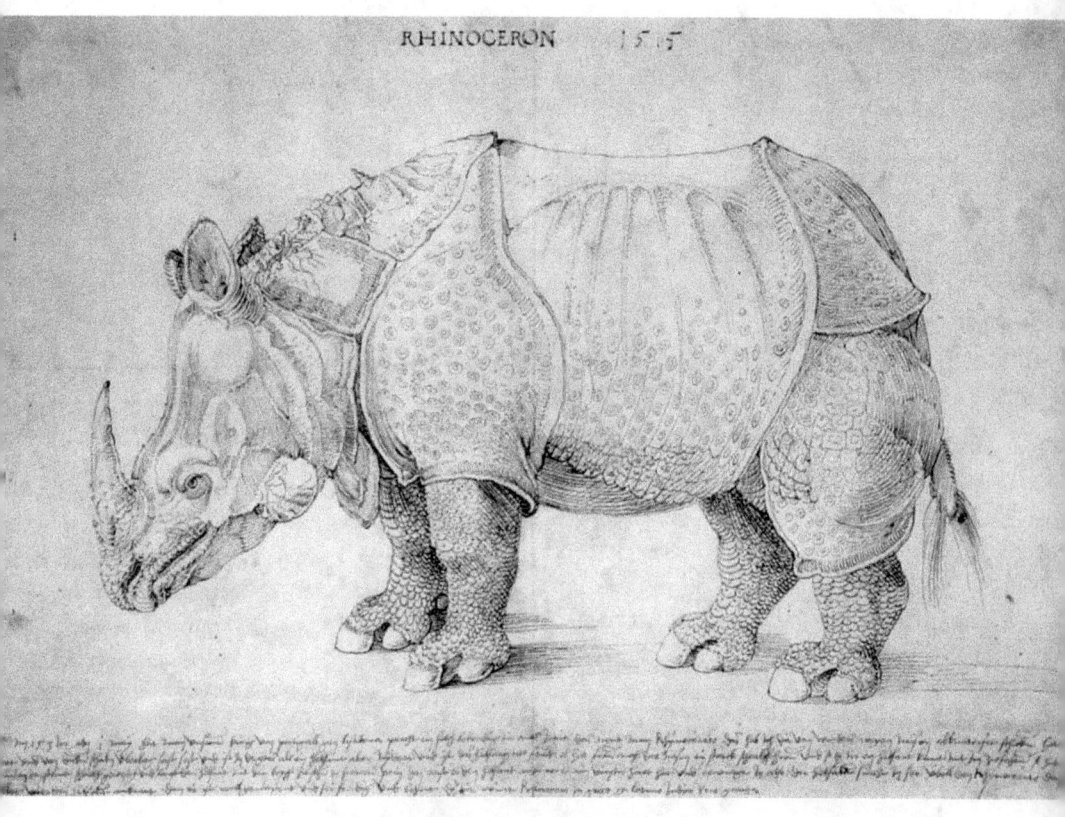

Albrecht Dürer, Rhinoceros

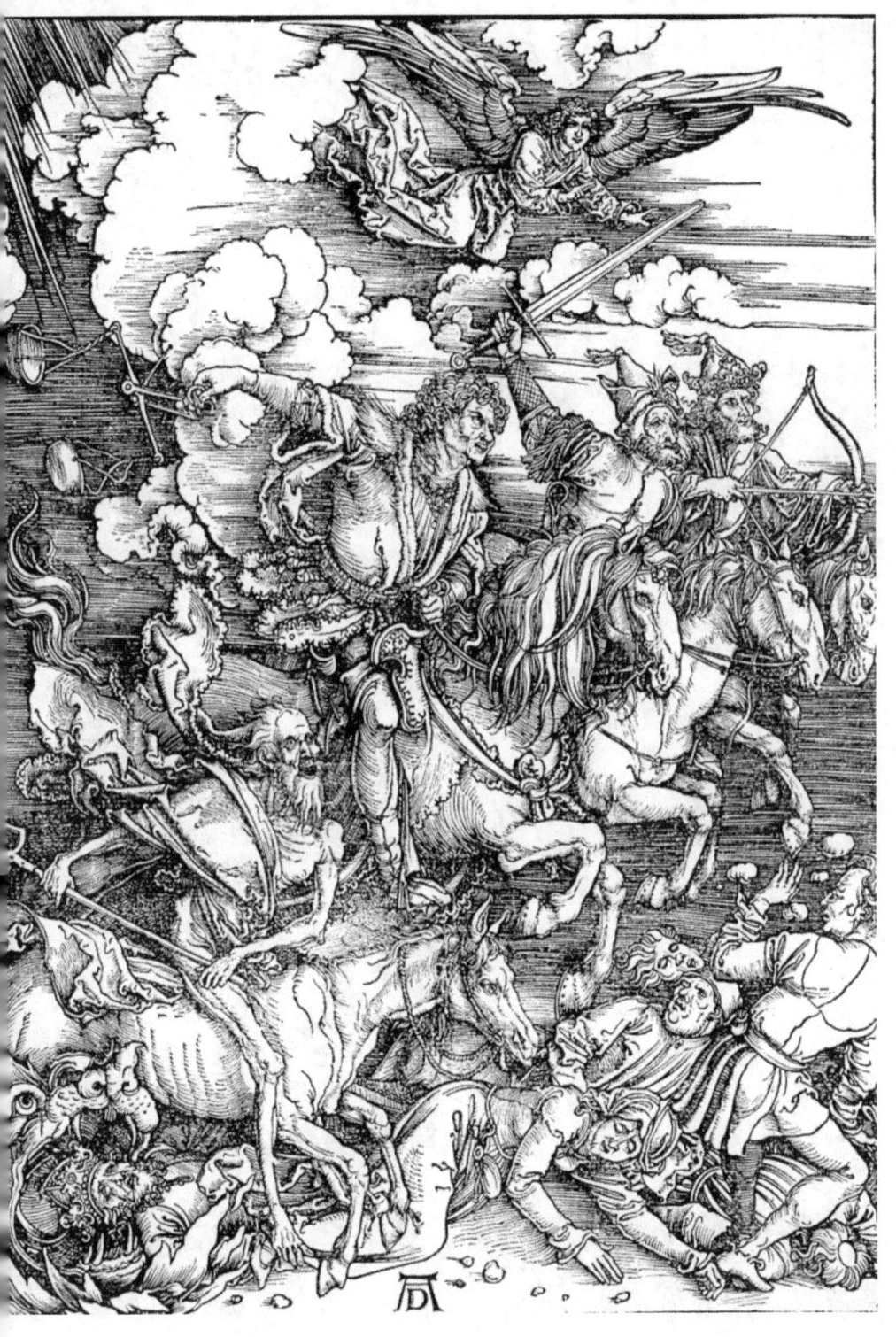

Albrecht Dürer, The Four Horseman of the Apocalypse, 1498

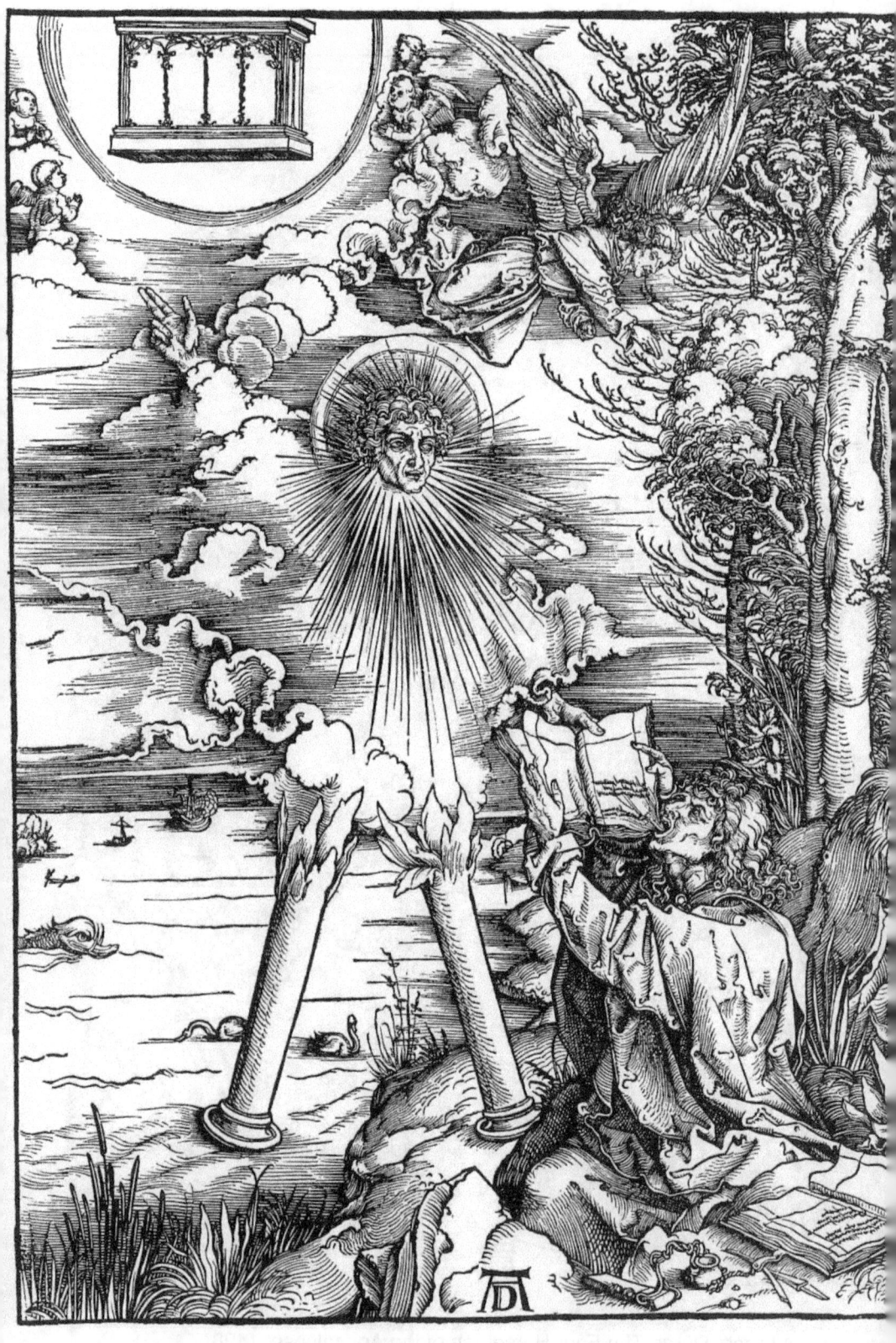

Albrecht Dürer, The Revelation of St John, 1498

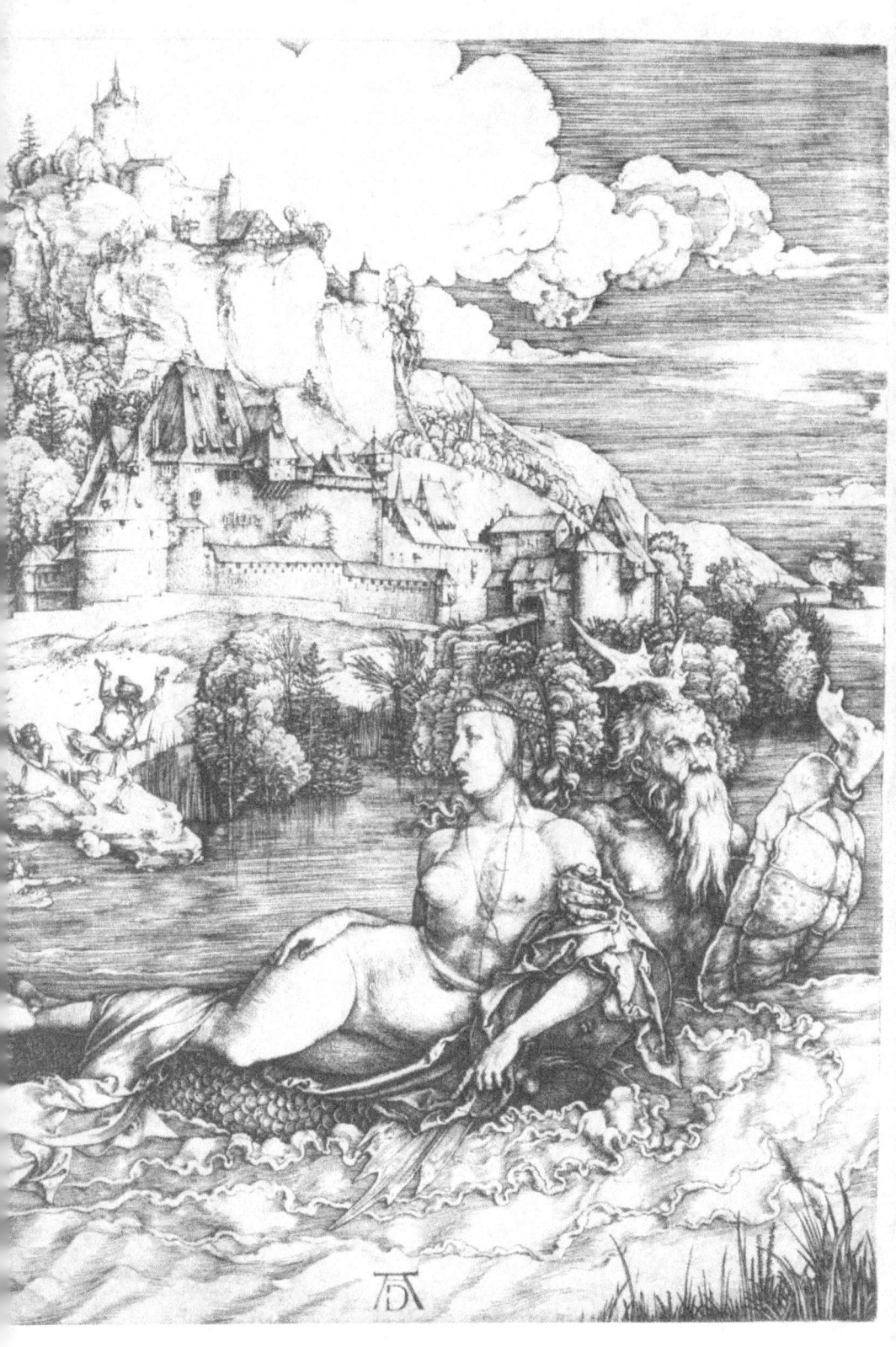

Albrecht Dürer, Sea Monster, 1498

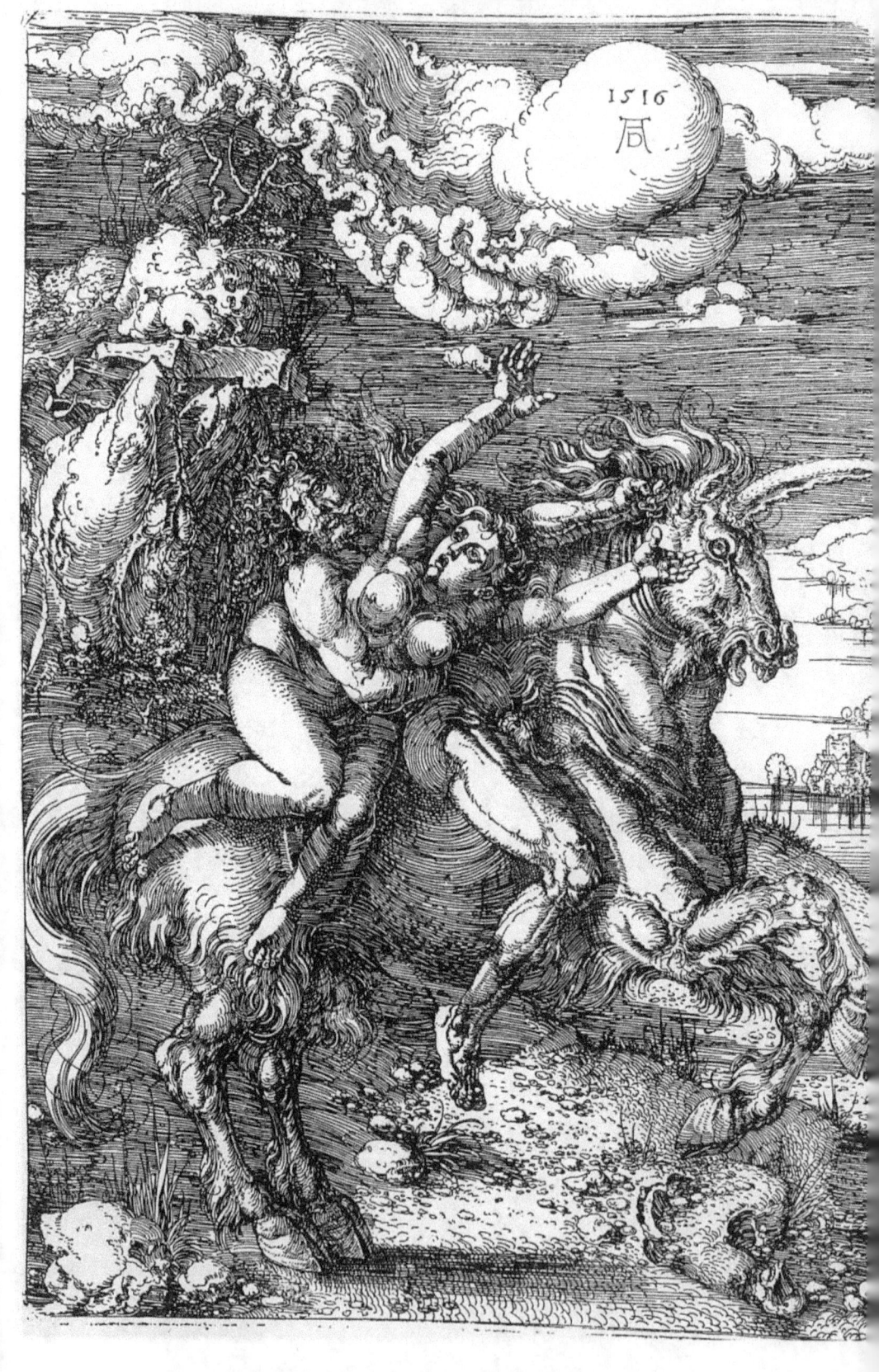

Albrecht Dürer, Abduction of the Unicorn, 1516,
Metropolitan Museum of Art, New York City

PART III

DÜRER AS A CREATOR

CHAPTER I

DÜRER'S PICTURES

I

Dürer's paintings have suffered more by the malignity of fortune than any of his other works. Several have disappeared entirely, and several are but wrecks of what they once were. Others are, as he tells us, "ordinary pictures," of which "I will in a year paint a pile which no one would believe it possible for one man to do in the time," and are perhaps more the work of assistants than of the master. Others, again, have since been repainted, more or less disastrously. Yet enough remain to show us that Dürer was not a painter born, in the sense that Titian and Correggio or Rembrandt and Rubens are; nay, not even in the sense that a Jan Van Eyck or a Mantegna is. Mantegna is certainly the painter with whom Dürer has most affinity, and whose method of employing pigment is least removed from his; but Mantegna is a born colourist – a man whose eye for colour is like a musician's ear for melody – while Dürer is at best with difficulty able to avoid glaring discords, and, if we are to judge by the "ordinary pictures," did not avoid them. Again, Mantegna is not so dependent on line as Dürer – nearly the whole of whose surface is produced by hatching with the brush point. These facts may, perhaps, account for the large portion of Dürer's time devoted to engraving. As an engraver he early found a style for himself, which he continued to develop to the end of his life. As a painter he was for ever experimenting, influenced now by Jacopo de' Barbari, again by Bellini and the pictures he saw at Venice, and yet again by those he saw in the Netherlands. As Velasquez, after each of his journeys to Italy, returns to attempt a mythological picture in the grand style, so Dürer turns to painting after his return from Venice or from the Netherlands; and his pictures divide themselves into three groups: those painted after or during his *Wanderjahre* and before he went to Venice in 1505, those painted there and during the next five years after his return, and those painted in the Netherlands or commenced immediately on his return thence.

II

The mediums of oil and tempera lend themselves to the production of broad-coloured surfaces that merge imperceptibly into one another. There are men the fundamental unit of whose picture language is a blot or shape; as children or as savages, they would find these most capable of expressing what they saw. There are others for whom the scratch or line is the fundamental unit, for whom every object is most naturally expressed by an outline. There are, of course, men who present us with every possible blend of these two fundamental forms of picture language.

The mediums of oils and tempera are especially adapted to the requirements of those who see things rather as a diaper of shapes than as a map of lines; while for these last the point of pen, burin, or etching-needle offers the most congenial implement.

Dürer was very greatly more inclined to express objects by a map of lines than as a diaper of coloured shapes; and for this reason I say that he was not a painter born. If this be true, as a painter he must have been at a disadvantage. In this preponderance of the draughtsman qualities he resembles many artists of the Florentine school, as also in his theoretic pre-occupation with perspective, proportion, architecture, and technical methods. We are impressed by a coldness of approach, an austerity, a dignity not altogether justified by the occasion, but as it were carried over from some precedent hour of spiritual elevation; the prophet's demeanour in between the days of visitation, a little too consciously careful not to compromise the divinity which informs him no longer. This tendency to fall back on manner greatly acquired indeed, but no longer consonant with the actual mood, which is really too vacant of import to parade such importance, is often a fault of natures whose native means of expression is the thin line, the geometer's precision, the architect's foresight in measurement. And by allowing for it I think we can explain the contradiction apparent between the critics' continual insistence on what they call Dürer's great thoughts, and the sparsity of intellectual creativeness which strikes one in turning over his engravings, so many are there of which either the occasion or the conception are altogether trivial when compared with the grandiose aspect of the composition or the impeccable mechanical performance. Dürer's literary remains sufficiently prove his mind to have been constantly exercised upon and around great thoughts, and their influence may be felt in the austerity and intensity of his noblest portraits and other creations. But "great thoughts" in respect of works of art either means the communication of a profound emotion by the creation of a suitable arabesque for a deeply significant subject, as in the flowing masses of Michelangelo's *Creation of Man*, or it means the pictorial enhancing of the telling incidents of a dramatic situation such as we find it in Rembrandt's treatment of the Crucifixion, Deposition, or Entombment. Now it seems to me the paucity of successes on these lines in one who nevertheless occasionally entirely succeeds, is what is most striking in Dürer. Perhaps when dealing with the graphic arts one should rather speak of great character than great thoughts; yet Dürer, while constantly impressing us as a great character, seems to be one who was all too rarely wholly himself. The abundant felicity in expression of Rembrandt or Shakespeare is altogether wanting. The imperial imposition of mood which Michelangelo affects is perhaps never quite certainly his, even in the *Melancholy*. Yet we feel that not only has he a capacity of the same order as those men, but that he is spiritually akin to them, despite his coldness, despite his ostentation.

But not only is Dürer praised for "great thoughts," but he is praised for realism, and sometimes accused of having delighted in ugliness; or, as it is more cautiously expressed, of having preferred truth to grace. This is a point which I consider may better be discussed in respect to his drawings than his pictures, which nearly always have some obvious conventional or traditional character, so that the word realism cannot be applied to them. Even in his portraits his signature or an inscription is often added in such a manner as insists that this is a painting, a panel; – not a view through a window, or an attempt to deceive the eye with a make-believe reality.

III

The altar-piece, consisting of a centre, the Virgin Mary adoring her baby son in the carpenter's shop at Nazareth, and two wings, St. Anthony and St. Sebastian, though the earliest of Dürer's pictures which has survived, is perhaps the most beautiful of them all, at least as far as the two wings are concerned. The centre has been considerably damaged by repainting, and was probably, owing to the greater complication of motives in it, never quite so successful. Whether at Venice or elsewhere, it would seem almost necessary that the young painter had seen and been impressed by pictures by Gentile Bellini and Andrea Mantegna, both of whom have painted in the same thin tempera on fine canvas, obtaining similar beauties of colour and surface. It is hardly possible to imagine one who had seen none but German or Flemish pictures painting the St. Sebastian. The treatment of the still life in the foreground is in itself almost a proof of this. Perhaps this thin, flat tempera treatment was that most suited to Dürer's native bias, and we should regret his having been tempted to overcome the more brilliant and exacting medium of oils. In any case he more than once reverted to it in portraits and studies, while the majority of the pictures painted before he went to Venice in 1506 have more or less kinship with it. The supposed portrait of Frederic the Wise is another masterpiece in this kind, and the *Hercules slaying the birds of the Stymphalian Lake* in the Germanic Museum, Nuremberg, 1500, was probably another. For though now considerably damaged by restorations and dirt, it suggests far greater pleasures than it actually imparts. The contrast between

> "The sea-worn face sad as mortality,
> Divine with yearning after fellowship,"

and the blond richly curling hair blown back from it, is extremely fine and entirely suited to the treatment; as is also the similar contrast between the richly inlaid bow, shield, and arrows, and the broad and flowing modulation of the energetic limbs and back.

The Paumgartner altar-piece, 1499, stands out from the "ordinary pictures" belonging to this early period. It consists of a charming and gay Nativity in the centre, and two knights in armour on the wings, probably portraits of the donors, Stephan and Lucas Paumgartner, figuring as warlike saints. Stephan, a

❊ 212

personal friend of Dürer's, figured again as St. George in the *Trinity and All Saints* picture painted in 1511. There were originally two panels with female saints beyond these again, but no trace of them remains. Now that the landscape backgrounds have been removed from the side panels, there is no reason to suppose that any one but Dürer had a hand in these works. But in writing to Heller, he tells him that it was unheard of to put so much work into an altar-piece as he was then putting into his *Coronation of the Virgin*, and we may feel certain that Dürer regarded this picture as in the altar-piece category. The two knights are represented against black grounds, and their silhouettes form a very fine arabesque, which the streamers of their lances, artificially arranged, complete and emphasise. This black ground points probably to the influence of Jacopo de' Barbari, whom Dürer had met and been mystified by.

No doubt there was much in such a background that appealed to the draughtsman in Dürer. It insisted on the outline which had probably been the starting-point of his conception. Nothing could be less painter-like, or make the modelling of figures more difficult, as Dürer, perhaps, realised when he later on painted the *Adam and Eve* at Madrid. These two warriors are, however, most successful and imposing, and immeasurably enhanced now that the spurious backgrounds, artfully concocted out of Dürer's own prints by an ingenious improver of his betters, have been removed. This person had also tinkered the centre picture, painting out two heraldic groups of donors, far smaller in scale than the actual personages of the scene, but very useful in the composition, as giving a more ample base to the masses of broken and fretted quality; useful also now as an additional proof of how free from the fetters of an impertinent logic of realism Dürer ever was. These little kneeling donors and their coats of arms emphasise the surface, and are delightful in their naïvety, while they serve to render the gay, almost gaudy panel more homely, and give it a place and a function in the world. For they help us to realise that it answered a demand, and was not the uncalled-for and slightly frigid excursion of the aesthetic imagination which it must otherwise appear. In the same way the brilliant *Adoration of the Magi* (dated 1504) in the Uffizi, also somewhat gaudy and frigid, could we but see it where it originally hung in Luther's church at Wittenberg, might invest itself with some charm that one vainly seeks in it now. The failure in emotion might seem more natural if we saw the wise Elector discussing his new purchase; we might have felt what Dürer meant when a year later he wrote from Venice: "I am a gentleman here and only a hanger-on at home." The expectation and prophecy of his success in those who surround a painter, – even if it be chiefly expressed by bitter rivalry, or the craft by which one greedy purchaser tries to over-reach another, even if he has to be careful not to eat at some tables for fear of being poisoned by a host whose ambition his present performance may have dashed – even expressed in this truly Venetian manner, the expectation and prophecy of his success in those about him make it easier for a painter to soar, and may touch his work with an indefinable glow that the approval of honest and astute electors or solid burghers may have been utterly powerless to impart.

IV

At Venice, perhaps the occasion for his journey thither, Dürer undertook a more important work than any he had yet attempted. *The Feast of the Rose Garlands* was painted for the high altar of the church of San Bartolommeo, belonging to the German Merchants' Exchange, and close to their Pondaco.[73] In it we find a very considerable influence of Italy in general, and Giovanni Bellini in particular; it is a splendid and pompous parade piece, and probably the portraits of the German merchants which it contained were the part of the work which was most successful, as it was certainly that most congenial to Dürer's genius. The *Christ among the Doctors*, dated 1506, and now in the Barberini Palace at Rome, might seem to have been painted chiefly to justify Giovanni Bellini's astonishment at the calligraphical painting of hair. It is one of those pictures of which a literary description would please more than the work itself. Though the contrast between the sweet childish face and those of the old worldly scribes is well conceived, it is in reality so violent as to be grotesque, and the play of hands produces the effect of a diagram explanatory of a conjuring trick, or a deaf and dumb alphabet, instead of conveying the inner sense of the scene represented after Rossetti's fashion, who so often succeeded in making hands speak. Another work, which dates from Venice, is the little *Crucifixion* (at Dresden.) Perhaps the landscape and suffering body are just sufficiently touched with acute emotion to make the arabesque of the two floating ends of the loin-cloth appear a little out of place; for in spite of the delicacy and all but tenderness which Dürer has for once attained to in the workmanship, one's satisfaction seems let and hindered.

V

Shortly after his return from Venice, Dürer completed two life-size panels representing Adam and Eve; there are drawings for them dated during his stay at Venice, but as a work of art they are far less interesting than the engraving of the same subject completed three years earlier. The treatment, even the conception, has been inadequately influenced by the proposed scale of the work. Probably they were like the earlier Hercules, done to please the artist himself rather than some patron; they are an effort to prove that he could do something which was after all too hard for him. Not only had he set himself the problem which the Greeks and Michelangelo, and Raphael with their aid alone, had solved, of finding proportions suitable to express harmoniously the infinite capacity for complex motion combined with that constancy of intention which gives dignity to men and women alone among animals; but the technical problems involved in representing life-size nude figures against a plain black ground were indeed an unconscious confession that Dürer did not understand paint. There is a copy of these panels, recently attributed to Baldung Grien, in the Pitti. Animals and birds have been added from drawings made by Dürer, but the picture is still farther from success, though Grien may not improbably have executed it with Dürer at his elbow. Dürer made one more attempt at representing a life-size nude, the *Lucretia*, finished in 1518, at a period when his powers seem to have been clouded, for the few pictures which belong to it are all inferior. However, studies for the figure exist dated 1508, so we may suppose it was a project brought back from Venice. His ill-success with this subject may remind us of Shakespeare's long pedantic exercise in rhyme on the same theme. The pictorial motive of Dürer's work is beautiful and worthy of a Greek: indeed it is identical with that of Watts' *Psyche*, of which the version in private hands is very superior to that in the Tate Gallery. The position of the bed, the idea of the draperies all are parallel. No doubt the lonely feather shed from Love's wing at which Psyche gazes is both more of a poet's and of a painter's invention than the cold steel of Lucretia's dagger. And in spite of his wide knowledge of Greek and Italian art, our English master could scarcely have produced a work of such classic dignity with the more violent motive of the dagger, which seems to call for "The torch that flames with many a lurid flake," or at least the torpid glow of smouldering embers, to light it in such a manner as would make a really pictorial treatment possible. No doubt Dürer has been misled by a too tyrannous notion as to what ought to be the physical build of so chaste a matron, and in his anxiety to make chastity self-evident, has forgotten to explain the need for it by such a degree of attractiveness as might tempt a tyrant to be dangerous. Just as Shakespeare, in attempting to exhaust every possible motive which the situation comports, has forgotten that for a character that can move us a selection is needed. Another elaborate piece of frigid invention is the *Massacre of the Ten Thousand Saints in the reign of Sapor II. of Persia*, in the Imperial Gallery at Vienna, dated 1508. However, in this case no doubt Dürer could plead that the subject was not of his own choice, for he was commissioned by the Elector, Frederic the Wise, whose wisdom probably did not extend to a knowledge of what subjects lend themselves to pictorial treatment. Still, making every allowance for these facts, it cannot be admitted that Dürer did the best possible with his subject. Probably it did not move him, and neither does he us. Peter Breughel and Albrecht Altdorfer would certainly have done far better so far as the conception of the picture is concerned, though neither of them had so much skill to waste on its realisation. Nevertheless, this tour *de force* is the picture of Dürer's most pleasing in surface and colour, with the exception of the Wings *of the Dresden Altar-piece*. It contains beautiful groups and figures, and is extremely well executed; so that it may amuse and delight the eye for a long time while the significance of the subject is forgotten.

VI

We now turn to the third and fourth of the half-dozen pictures of Dürer, which stand out from all the rest by their elaboration and importance. The *Coronation of the Virgin* (*see* p. 97), painted as the centre panel of the altar-piece commissioned by Jacob Heller at

Frankfort, was unfortunately burnt with the palace at Munich on the night of April 9, 1674; the Elector Maximilian of Bavaria having forced or cajoled the Dominicans, to whose church Heller had left it, to sell it to him. It is now represented by a copy made by Paul Juvenal in its original position, where the almost ruined portraits of Heller and his wife are supposed to have been partly Dürer's, though the other panels are obviously the work of assistants. This work exists for us in a series of magnificent brush drawings in black and white line on grey paper, rather than in the copy, and we can in a measure imagine its appearance by the perfectly-preserved *Trinity and All Saints* commenced immediately after it for Matthew Landauer, and now in the Imperial Gallery at Vienna. Nothing can surpass this last picture in elaboration and finish; the colour, if not beautiful, is rich and luminous; and though it is separate faces and draperies which chiefly delight the eye, the composition of the whole is an adequate adaptation of the traditional treatment for such themes which had been handed down through the middle ages. It invites comparison rather with the similar subjects painted by Fra Angelico than with the *Disputa* of Raphael, to which German critics compare it; however, it possesses as little of Angelico's sweet blissfulness as the Dominican painter possessed of Dürer's accuracy of hand and searching intensity of visual realisation. Both painters are interested in individuals, and, representing crowds of faces, make every one a portrait; both evince a dramatic sense of propriety in gesture, both revel in bright, clear colours, especially azure; but as the light in Dürer's masterpiece has a rosy hotness, which ill bears comparison with the virginal pearliness of Angelico's heaven, so the costumes and the figures of the Florentine are doll-like, when compared with the unmistakable quality of the stuffs in which the fully-resurrected bodies of Dürer's saints rumple and rustle. The wings of his angels are at least those of birds, though coloured to fancy, while Angelico's are of pasteboard tinsel and paint. But in spite of the comparative genuineness of his upholstery, as a vision of heaven there can be no hesitation in preferring that of the Florentine.

In a frame designed by Dürer and carved under his supervision, this monument to thoroughness and skill was ensconced in a little chapel dedicated to All Saints, which in style approaches our Tudor buildings. There the frame remained till lately with a poor copy of the picture and an inscription in old German to this effect: ('Matthew Landauer completed the dedication of this chapel of the twelve brethren, together with the foundation attached to it, and this picture, in the year 1511 after the birth of Christ,')

Dürer signed his picture with the same Latin formula as that of the *Coronation*:

> "Albrecht Dürer of Nuremberg did this the year from when the Virgin brought forth 1511."

VII

Of all Dürer's paintings of the Madonna, there is only one which, by its superb design, deserves special notice among his masterpieces. This *Madonna with the Iris* exists in two versions, both unfinished; one the property of Sir Frederick Cook, the other at Prague, in the Rudolphium. This latter Mr. Campbell Dodgson considers to be a poor copy. The panel is badly cracked, and weeds and long grasses have been added, apparently with a view to masking the cracks. Judging from a photograph alone, many of these additions seem so appropriately placed and freely sketched that I feel it at least to be possibly a work by the master himself. On the other hand, Sir Frederick's picture is so sleepy and clumsy in handling, that though it is unfinished, and perhaps in part damaged by some restorer, I feel great hesitation in regarding it as Dürer's handiwork. In both cases the magnificent design is his, and that alone in either is fully representative of him. Mr. Campbell Dodgson ventures to criticise the profusion of drapery as excessive, but my feeling, I must confess, endorses Dürer's in this, rather than that of his learned critic. To me this profusion, and the grandeur it gives as a mass in the design, is of the very essence of what is most peculiarly creative in Dürer's imagination.

The last picture of which it is necessary to speak is that of the *Four Apostles* or the *Four Preachers*, as they have been more appropriately called; it was perhaps the last he painted, and is in many respects the most successful. It is the only one by which the comparison with Raphael, so dear to German critics, seems at all warranted: there is certainly some kinship between Dürer's St. John and St. Paul and apostolic figures in the cartoons or on the Vatican walls. The German artist's manner is less rhetorical, but his conception is hardly less grandiose; and his taste does not so closely border on over-emphasis, but neither is it so conscious or so fluent. Technically it seems to me that the chief influence is a recollection of the large canvases of Jan and Hubert Van Eyck and Hubert Van der Goes which Dürer had admired in the Netherlands; these had strengthened and directed the bias of his self-culture towards simple masses on a large scale.[74] He may very well have sought to combine what he learnt from them with hints he found in the engravings after Raphael which he obtained in Antwerp. His increasing sickness may probably account for the fact that the white mantle of St. Paul is the only portion quite finished. The assertion of the writing-master, Johann Neudörffer, who in his youth had known Dürer, that the four figures are typical of the four temperaments, the sanguine, the choleric, the phlegmatic, and the melancholic, – into which categories an amateurish psychology arbitrarily divided human characters, – is as likely to be correct as it is certain that it adds nothing to the power and beauty of the presentation. Though Dürer in his work on human proportions describes the physical build of these different types, we do not know exactly what degree of precision he imagined it possible to attain in discerning them, or to what extent their names were merely convenient handles for certain types which he had chosen æsthetically. To us to-day this classification is merely a trace of an obsolete pedantry, which it would be a vain curiosity to attempt to follow with the object of identifying its imaginary bases.

The four preachers have all the air of being striking likenesses of actual people which it is possible for work so broadly and grandly conceived to have. These panels are interesting, even more than by their actual success, as showing us what a scholar Dürer was to the end; how he learned from every defeat as well as every victory, and constantly approached a conception and a rendering of human beauty which seems intimately connected with man's fullest intellectual and spiritual freedom – a conception and rendering of human beauty which Raphael himself had to learn from the Greeks and Michelangelo. The work has suffered, it is supposed, from restorers, and also from the Munich monarch, Maximilian, who had the tremendous texts (see page 177) which Dürer had inscribed beneath the two panels sawn off in order to spare the feelings of the Jesuits, who were dominant at his court, for their conception of religion did not consist with terrors to come for those who, abuse their trust as governors and directors of mankind.

Lastly, mention must be made of Dürer's monochrome masterpiece, The Road to Calvary 15.27 (see illus.), in the collection of Sir Frederick Cook. A poor copy of this work is at Dresden, a better one at Bergamo. The effect of it, and several elaborate water-colour designs of the same class, is akin to the peculiar richness of chased metal work; glinting light hovers over crowds of little figures.

CHAPTER II

DÜRER'S PORTRAITS

I

If Dürer's pictures are as a whole the least satisfactory section of his work, in his portraits he makes us abundant amends for the time he might otherwise have been reproached for wasting to obtain a vain mastery over brushes and pigment.

Unfortunately it is probable that many even of these have been lost or destroyed, while of his most interesting sitters we have nothing but drawings. He did not paint his friend, the boisterous and learned Pirkheimer; and what would we not give for a painted portrait of Erasmus, or a portrait of Kratzer, the astronomer royal, to compare with the two masterpieces by Holbein in the Louvre? Even the posthumous portrait of his Imperial patron Maximilian is less interesting than the drawings from which it was done, the eccentric sitter not having the time to spare for so sensible a monument.

II

However, Dürer had one sitter who was perhaps the most beautiful of all the sons of men, whose features combined in an equal measure nobleness of character, intellectual intensity and physical beauty; and, finding him also most patient and accessible, he painted him frequently. The two earliest portraits of himself are the drawings which show him at the ages of thirteen and nineteen(?) respectively. Then, as a young man with a sprouting chin, we have the picture till recently at Leipzig of which Goethe's enthusiastic description has already been quoted (p. 62). It is probable that neither Titian nor Holbein could have shown at so early an age a portrait so admirably conceived and executed. It is a masterpiece, even now that the inevitable improvements which those who lack all relish of genius rarely lack the opportunity, never the inclination, to add to a masterpiece, have confused the drawing of the eyes, and reduced the bloom and delicacy that the features traced by a master hand, even when they become an almost complete wreck, often retain; for time and fortune are not so conscientiously destructive as the imbecility of the incapable. Next we have a portrait of Dürer when only five years older, in perfect preservation, – that in the Prado at Madrid. This charming picture must certainly have drawn a sonnet from the Shakespeare who wrote *Love's Labour Lost*, could he have seen it. For it presents a young dandy, the delicacy and sensitiveness of whose features seem to demand and warrant the butterfly-like display of the white and black costume hemmed with gold, and of a cap worthy to crown those flowing honey-coloured locks. There is a good copy of this delightful work in the Uffizi, where, in a congregation of self-painted artists, it does all but justice to the most beautiful of them all. For fineness of touch the original has never been surpassed by any hand of European or even Chinese master. Next there are the dapper little full-length portraits which Dürer inserted in his chief paintings. He stands beside his friend Pirkheimer at the back of the adoring crowd in the *Feast of the Roses*, and again in the midst of the mountain slope, where on all sides of them the ten thousand saints suffer martyrdom. Dürer stands alone beside an inscription in a gentle pastoral landscape beneath the vision of the Virgin's Assumption seen over the heads of the Apostles, who gaze up in rapture; and again he is alone beside a broad peaceful river beneath the vision of the Holy Trinity and All Saints. I know of no parallel to these little portraits. Rembrandt and Botticelli and many others have introduced portraits of themselves into religious pictures, but always in disguise, as a personage in the crowd or an actor in the scene. Only the master who was really most exceptional for his good looks, has had the kindness, in spite of every incongruity, to present himself before us on all important occasions, like the court beauty in whom it is charity rather than vanity to appear in public. It is expected that the very beautiful be gracious thus. Emerson tells us that two centuries ago the Town Council of Montpelier passed a law to constrain two beautiful sisters to sit for a certain time on their balcony every other day, that all might enjoy the sight of what was most beautiful in their town. It was one of the most gracious traits of Jeanne d'Arc's character that she liked to wear beautiful clothes, because it pleased the poor people to see her thus. And Palm Sunday commemorates another historical example of such grace and truth. Dürer's face had a striking resemblance to the traditional type for Jesus, adding to it just that element of individual peculiarity, the absence of which makes it ever liable to appear a little vacant and unconvincing. The perception of this would seem to have dictated the general arrangement of Dürer's crowning portrait of himself, that at Munich dated 1500 (see illus.), "Before which" (Mr. Ricketts writes in his recently published volume on the Prado) "one forgets all other portraits whatsoever, in the sense that this perfect realisation of one of the world's greatest men is equal to the occasion." The most exhaustive visual power and executive capacity meet in this picture, which would seem to have traversed the many perils to which it has been exposed without really suffering so much as their enumeration makes one expect. Thausing tells us:

> The following is the story of the picture's wanderings, as told at Nuremberg. It was lent by the magistrates, after they had taken the precaution of placing a seal and strings on the back of the panel, to the painter and engraver Kügner, to copy. He, however, carefully sawed the panel in half (layer-wise) and glued to the authentic back his miserable copy, which now hangs in the Town Hall. The original he sold, and it eventually came into the possession of King Ludwig I., before Nuremberg belonged to Bavaria.

He suggests that the colour was once bright and varied, and that by varnish and glazes it has been reduced to its present harmonious condition. The hair is certainly much darker than the other portraits would have led one to expect, and the almost walnut brown of the general colour scheme is unique in Dürer's work. However, if some such transmogrification has been effected, it is marvellous that it should have obliterated so little of the inimitable handiwork of the master. Thausing considered the date (1500), monogram and inscription on the back to be forgeries, and it certainly looks as if it ought to come nearer to the portrait in the *Feast of the Rose Garlands* (1506) than to that at Madrid (1498). A genuine scalloped tablet is faintly visible under the dark glazes which cover the background; and this, no doubt, bears the original inscription and date. What may not have happened to a picture after or before it left the artist's studio? Critics are too quick to determine that such changes have been introduced by others. In this case we must remember how experimental Dürer was, even with regard to his engravings on metal. He tries iron plates and etching, and finally settles on a method of commencing with etching and finishing with the burin; and this was in a medium in which he soon found himself at home. But with painting he was vastly more experimental, and never satisfied with his results, as he told Melanchthon (see p. 187). Then we must remember that this picture probably was during Dürer's lifetime, if not in his own possession, at least never out of his reach; and no

※ 225

doubt he was aware that it was the grandest and most perfectly finished of all his portraits – therefore, as he came more and more, especially after his visit to the Netherlands, to desire and seek after simplicity, he may himself have added the dark glazes. If the original inscription contained a dedication to Pirkheimer or some other notable Nuremberger, there was every reason for the artist who stole the picture to obliterate this and add a new one: or this may have been done when it became the property of the town, for those who sold it may have wished that it should not be known that it might have been an heirloom in their family. Infinite are the possibilities, those only decide in such cases who have a personal motive for doing so; "la rage de conclure" (as Flaubert saw) is the pitfall of those who are vain of their knowledge.

III

Though fearing that it will appear but tedious, I will now attempt briefly to describe in succession the remaining master portraits which we owe to Dürer, and the effect that each produces. It is by these works and not by his creative pictures that his ranks among the greatest names of painting. These might be compared with the very finest portraits by Raphael and Holbein, and the precedence would remain a question of personal predilection; since nothing reasoned, no distinguishable superiority over Dürer in vision or execution could be urged for either. Rather, if mere capacity were regarded, he must have the palm; nor did either of his compeers light upon a happier subject than was Dürer's when he represented himself; nor did they achieve nobler designs. In effect upon our emotions and sensations, these portraits may compete with the masterpieces of Titian and Rembrandt, though the method of expression is in their case too different to render comparison possible. Whatever in the glow of light, in the power of shadow, to envelop and enhance the features portrayed, is theirs and not his, his superiority of searching insight, united with its equivalent of unique facility in definition, seems more than to outweigh. Before he left for Venice, besides the renderings of himself already mentioned, Dürer had painted his father twice, in 1494 and in 1497. The latter was the pair to and compeer of his own portrait at Madrid,; and, hitherto unknown, was lent last year by Lord Northampton to the Royal Academy, and has since been bought for the National Gallery. This beautiful work is unique even among the works of the master, and is not so much the worse for repainting as some make out. The majority of Dürer's portraits stand alone. In each the Esthetic problem has been approached and solved in a strikingly different manner. This picture and its fellow, the portrait of the painter at Madrid, the *Oswolt Krel*, the portrait of a lady seen against the sea at Berlin, the *Wolgemut*, and Dürer's own portrait at Munich, though seen by the same absorbing eyes, are rendered each in quite a different manner. No man has ever been better gifted for portraying a likeness than Dürer; but the absence of a native comprehension of pigment made him ever restless, and it might be possible to maintain that each of these pictures presented us with a differing strategy to enforce pigment, to subserve the purposes of a draughtsman. Still this would seem to imply a greater sacrifice of ease and directness than those brilliant masterpieces can be charged with. They none of them lack beauty of colour, of surface, or of handling, though each so unlike the other. In this portrait of his father, Dürer has developed a shaken brushline, admirably adapted to suggest the wrinkled features of an old man, but in complete contrast to the rapid sweep of the caligraphic work in the *Oswolt Krel*; and it is to be noticed how in both pictures the touch seems to have been invented to facilitate the rendering of the peculiar curves and lines of the sitter's features, and further variations of it developed to express the

❈ 227

draperies and other component parts of the picture. It is this inventiveness in handling which most distinguishes Dürer from painters like Raphael and Holbein, and makes his work comparable with the masterpieces of Rembrandt and Titian, in spite of the extreme opposition in aspect between their work and his.

The noble portrait of a middle-aged man, No. 557c, in the Royal Gallery at Berlin, (supposed to represent Frederick the Wise, Elector of Saxony, Dürer's first patron), gives us a master portrait, in which the technical treatment is comparable to that of the early triptych at Dresden, and which is a monument of sober power and distinction, though again very difficult to compare with the other splendid portraits by the same hand which hang beside or near it in that Gallery.

The vivid *Oswolt Krel* at Munich shows the peculiarity of Dürer's caligraphic touch better than perhaps any other of his portraits. The finish is not carried so far as in the Madrid portrait of himself, where even the texture of the gloves has been softened by touches of the thumb, and the absence of these extra refinements leaves it the most spontaneous and vigorously bold of all Dürer's paintings. The concentrated energy of the sitter's features demanded such a treatment; he seems to burn with the inconsiderate atheism of a Marlowe. Young, and less surprised than indignant to be alone awake in a sleepy and bigoted world, he seems convinced of a mission to chastise, *even* to scandalise his easy-going neighbours. Let us hope he met with better luck than the Marlowes, Shelleys, and Rimbauds, whose tragedies we have read; for one can but regret, as one meets his glance so much fiercer than need be, that he is not known to history.

The fine portrait of Hans Tucher, 1499, in the Grand Ducal Museum at Weimar should, judging from a photograph alone, be mentioned here. It has obvious affinities with the *Oswolt Krel*, but the caligraphic method is again modified in harmony with the character of the sitter's features. The companion piece, representing Felicitas Tucherin, would seem at some period to have been restored to the insignificance and obscurity that belonged to the sitter before Dürer painted her.

IV

The portraits which Dürer painted at Venice, or soon after his return, betray the influence of other masterpieces on his own. Mr. Ricketts has pointed to that of Antonello da Messina in the portraits of young men at Vienna (1505) and at Hampton Court (1506). The former of these has an allegorical sketch of Avarice, painted on the back in a thick impasto, such as seems almost a presage of after developments of the Venetian school, and may possibly show the influence of some early experiment by Giorgione which Dürer wished to show that he could imitate if he liked. The latter represents a personage who appears on the left of the *Feast of Rose Wreaths* in exactly the same cap and with the same fastening to his jerkin, crossing his white shirt.

Not improbably Dürer may have painted separate portraits of nearly all the members of the German Guild at Venice who appear in the *Rose Garlands*. In any case much of his work during his stay there has disappeared. It was here that he painted that beautiful head of a woman (No. 557 G in the Berlin Gallery) with soft, almost Leonardesque shadows, seen against the luminous hazy sea and sky, which remains absolutely unique in method and effect among his works, and makes one ask oneself unanswerable questions as to what might not have been the result if he could but have brought himself to accept the offered citizenship and salary, and stop on at Venice. A Dürer, not only secluded from Luther and his troubling denunciations, but living to see Titian and Giorgione's early masterpieces, perhaps forming friendships with them, and later visiting Rome, standing in the

Sistine Chapel, seated in the Stanze between the School of Athens and the Disputa! I at least cannot console myself for these missed opportunities, as so many of his critics and biographers have done, by saying that doubtless had he stayed he would have been spoiled like those second-class German and Dutch painters, for whom the siren art of Italy proved a baneful influence. One could almost weep to think of what has been probably lost to the world because Dürer could not bring himself to stay on at Venice. It *was* here he painted the tiny panel representing the head of a girl in gay apparel dated 1507 (in the Berlin Gallery), that makes one think, even more than do Holbein's *Venus* and *Lais* at Basle, of the triumphs that were reserved for Italians in the treatment of similar subjects.

After his return the influence of Venetian methods gradually waned, till we find in the masterly and refined portrait of *Wolgemut* (1516); something of a return to the caligraphic method so noticeable in the *Oswolt Krel*. About the same time Dürer recommenced painting in tempera in a manner resembling the early Dresden *Madonna* and the *Hercules*, as we see by the rather unpleasant heads of Apostles in the Uffizi and the tine one of an old man in a vermilion cap in the Louvre, &c. &c.

V

On his arrival at Antwerp in 1521 Dürer commenced the third and last group of master-portraits; foremost is the superb head and bust at Madrid, supposed to represent Hans Imhof, a patrician of Dürer's native town and his banker while at Antwerp; of the same date are the triumphant renderings of the grave and youthful Bernard van Orley (at Dresden) and that of a middle-aged man – lost for the National Gallery, and now in the possession of Mrs. Gardner, of Boston. All three were probably painted at Antwerp.

It may be that the portrait of Imhof and the report of the honours and commissions showered on their painter while in the Netherlands, woke the Nuremberg Councillors up, for we have portraits of three of them dated 1526 – Jacob Muffel, Hieronymus Holzschuher, (both in the Royal Gallery, Berlin,) and the eccentric and unpleasing medallion representing Johannes Kleeberger, at Vienna. With the exception of this last, this group is composed of masterpieces absolutely unrivalled for intensity and dignity of power. Van Eyck painted with inhuman indifference a few ugly grotesque but otherwise uninteresting people. All but a very few of Holbein's best portraits pale before these instances of searching insight; and, north of the Alps at least, there are no others which can be compared to them. The *Hans Imhof* shows a shrewd and forbidding schemer for gain on a large scale – a face which produces the impression of a trap or closed strong box, but, being so alert and intelligent, seems to demand some sort of commiseration for the constraint put upon its humanity in the creation of a master, a tyrant over himself first and afterwards over an ever-widening circle of others. The unknown master who is represented in Mrs. Gardner's beautiful picture is less forbidding, though not less patently a moulder of destiny. *Jacob Muffel* has a more open face, a more serene gaze; but his mouth too has the firmness acquired by those who live always in the presence of enemies, or are at least aware that "a little folding of the hands" may be fatal to all their most cherished purposes. The last of these masters of themselves and of their fortunes in hazardous and change-fraught times is *Hieronymus Holzschuher*, Dürer's friend. Only less felicitous because less harmonious in colour than the three former, this vivacious portrait of a ruddy, jovial, and white-haired patrician seen against a bright blue background might produce the effect of a Father Christmas, were it not for the resolute mouth and the puissant side-glance of the eyes. Bernard van Orley, the only youthful person immortalised in this group, has a gentle, responsible air which his features are a little too heavy to enhance.

I have now mentioned the chief of his portraits, which are the best of his painting, and by which he ranks for the directness and power of his workmanship and of his visual analysis in the company of the very greatest. Raphael and Holbein have alone produced portraits which, as they can be compared to Dürer's, might also be held to rival them; Titian, Rubens, Velasquez, Rembrandt, Van Dyck, Reynolds have done as splendidly, but the material they used and the aims they set themselves were too different to make a comparison serviceable. These men are pre-eminent among those who have produced portraits which, while unsurpassed for technical excellences, present to us individuals whose beauty or the character it expresses are equally exceptional.

CHAPTER III

DÜRER'S DRAWINGS

I

Perhaps Dürer is more felicitous as a draughtsman than in any other branch of art. The power of nearly all first-rate artists is more wholly live and effective in their drawings than in elaborated works. Dürer himself says:

An artist of understanding and experience can show more of his great power and art in small things, roughly and rudely done, than many another in his great work. Powerful artists alone will understand that in this strange saying I speak truth. For this reason a man may often draw something with his pen on a half sheet of paper in one day, or cut it with his graver on a small block of wood, and it shall be fuller of art and better than another's great work whereon he hath spent a whole year's careful labour.

But it is possible to go far beyond this and say not only "another's great work," but his own great work.

In the first chapter of this work I said that the standard in works of art is not truth but sincerity; that if the artist tells us what he feels to be beautiful, it does not matter how much or how little comparison it will bear with the actual objects represented. And from this fact, that sincerity not truth is of prime importance in matters of expression, results the strange truth that Dürer says will be recognised by powerful artists alone (see page 227). Any one who recognises how often the sketches and roughs of artists, especially of those who are in a peculiar degree creators, excel their finished works in those points which are the distinctive excellences of such men, will grant this at once. Only to turn to the sketch (inscribed *Memento Mei 1505*) of *Death* on horseback with a scythe, or the pen-portrait of Dürer leaning on his hand, will be enough to convince those who alone can be convinced on these points. For any who need to explain to themselves the character of such sketches – as the authoress of a recent little book on Dürer does that of the pen drawing "in which the boy's chin rests on his hand" by telling us that "it is unfinished and was evidently discarded as a failure," – any who must be at such pains in a case of this sort is one of those who can never understand wherein the great power of a work of art resides. Such people may get great pleasure from works of art; only I am content to remain convinced that the pleasure they get has no kind of kinship with that which I myself obtain, or that which the greatest artists most constantly seek to give. This marvellous portrait of himself as a lad of from seventeen to nineteen years of age is just one of those things "roughly and rudely done," of which Dürer speaks. There is probably no parallel to it for mastery or power among works produced by artists so youthful.

There is often some virtue in spontaneity which is difficult to define; perhaps it bears more convincing witness to the artist's integrity than slower and longer labours, from which it is difficult to ward all duplicity of intention. The finishing-touch is too often a Judas' kiss. "Blessed are the pure in heart" is absolutely true in art. (Of course, I do not use purity in the narrow sense which is confined to avoidance of certain sensual subjects and seductive intentions.) It is only poverty of imagination which taboos subject-matter, and lack of charity that believes there are themes which cannot be treated with any but ignoble intentions. But the virtue in a spontaneous drawing is akin to that single devotion to whatever is best, which true purity is; as the refinement of economy which results in the finished work is akin to that delicate repugnance to all waste, which is true chastity. A sketch by Rembrandt of a naked servant girl on a bed is as "simple as the infancy of truth" – as single in intention. A Greek statue of a raimentless Apollo is pre-eminently chaste. But it does not follow that Rembrandt was in his life eminently pure, or the Greek sculptor signal for chastity. Drawings rapidly executed have often a lyrical, rapturous, exultant purity, and are for that reason, to those whose eyes are blinded neither by prejudice nor by misfortune, as captivating as are healthy, gleeful children to those whose hearts are free. And while the joy that a child's glee gives is for a time, that which a drawing gives may well be for ever.

We say a "spirited sketch" as we say "a spirited horse"; but works of art are instinct with a vast variety of spirits and exert manifold influences. It is a poverty of language which has confined the use of this word to one of the most obvious and least estimable. It can be never too much insisted on that a work of art is something that exerts an influence, and that its whole merit lies in the quality and degree of the influence exerted; for those who are not moved by it, it is no more than a written sentence to one who cannot read.

II

Many people in turning over a collection of Dürer's drawings would be constantly crying, "How marvellously realistic!" and would glow with enthusiasm and smile with gratitude for the perception which these words expressed. Others would say "merely realistic"; and the words would convey, if not disapprobation for something shocking, at least indifference. In both cases the word "realistic" would, I take it, mean that the objects which the pen, brush, or charcoal strokes represented were described with great particularity. And in the first case delight would have been felt at recognising the fulness of detailed information conveyed about the objects drawn – that each drawing represented not a generalisation, but an individual. In the other case the mind would have been repelled by the infatuated insistence on insignificant or negligible details, the absence of their classification and subordination to ideas. The first of these two frames of mind is that of Paul Pry, who is delighted to see, to touch, or behold, for whom everything is a discovery; and there are members of this class of temperament who in middle life continue to make the same discoveries every day with zest and a wonder equal to that which they felt when children. The second of these frames of mind is that of the man with a system or in search of a system, who desires to control, or, if he cannot do that, at least to be taken into the confidence of the controller, or to gain a position from which he can oversee him, and approve or disapprove. Now neither of these judgments is in itself aesthetic, or implies a comprehension of Dürer as an artist.

The man who cries out: "Just look how that is done!" "Who could have believed a single line could have expressed so much?" judges as an artist, a craftsman. The man who, like Jean Francois Millet, exclaims: "How fine! How grand! How delicate! How beautiful!" judges as a creator. He sees that "it is good." An artist – a creator – may possess either or even both the two former temperaments; but as an artist he must be governed by the latter two, either singly or combined. Dürer, doubtless, had a considerable share in all four of these points of view. He delighted in objects as such, in the new and the strange as new and strange, in the intricate as intricate, in the powerful as powerful. And above all in his drawings does he manifest this direct and childish interest and curiosity. He was also in search of a system, of an intellectual key or plan of things; and in the many drawings he devoted to explaining or developing his ideas of proportion, of perspective, of architecture, he shows this bias strongly. But nearly every drawing by him, or attributed to him, manifests the third of these temperaments. The never-ceasing economy and daring of the invention displayed in his touch, or, as he would have said, "in his hand," is almost as signal as his perfect assurance and composure. And when one reflects that he was not, like Rembrandt, an artist who made great or habitual use of the spaces of shade and light, but that his workmanship is almost entirely confined to the expressive power of lines, wonder is only increased. Of the fourth character that creates and estimates value, though in certain works Dürer rises to supreme heights, though in almost all his important works he appeases expectation, yet often where he could surely have done much better he seems to have been content not to exert his rarest gifts, but rather to play with or parade those that are secondary. Not only is this so in drawings like the *Dance of Monkeys* at Basle, done to content his friend the reformer Felix Frey (see page 168), and in the borders designed to amuse Maximilian during the hours that custom ordained he should pretend to give to prayer; but there are drawings which were not apparently thrown as sops to the idleness of others, but done to content some half-vacant mood of his own (see Lippmann, 41, 83, 394, 4.20, 333).

In such drawings the economy and daring of the strokes is always admirable, can only be compared to that in drawings by Rembrandt and Hokusai; but the occasion is often idle, or treated with a condescension which well-nigh amounts to indifference. There is no impressiveness of allure, no intention in the proportions or disposition on the paper such as Erasmus justly praised in the engravings on copper, probably recollecting something which Dürer himself had said (see page 186).

Yet in his portrait heads the right proportions are nearly always found; and in many cases I believe it is no one but the artist himself who has cut down such drawings after they were completed, to find a more harmonious or impressive proportion. And often these drawings are as perfect in the harmony between the means employed and the aspect chosen, and in the proportion between the head and the framing line and the spaces it encloses, as Holbein himself could have made them; while they far surpass his best in brilliancy and intensity.

III

Something must be said of Dürer's employment of the water-colours, pen-and-ink, silver-point, charcoal, chalk, &c., with which he made his drawings. He is a complete master of each and all these mediums, in so far as the line or stroke may be regarded as the fundamental unit; he is equally effective with the broad, soft line of chalk, or the broad broken charcoal line, as with the fine pen stroke, the delicate silver-point, or the supple and tapering stroke produced by the camel's hair brush. But when one comes to broad washes, large masses of light and shade, the expression of atmosphere, of bloom, of light, he is wanting in proportion as these effects become vague, cloudy, indefinite, mist-like. His success lies rather in the definite reflections on polished surfaces; he never reproduces for us the bloom on peach or flesh or petal. He does not revel, like Rembrandt, in the veils and mysteries of lucent atmosphere or muffling shadow. The emotions for which such things produce the most harmonious surroundings he hardly ever attempts to appeal to; he is mournful and compassionate, or indignant, for the sufferings, of his Man of Sorrows; not tender, romantic, or awesome. Only with the tapering tenuity and delicate spring of the pure line will he sometimes attain to an infantile or virginal freshness that is akin to the tenderness of the bloom on flowers, or the light of dawn on an autumn morning.[75]

In the same way, when he is tragic, it is not with thick clouds rent in the fury of their flight, or with the light from shaken torches cast and scattered like spume-flakes from the angry waves; nor is it with the accumulated night that gives intense significance to a single tranquil ray. Only by a Rembrandt, to whom these means are daily present, could a subject like the *Massacre of the Ten Thousand* have been treated with dramatic propriety; unless, indeed, Michelangelo, in a grey dawn, should have twisted and wrung with manifold pain a tribe of giants, stark, and herded in some leafless primeval valley. With Dürer the occasion was merely one on which to coldly invent variations, as though this human suffering was a motive for *an* arabesque. Yet even from the days when he copied Andrea Mantegna's struggling sea-monsters, or when he drew the stern matured warrior angels of his Apocalypse fighting, with their historied faces like men hardened by deceptions practised upon them, like men who have forbidden salt tears and clenched their teeth and closed their hearts, who see, who hate; even from these early days, the energy of his line was capable of all this, and his spontaneous sense of arabesque could become menacing and explosive. There are two or three drawings of angry, crying cupids (Lipp., 153 and 446), prepared for some intended picture of the Crucifixion, where he has made the motive of the winged infants head, usually associated with bliss and scattered rose-leaves, become terrible and stormy. And the *Agony in the Garden*, etched on iron, contains a tree tortured by the wind, as marvellous for rhythm, power, and invention as the blast-whipped brambles and naked bushes that crest a scarped brow above the jealous husband who stabs his wife, in Titian's fresco at Padua. Again, the unspeakable tragedy of the stooping figure of Jesus, who is being dragged by His hair up the steps to Annas' throne, in the *Little Passion*, is rendered by lines instinct with the highest dramatic power. These are a draughtsman's creations; though they are less abundant in Dürer's work than one could wish, still only the greatest produce such effects; only Michelangelo, Titian, and Rembrandt can be said to have equalled or surpassed Dürer in this kind, rarely though it be that he competes with them.

It is for the intense energy of his line, combined with its unique assurance, that Dürer is most remarkable. The same amount of detail, the same correctness in the articulation and relation between stem and leaf, arm and hand, or what not, might be attained by an insipid workmanship with lifeless lines, in patient drudgery. It is this fact that those who praise art merely as an imitation constantly forget. There is often as much invention in the way details are expressed by the strokes of pen or brush, as there could be in the grouping of a crowd; the deftness, the economy of the touches, counts for more in the inspiriting effect than the truth of the imitation. A photograph from nature never conveys this, the chief and most fundamental merit of art. Reynolds says:

> Rembrandt, in older to take advantage of an accident, appears often to have used the pallet-knife to lay his colours on the canvas instead of the pencil. Whether it is the knife or any other instrument, *it suffices, if it is something that does not follow exactly the will. Accident, in the hands of* an artist *who knows horn to take the advantage of its hints, will often produce bold and capricious beauties of handling,* and facility such as he would not have thought of or ventured with his pencil, under the regular restraint of his hand.[76]

In such a sketch as the *Memento Mei*, 1505, (*Death* riding on horseback,) all those who have sense for such things will perceive how the rough paper, combined with the broken charcoal line, lends itself to qualities of a precisely similar nature to those described by Reynolds as obtained by Rembrandt's use of the pallet-knife. Yet, just as, in the use of charcoal, the "something that does not follow exactly the will" is infinitely more subtle than in the use of the palette-knife to represent rocks or stumps of trees, so in the pen or silver-point line this element, though reduced and refined till it is hardly perceptible, still exists, and Dürer takes "the advantage of its hints." And not only does he do' this, but he foresees their occurrence, and relies on them to render such things as crumpled skin, as in the sketches for Adam's hand holding the apple. (Lipp. 234). The operation is so rapid, so instantaneous, that it must be called an instinct, or at least a habit become second nature, while in the instance chosen by Reynolds, it is obvious and can be imagined step by step; but in every case it is this capacity to take advantage of the accident, and foresee and calculate upon its probable occurrences, that makes the handling of any material inventive, bold, and inimitable. It is in these qualities that an artist is the scholar of the materials he employs, and goes to school to the capacities of his own hand, being taught both by their failure to obey his will here, and by their facility in rendering his subtlest intentions there. And when he has mastered all they have to teach him, he can make their awkwardness and defects expressive; as stammerers sometimes take advantage of their impediment so that in itself it becomes an element of eloquence, of charm, or even of explicitness; while the extra attention rendered enables them to fetch about and dare to express things that the fluent would feel to be impossible and never attempt.

IV

Lastly, it is in his drawings, perhaps, even more than in his copper engravings, that Dürer proves himself a master of "the art of seeing nature," as Reynolds phrased it; and the following sentence makes clear what is meant, for he says of painting "perhaps it ought to be as far removed from the vulgar idea of imitation, as the refined, civilised state in which we live is removed from a gross state of nature";[77] and again: "If we suppose a view of nature, represented with all the truth of the camera obscura, and the same scene represented by a great artist, how little and how mean will the one appear in comparison of the other, where no superiority is supposed from the choice of the subject."[78] Not only is outward nature infinitely varied, infinitely composite; but human nature – receptive and creative – is so too, and after we have gazed at an object for a few moments, we no longer see it the same as it was revealed to our first glance. Not only has its appearance changed for us, but the effect that it produces on our emotions and intelligence is no longer the same. Each successful mind, according to its degree of culture, arrives finally at a perception of every class of objects presented to it which is most in agreement with its own nature – that is, calls forth or nourishes its most cherished energies and efforts, while harmonising with its choicest memories. All objects in regard to which it cannot arrive at such a result oppress, depress, or even torment it. At least this is the case with our highest and most creative moods; but every man of parts has a vast range of moods, descending from this to the almost vacant contemplation of a cow – the innocence of whose eye, which perceives what is before it without transmuting it by recollection or creative effort, must appear almost ideal to the up-to-date critic who has recently revealed the innocent confusion of his mind in a ponderous tome on nineteenth-century art. The art of seeing nature, then, consists in being able to recognise how an object appears in harmony with any given mood; and the artist must employ his materials to suggest that appearance with the least expenditure of painful effort. The highest art sees all things in harmony with man's most elevated moods; the lowest sees nature much as Dutch painters and cows do. Now we can understand what Goethe means when he says that "Albrecht Dürer enjoyed the advantages of a profound realistic perception, and an affectionate human sympathy with all present conditions." The man who continued to feel, after he had become a Lutheran, the beauty of the art that honoured the Virgin, the man who cannot help laughing at the most "lying, thievish rascals" whenever they talk to him because "they know that their knavery is no secret, but 'they don't mind,'" is affectionate; he is amused by monkeys and the rhino-ceros; he can bear with Pirkheimer's bad temper; he looks out of kindly eyes that allow their perception of strangeness or oddity to redeem the impression that might otherwise have been produced by vice, or uncouthness, or sullen frowns.

I have supposed that a realistic perception was one which saw things with great particularity; and the words "a profound realistic perception" to Goethe's mind probably conveyed the idea of such a perception, in profound accord with human nature, that is where the human recognition, delight and acceptance followed the perception even to the smallest details, without growing weary or failing to find at least a hope of significance in them. If this was what the great critic meant, those who turn over a collection of Dürer's drawings will feel that they are profoundly realistic (realistic in a profoundly human sense), and that their author enjoyed an affectionate human sympathy with all present conditions; and by these two qualities is infinitely distinguished from all possessors of so-called innocent eyes, whether quadruped or biped.

It is well to notice wherein this notion of Goethe's differs from the conventional notions which make up everybody's criticism. For instance, "In all his pictures he confined himself to facts," says Sir Martin Conway,[79] and then immediately qualifies this by adding, "He painted events as truly as his imagination could conceive them." We may safely say that no painter of the first rank has ever confined himself to facts. Nor can we take the second sentence as it stands. Any one who looks at the Trinity in the Imperial Gallery at Vienna will see at once that the artist who painted it did not shut his eyes and try to conjure up a vision of the scene to be represented; the ordering of the picture shows plainly throughout that a foregone conventional arrangement, joined with the convenience of the methods of representation to be employed, dictated nearly the whole composition, and that the details, costumes, &c., were gradually added, being chosen to enhance the congruity or variety of what was already given. Perhaps it was never a prime object with Dürer to conceive the event, it was rather the picture that he attempted to conceive; it is Rembrandt who attempts to conceive events, not Dürer. He is very far from being a realist in this sense: though certain of his etchings possess a considerable degree of such realism, it is not what characterises him as a creator or inventor. But a "profound realistic perception" almost unequalled he did possess; what he saw he painted not as he saw it, not where he saw it, but as it appeared to him to really be. So he painted real girls, plain, ugly or pretty as the case might be, for angels, and put them in the sky; but for their wings he would draw on his fancy. Often the folds of a piece of drapery so delighted him that they are continued for their own sake and float out where there is no wind to support them, or he would develop their intricacies beyond every possibility of conceivable train or other superfluity of real garments; and it is this necessity to be richer and more magnific- ent than probability permits which brings us to the creator in Dürer; not only had he a profound realistic perception of what the world was like, but he had an imagination that suggested to him that many things could be played with, embroidered upon, made handsomer, richer or more impressive. When Goethe adds that "he was retarded by a gloomy fantasy devoid of form or foundation," we perceive that the great critic is speaking petulantly or without sufficient knowledge. Dürer's gloomy fantasy, the grotesque element in his pictures and prints, was not his own creation, it is not peculiar to him, he accepted it from tradition and custom (see Plate "Descent into Hell"). What is really characteristic of him is the richness displayed in devils' scales and wings, in curling hair or crumpled drapery, or flame, or smoke, or cloud, or halo; and, still more particularly, his is the energy of line or fertility of invention with which all these are displayed, and the dignity or austerity which results from the general proportion of the masses and main lines of his composition.

❉ 244

V

For the illustration of this volume I have chosen a larger
proportion of drawings than of any other class of work; both
because Dürer's drawings are less widely known than his
engravings on metal, and because, though his fame may perhaps
rest almost equally on these latter, and they may rightly be
considered more unique in character, yet his drawings show the
splendid creativeness of his handling of materials in greater
variety. One engraving on copper is like another in the essential
problem that it offered to the craftsman to resolve; but every
different medium in which Dürer made drawings, and every
variety of surface on which he drew, offered a different problem,
and perhaps no other artist can compare with him in the great
variety of such problems which he has solved with felicity. And
this power of his to modify his method with changing conditions
is, as we have seen, from the technical side the highest and
greatest quality that an artist can possess. It only fails him when
he has to deal with oil paintings, and even there he shows a
corresponding sense of the nature of the problems involved, if he
shows less felicity on the whole in solving them; and perhaps
could he have stayed at Venice and have had the results of
Giorgione's and Titian's experiments to suggest the right road, we
should have been scarcely able to perceive that he was less gifted
as a painter than as draughtsman. As it is, he has given us water-
colour sketches in which the blot is used to render the foliage of
trees in a manner till then unprecedented. (Lipp. 132, &c.) He can
rival Watteau in the use of soft chalk, Leonardo in the use of the
pen, and Van Eyck in the use of the brush point; and there are
examples of every intermediate treatment to form a chain across
the gulf that separates these widely differing modes of graphic
expression. There can be no need to point the application of these
remarks to the individual drawings here reproduced; those who
are capable of recognising it will do so without difficulty.

VI

In conclusion, Dürer appears as a draughtsman of unrivalled powers. And when one looks on his drawings as what they most truly were, his preparation for the tasks set him by the conditions of his life, there is room for nothing but unmixed admiration. It is only when one asks whether those tasks might not have been more worthy of such high gifts that one is conscious of deficiency or misfortune. And can one help asking whether the Emperor Max might not have given Dürer his Bible or his Virgil to illustrate, instead of demanding to have the borders of his "Book of Hours" rendered amusing with fantastic and curious arabesques; whether Dürer's learned friends, instead of requiring from him recondite or ceremonious allegories, might not have demanded title-pages of classic propriety; or whether the imperial bent of his own imagination might not have rendered their demands malleable, and bid them call for a series of woodcuts, engravings or drawings, which could rival Rembrandt's etchings in significance of subject-matter and imaginative treatment, as they rival them in executive power? In his portraits – the large majority of which have come down to us only as drawings, the majority of which were never anything else – the demand made upon him was worthy; but even here Holbein, a man of lesser gift and power, has perhaps succeeded in leaving a more dignified, a more satisfying series; one containing, if not so many masterpieces, fewer on which an accidental or trivial subject or mood has left its impress. Yet, in spite of this, it is Dürer's, not Rembrandt's, not Holbein's character, that impresses us as most serious, most worthy to be held as a model. It is before his portrait of himself that Mr. Ricketts "forgets all other portraits whatsoever, in the sense that this perfect realisation of one of the world's greatest men is worthy of the occasion." So that we feel bound to attribute our dissatisfaction to something in his circumstances having hindered and hampered the flow of what was finest in his nature into his work. From Venice he wrote: "I am a gentleman here, but only a hanger-on at home." Germany was a better home for a great character, a great personality, than for a great artist: Dürer the artist was never quite at home there, never a gentleman among his peers. The good and solid burghers rated him as a good and solid burgher, worth so much per annum; never as endowed with the rank of his unique gift. It was only at Venice and Antwerp that he was welcomed as the Albert Dürer whom we to-day know, love, and honour.

CHAPTER IV

DÜRER'S METAL ENGRAVINGS

I

For the artist or designer the chief difference between the
engraving done on a wood block and that done on metal lies in
the thickness of the line. The engraved line in a wood block is in
relief, that on a metal plate is entrenched; the ink in the one case
is applied to the crest of a ridge, in the other it fills a groove into
which the surface of the paper is squeezed. Though lines almost
as fine as those possible on metal have been achieved by wood
engravers, in doing this they force the nature of their medium,
whereas on a copper plate fine lines come naturally. Perhaps no
section of Dürer's work reveals his unique powers so thoroughly
as his engravings on metal. They were entirely his own work
both in design and execution; and no expenditure of pains or
patience seems to have limited his intentions, or to have hindered
his execution or rendered it less vital. And perhaps it is this fact
which witnesses with our spirit and bids us recognise the master:
rather than the comprehension of natural forms which he evinces,
subtle and vigorous though it be; or than the symbols and types
which he composed from such forms for the traditional and novel

ideas of his day. And this unweariable assiduity of his is continually employed in the discovery of very noble arabesques of line and patterns in black and white, more varied than the grain in satin wood or the clustering and dispersion of the stars. Intensity of application, constancy of purpose, when revealed to us by beautifully variegated surfaces, the result of human toil, may well impress us, may rightly impress us, more than quaint and antiquated notions about the four temperaments, or about witches and their sabbaths, or about virtues and vices embodied in misconceptions of the characters of pagan divinities, and in legends about them which scholars had just begun to translate with great difficulty and very ill. It is the astonishing assurance of the central human will for perfection that awes us; this perception that flinches at no difficulty, this perception of how greatly beauty deserves to be embodied in human creations and given permanence to.

II

In the encomium which Erasmus wrote of Albert Dürer he dealt, as one sees by the passage quoted (p. 186), with Dürer's engraved work almost exclusively. Perhaps the great humanist had seen no paintings by Dürer, and very likely had heard Dürer himself disparage them, as Melanchthon tells us was his wont (p. 187). We know that Dürer gave Erasmus some of his engravings, and we may feel sure that he was questioned pretty closely as to what were the aims of his art, and wherein he seemed to himself to have best succeeded. The sentence I underlined (on p. 186) gives us probably some reflection of Dürer's reply. We must remember that Erasmus, from his classical knowledge as to how Apelles was praised, was full of the idea that art was an imitation, and may probably have refused to understand what Dürer may very likely have told him in modification of this view; or he may by citing his Greek and Latin sources have prevented the reverent Dürer from being outspoken on the point. But though most of his praise seems mere literary commonplace, the sentence underlined strikes us as having another source.

"He reproduces not merely the natural aspect of a thing, but also observes the laws of perfect symmetry and harmony with regard to the position of it." How one would like to have heard Dürer, as Erasmus may probably have heard him, explain the principles on which he composed! No doubt there is no very radical difference between his sense of composition and that of other great artists. But to hear one so preoccupied with explaining his processes to himself discourse on this difficult subject would be great gain. For though there are doubtless no absolute rules, and the appeal is always to a refined sense for proportion, – yet to hear a creator speak of such things is to have this sense, as it were, washed and rendered delicate once more. We can but regret that Erasmus has not saved us something fuller than this hint. In the same way, how tempting is the criticism that Camerarius gives of Mantegna, – we feel that Dürer's own is behind it; but as it stands it is disjointed and absurd, like some of the incomplete and confused parables which give us a glimpse of how much more was lost than was preserved by the reporters of the sayings of Jesus. It is the same thing with the reported sayings of Michelangelo, and indeed of all other great men. It is impossible to accept "his hand was not trained to follow the perception and nimbleness of his mind" as Dürer's dictum on Mantegna; but how suggestive is the allusion to "broken and scattered statues set up as examples of art," for artists to form themselves upon! Yet the fact that Dürer missed coming into contact not only with Mantegna but with Titian, Leonardo, Raphael, Michelangelo, is indeed the saddest fact in regard to his life. We can well believe that he felt it in Mantegna's case. Ah!

Why could he not bring himself to accept the overtures made to him, and become a citizen of Venice?

III

The subjects of these engravings are even generally trivial or antiquated, either in themselves or by the way they are approached. Perhaps alone among them the figure of Jesus, as it is drawn in the various series on copper and wood illustrating the Passion, is conceived in a manner which touches us to-day with the directness of a revelation; and even this cannot be compared to the same figure in Rembrandt etchings and drawings, either for essential adequacy, or for various and convincing application. No, we must consent to let the expression "great thoughts" drop out of our appreciation of Dürer's works, and be replaced by the "great character" latent in them.

However, one among Dürer's engravings on copper stands out from among the rest, and indeed from all his works. In the *Melancholy* the composition is not more dignified in its spacing and proportion; the arabesque of line is not richer or sweeter, the variations from black to white are not more handsome, than in some half dozen of his other engravings. No, by its conception alone the *Melancholy* attains to its unique impressiveness. And it is the impressiveness of an image, not the impressiveness of an idea or situation, as in the case of the *Knight, Death, and the Devil,* by which almost as much bad literature has been inspired. There is nothing to choose between the workmanship of the two plates; both are absolutely impeccable, and outside the work of Dürer himself, unrivalled. The *Melancholy* is the only creation by a German which appears to me to invite and sustain comparison with the works of the greatest Italian. In it we have the impressiveness that belongs only to the image, the thing conceived for mental vision, and addressed to the eye exclusively. If there was an allegory, or if the plate formed (as has been imagined) one of a series representative of the four temperaments, the eye and the visual imagination are addressed with such force and felicity that the inquiries which attempt to answer these questions must for ever appear impertinent. They may add some languid interest to the contemplation which is sated with admiring the impeccable mastery of the Knight; for that plate always seems to me the mere illustration of a literary idea, a sheer statement of items which require to be connected by some story, and some of which have the crude obviousness of folk-lore symbols, without their racy and genial naïvety. They have not been fused in the rapture of some unique mood, not focussed by the intensity of an emotion. With the *Melancholy* all is different; perhaps among all his works only Dürer's most haunting portrait of himself has an equal or even similar power to bind us in its spell. For this reason I attempt the following comparison between the *Sibyls* of the Sistine Chapel and the *Melancholy* a comparison which I do not suppose to have any other value or force than that of a stimulant to the imagination which the works themselves address.

The impetuosity of his Southern blood drives Michelangelo to betray his intention of impressing in the pose and build of his Sibyls. Large and exceptional women, "limbed" and thewed as gods are, with an habitual command of gesture, they lift down or open their books or unwind their scrolls like those accustomed to be the cynosure of many eyes, who have lived before crowds of inferiors, a spectacle of dignity from their childhood upwards. On the other hand, the pose and build of the *Melancholy* must have been those of many a matron in Nuremberg. It is not till we come to the face that we find traits that correspond with the obvious symbolism of the wings and wreath, or the serious richness of the black and white effect of the composition; but that face holds our attention as not even the Sibylla Delphica cannot by beauty, not by conscious inspiration, but by the spell of unanswerable thought, by the power to brood, by the patience that can and dare go unresolved for many years. Everything is begun about her; she cannot see unto the end; she is powerful, she is capable in many works, she has borne children, she rests from her labours, and her thought wanders, sleeps or dreams. The spirit of the North, with its industry, its cool-headed calculation, its abundance in contrivance, its elaboration of duty and accumulation of possessions – there she sits, absorbed, unsatisfied. Impetuosity and the frank avowal of intention are themselves an expression of the will to create that which is desirable; they can but form the habit of every artist under happy circumstances. They proceed on the expectation of immediate effectiveness, they belong to power in action; while, if beauty be not impetuous, she is frank, and adds to the avowal of her intention the promise of its fulfilment. The work of art and the artist are essentially open; they promise intimacy, and fulfil that promise with entirety when successful. Nor is anything so impressive as intimacy which implies a perfect sincerity, a complete revelation, a gift without reserve, increase without let. But the circumstances of the artist never are happy: even Michelangelo's were not. An intense brooding melancholy arises from the repressed and baffled desire to create; and in some measure this gloom of failure underlying their success is a necessary character of all lovely and spiritual creations in this world. Now Michelangelo's works, because of their Southern impetuosity and volubility, are not so instinct with this divine sorrow, this immobility of the soul face to face with evil, as is Dürer's *Melancholy*. He inspires and exhilarates us more, but takes us out of ourselves rather than leads us home.

Here is Dürer's success: let and hindered as it really is, he makes us feel the inalienable constancy of rational desire, watching adverse circumstance as one beast of prey watches another. She keeps hold on the bird she has caught, the ideal that perhaps she will never fully enjoy. Michelangelo pictures for us freedom from trammels, the freedom that action, thought and ecstasy give, the freedom that is granted to beauty by all who recognise it; Dürer shows us the constancy that bridges the intervals between such free hours, that gives continuity to man's necessarily spasmodic effort. Thus he typifies for us the Northern genius: as Michelangelo's athletes might typify by their naked beauty and the unexplained impressiveness of their gestures, the genius of the sudden South – sudden in action, sudden in thought, suddenly mature, suddenly asleep – as day changes to night and night to day the more rapidly as the tropics are approached.

Instances of the highest imaginative power are rare in Dürer's work. The *Melancholy* has had a world-wide success. The *Knight, Death and the Devil* has one almost equal, but which is based on the facility with which it is associated with certain ideas dear to Christian culture, rather than on the creation of the mood in which these ideas arise. It does not move us until we know that it is an illustration of Erasmus's Christian Knight. Then all its dignity and mastery and the supremacy of the gifts employed on it are brought into touch with the idea, and each admirer operates, according to his imaginativeness, something of the transformation which Dürer had let slip or cool down before realising it.

IV

Among the prints with lesser reputations are several which attain a far higher success. There is the iron plate of the *Agony in the Garden*, B. 19, already mentioned (p. 235), in which the storm-tortured tree and the broken light and shade are full of dramatic power, the *Angel with the Sudarium*, B. 26, where the arabesque of the folds of drapery and cloud unite with the daring invention of the central figure to create a mood entirely consonant with the subject. There is the woman carried off by a man on an unicorn, in which the turbulence of the subject is expressed with unrivalled force by the rich and beautiful arabesque and black and white pattern.

B. Nos. 4, 5, 6, 8, 9, 10, 11, 14, 16, 18, of the *Little Passion*, on copper, are all of them noteworthy successes of more or less the same kind; and in these, too, we come upon that racy sense for narration which can enhance dramatic import by emphasising some seemingly trivial circumstance, as in the gouty stiffness of one of Christ's scourgers in the *Flagellation*, or the abnormal ugliness of the man who with such perfect gravity holds the basin while Pilate *washes his hands:* while in the *Crown of Thorns* and *Descent into Hades* we have peculiarly fine and suitable black and white patterns, and in the *Peter and John at the Beautiful Gate and the Ecce Homo* figures of monumental dignity in tiny gems of glowing engraver's work. The repose and serenity of the lovely little *St. Antony*; the subsidence of commotion in the noonday victory of the little *St. George on foot*, B. 53 – perhaps the most perfect diamond in the whole brilliant chain of little plates, or the staid naïvety of the enchanting *Apollo and Diana*, B. 68; who shall prefer among these things? Every time we go through them we choose out another until we return to the most popular and slightly obvious *St. George on Horseback*, B. 54. Next come the dainty series of little plates in honour of Our Lady the Mother of God, commencing before Dürer made a rule of dating his plates; before 1503 and continuing till after 1520, in which the last are the least worthy. Among these the Virgin embracing her Child at the foot of a tree, B. 34, dated 1513; The Virgin standing on the crescent moon, her baby in one arm, her sceptre in the other hand and the stars of her crown blown sideways as she bows her head, B. 32, dated 1516, and the stately and monumental Virgin seated by a wall, B. 40, dated 1514, are at present my favourites. And to these succeeded the noble army of Apostles and Martyrs of which the more part are dated from 1521 to 1526, though two, B. 48 and 50, fall as early as 1514.

Then amongst the most perfect larger plates I cannot refrain from mentioning the *St. Jerome*, B. 60, with its homely seclusion as of Dürer's own best parlour in summer time which not even the presence of a lion can disturb; the idyllic and captivating *St. Hubert*, B. 57; the august and tranquil *Cannon*, B. 99: and lastly, perhaps, in the little *Horse*, B. 96, we come upon a theme and motive of the kind best suited to Dürer's peculiar powers, in which he produces an effect really comparable to those of the old Greek masters, about whose lost works he was so eager for scraps of information, and whose fame haunted him even into his slumbers, so that he dreamed of them and of those who should "give a future to their past." This delightful work may illustrate an allegory now grown dark or some misconception of a Grecian story; but though the relation between the items that compose it should remain for ever unexplained, its beauty, like that of some Greek sculpture that has been admired under many names, continues its spell, and speaks of how the simplicity, austerity and noble proportions of classical art were potent with the spirit of the great Nuremberg artist, and occasionally had free way with him, in spite of all there was in his circumstances and origins to impede or divert them. (See also the spirited drawing, Lipp. 366.)

V

It would be idle to attempt to say something about every masterpiece in Dürer's splendidly copious work on metal plates. There is perhaps not one of these engravings that is not vital upon one side or another, amazingly few that are not vital upon many. One other work, however, which has been much criticised and generally misunderstood, it may be as well to examine at more length, especially as it illustrates what was often Dürer's practice in regard to his theories about proportion, with which my next Part will deal. I speak of the *Great Fortune* or *Nemesis* (B. 77). His practice at other times is illustrated by the splendid *Adam and Eve* (B. 1), over the production of which the nature of the canon he suggested was perhaps first thoroughly worked out. But before this and afterwards too he no doubt frequently followed the advice he gives in the following passage.

To him that setteth himself to draw figures according to this book, not being well taught beforehand, the matter will at first become hard. Let him then put a man before him, who agreeth, as nearly as may be, *with the proportions he desireth*; and let him draw him in outline according to his knowledge and power. And a man is held to have done well if he attain accurately to copy a figure according to the life, so that his drawing resembleth the figure and is like unto nature. *And in particular if the thing copied as beautiful; then is the copy held to be artistic*, and, as it deserveth, it is highly praised.

Dürer himself would seem to have very often followed his own advice in this. The *Great Fortune* or Nemesis is a case in point. The remarks of critics on this superb engraving are very strange and wide. Professor Thausing said, "Embodied in this powerful female form, the Northern worship of nature here makes its first conscious and triumphant appearance in the history of art." With the work of the great Jan Van Eyck in one's mind's eye, of course this will appear one of those little lapses of memory so convenient to German national sentiment. "Everything that, according to our aesthetic formalism based on the antique, we should consider beautiful, is sacrificed to truth." (I have already pointed out that this use of the word "truth" in matters of art constitutes a fallacy) "And yet our taste must bow before the imperishable fidelity to nature displayed in these forms, the fulness of life that animates these limbs." Of course, "imperishable fidelity to nature" and "taste that bows before it" are merely the figures of a clumsy rhetoric. But the idea they imply is one of the most common of vulgar errors in regard to works of art. In the first place one must remind our enthusiastic German that it is an engraving and not a woman that we are discussing; and that this engraving is extremely beautiful in arabesque and black and white pattern, rich, rhythmical and harmonious; and that there is no reason why our taste should be violated in having to bow submissively before such beauties as these, which it is a pleasure to worship. Now we come to the subject as presented to the intelligence, after the quick receptive eye has been satiated with beauty. Our German guide exclaims, "Not misled by cold definite rules of proportion, he gave himself up to unrestrained realism in the presentation of the female form." Our first remark is, that though the treatment of this female form may perhaps be called realistic, this adjective cannot be made to apply to the figure as a whole. This massively built matron is winged; she stands on a small globe suspended in the heavens, which have opened and are furled up like a garment in a manner entirely conventional. She carries a scarf which behaves as no fabric known to me would behave even under such exceptional and thrilling circumstances.

Dr. Carl Giehlow has recently suggested that this splendid engraving illustrates the following Latin verses by Poliziano:

Est dea, quse vacuo sublimis in aëre pendens
It nimbo succincta latus, sed candida pallam,
Sed radiata comam, ac stridentibus insonat alis.
Haec spes immodicas premit, haec infesta superbis
Imminet, huic celsas hominum contundere mentes
Incessusque datum et nimios turbare paratus.
Quam veteres Nemesin genitam de nocte silenti
Oceano discere patri. Stant sidera fronti.
Frena manu pateramque gerit, semperque verendum
Ridet et insanis obstat contraria coeptis.
Improba vota domans ac summis ima revolvens
Miscet et alterna nostros vice temperat actus.
Atque hue atque illuc ventorum turbine fertur.

There is a goddess, who, aloft in the empty air, advances girdled about with a cloud, but with a shining white cloak and a glory in her hair, and makes a rushing with her wings. She it is who crushes extravagant hopes, who threatens the proud, to whom is given to beat down the haughty spirit and the haughty step, and to confound over-great possessions. Her the men of old called Nemesis, born to Ocean from the womb of silent Night. Stars stand upon her forehead. In her hand she bears bridles and a chalice, and smiles for ever with an awful smile, and stands resisting mad designs. Turning to nought the prayers of the wicked and setting the low above the high she puts one in the other's place and rules the scenes of life with alternation. And she is borne hither and thither on the wings of the whirlwind.

If this suggestion is a good one it shows us that Dürer was no more consistently literal than he was realistic. The most striking features of his illustration are just those to which his text offers no counterpart, i.e., the nudity and physical maturity of his goddess. Neither has he girdled her about with cloud nor stood stars upon her forehead. I must confess that I find it hard to believe that there was any close connection present to his mind between his engraving and these verses.

In a former chapter I have spoken of the fashion in female dress then prevalent; how it underlined whatever is most essential in the physical attributes of womanhood, and how probably something of good taste is shown in this fashion (see pp. 92 and 93). What I there said will explain Dürer's choice in this matter; and also that what Thausing felt bow in him was not taste, but his prejudices in regard to womanly attractiveness, and his misconception as to where the beauty of an engraving should be looked for and in what it consists. These same prejudices and misconceptions render Mrs. Heaton (as is only natural in one of the weaker sex) very bold. She says, "A large naked winged woman, whose ugliness is perfectly repulsive." This object, I must confess, appears to me, a coarse male, "welcome to contemplation of the mind and eye." The splendid Venus in Titian's *Sacred and Profane Love*, or his *Ariadne* at Madrid; or Raphael's *Galatea*; or Michelangelo's *Eve* (on the Sistine vault) are all of them doubtless far more akin to the *Aphrodite* of Praxiteles, or to her who crouches in the Louvre, than is this *Nemesis*; but we must not forget that they are works on a scale more comparable with a marble statue; and that in works of which the scale is more similar to that of our engraving, Greek taste was often far more with Dürer than with Thausing. This is an important point, though one which is rarely appreciated. However, there is no reason why we should condemn "misled by cold definite rules of taste" even such pictures as Rembrandt's *Bathing Woman* in the Louvre, though here the proportions of the work are heroic. Oil painting was an art not practised by the Greeks, and this medium lends itself to beauties which their materials put entirely out of reach. Besides, Rembrandt appealed to an audience who had been educated by Christian ideals to appreciate a pathos produced by the juxtaposition of the fact with the ideal, and of the creature with the creator, to appeal to which a Greek would have had to be far more circumspect in his address – even if he had, through an exceptional docility and receptiveness of character, come under its influence himself. These considerations when apprehended will, I believe, suffice to dispel both prejudice and misconception in regard to this matter; and we shall find in Professor Thausing's remarks relative to the treatment of the "female form divine" in this engraving no additional reason for considering it a comparatively early work. And we shall only smile when he tells us "The *Nemesis* to a certain *degree* (sic) marks the extreme *point* (sic) reached by Dürer in his unbiased study of the nude. His further progress became more and more influenced by his researches into the proportions of the human body." The bias will appear to us of rather more recent date, and we shall be ready to consider with an open mind how far Dürer's practice was influenced for good or evil by his researches into the proportions of the human body.

CHAPTER V

DÜRER'S WOODCUTS

It is now generally accepted that Dürer did not himself engrave on wood. In his earliest blocks he shows a greater respect for the limitations of this means of expression than later on. The earliest wood blocks, though no doubt they aimed at being facsimiles, were not such in fact; but the engraver took certain liberties for his own convenience, and probably did not attempt to render what Dürer calls "the hand" of the designer. "The hand" was equivalent to what modern artists call "the touch," and meant the peculiar character recognisable in the vast majority of the strokes or marks which each artist uses in drawing or painting. Dürer affected extremely curved and rapid strokes, Mantegna the deliberate straight line, Rembrandt the straight stroke used so as to seem a continual improvisation; though indeed he varies the character of his touch more continually and more vastly than any other master, yet in his drawings and etchings the majority of the strokes are straight. Already in the woodcuts provided by Michael Wolgemut, Dürer's master, to illustrate books, there is a general attempt to render cross hatching: and the eyes and hair, though still those of an engraver, are frequently modified to some extent in deference to the character given by the draughtsman. Still, no one with practical experience would consider these woodcuts as adequate facsimiles: which makes the question of their attribution to Wolgemut, or his partner and step-son, Pleydenwurff, of still less interest and importance than it is on all other grounds. So conscious an exception as the soul of the accurate Albert Dürer was, could not be expected to endure a partner in his creations, especially one whose character was revealed chiefly by the clumsy compromises convenient to lack of skill. Doubtless the demand for "his hand" was a new factor in the education of the engraver, as constant and as imperturbable as the action of a copious stream, which, having its source in lonely heights, wears a channel through the hardest rock, the most sullen soils. It may have been the pitiless tyranny of the master's will for perfection which drove Hieronymus Andreae, "the most famous of Dürer's wood engravers," into religious and even civil rebellion, joining hands with levelling fanatics and taking active part in the Peasant War. Dürer probably would have commanded too much reverence and affection for these rebellions to be directed against him; but an insupportably heavy yoke is not rendered lighter because it is imposed by a loved hand, – though every other burden and restraint may in such a case be shaken off and resented before that which is the real cause of oppression. Dürer's wood cutters had no doubt to resign any indolence, any impatience, or whatever else it might be that had otherwise stamped a personal character on their work; and all remonstrance must have been shamed by the evident fact that the young master spared himself not a whit more. The perseverance and docility which made such engraving possible was perhaps the greatest aid that Dürer drew from German character; it was not only an aid, but an example to and restraint upon that haughty spirit of his that restively ever again vows never to take so much pains over another picture to be so poorly paid (see page 103); that complains of failure and discouragement after years of repeatedly more world-wide successes (see page 187). These are not German traits, but it may have been the German blood he inherited from his mother and the example of his friends, fellow-workers, and helpers, which enabled him to get the better of such petulant and gloomy outbursts, and return to the day of small things with the will to continue and endure.

The difference introduced by the engravers becoming more and more capable of rendering Dürer's hand is well illustrated by comparing the frontispiece to the *Apocalypse*, added about 1511, with the other cuts which had appeared in 1498. Doubtless Dürer's hand had changed its character considerably during this period of constant and rapid development, and it requires tact and knowledge to separate the differences due to the creator from those due to the engraver. Dürer's drawings differed as widely from the earlier drawings as does the engraving from the earlier blocks. But, as we may see by early drawings done as preliminary studies for engravings, the method of his pen strokes had changed less than the character of the forms they rendered; the conception of the design as a whole had advanced more rapidly than the skill and sleight of hand which expressed it. The engraver has by 1511 become capable of expressing a greater variety of speed in the stroke, makes it taper more finely, and can follow the tongue-like lap and flicker as the pen rises and dips again before leaving the surface of the block (as in the outer ends of the strokes that represent the radiance of the Virgin's glory). Holbein, later on, was to obtain a yet more wonderful fidelity from Lutzelburger, the engraver of his *Dunce of Death*.

Still it were misleading to suppose that Dürer's disregard for the facilities and limitations of wood-cutting went the lengths that the demands made upon modern skill have gone. Not only has the line been reproduced, but it has been drawn not with a full pen or brush, but in pencil or with watered ink; and the delicate tones thus produced have been demanded of and rendered by human skill. Dürer always uses a clear definite stroke; and in thus limiting himself he shows an appreciation of the medium to be used in reproducing his drawing, and recognises its limits to a large extent, though this is the only limitation he accepts. Less

and less does he consider the possibilities which engraving offers
for the use of a white line on black Doing his drawing with a
black line, he contents himself with the qualities that the resources
and facilities of the full pen line give: and his design is for a
drawing which can be cut on wood, not for something that first
really exists in the print; the prints are copies of his drawings. His
drawings were not prepared to receive additions in the course of
cutting, such as could only be rendered by the engraver.
Faithfulness was the only virtue he required of Hieronymus
Andreae. Yet even in such drawings as Dürer's no doubt were,
there would have been some qualities, some defects perhaps, that
the print does not possess. For a print, from the mode of inking,
has a breadth and unity which the drawing never can have. Even
in drawings made with full flowing brush or pen, there will be
modulations in the strength of the ink, or occasioned by the
surface of the wood or paper, in every stroke, by which the,
sensitive artist in the heat of work cannot help being influenced,
and which will lead him to give a bloom, a delicacy, to his
drawing, such as a print can never possess. And, on the other
hand, the unity of the print can never be quite realised in the
drawing, however much the artist may strive to attain it, because
the conditions must change, however slightly, for strokes
produced in succession; while in a print all are produced together,
and variations, if variations there are, occur over wide spaces and
not between stroke and stroke. It is considerations, of this kind
that in the last resort determine the quality of works of art. The
artist is taught, though often unconsciously, by the means he
employs, but the diligent man who is not by nature an artist
never can learn these things: he can Imitate the manner and form,
never the grace, the bloom, and the life.

II

Dürer's first important issue of woodcuts was the *Apocalypse*. A great deal has been written in praise of this production as a political pamphlet against the corrupt Papacy. It was undoubtedly the most important series of woodcuts that had ever appeared, by the size, number and elaboration of the designs. It also undoubtedly attacks ecclesiastical corruption, but not ecclesiastical only. Whether to Dürer and his friends it appeared even chiefly directed against prelates, or even against those who sat in high places; whether the popes, bishops and figures typical of the Church seemed to him to illustrate the moral in any pre-eminent degree, may be doubted. Still more doubtful is it whether there was any objection to papacy or priesthood as institutions connected with these figures in his mind. Unworthy popes, unworthy bishops, and an unworthy Rome were censured: but not popes, bishops, or Rome as the capital see of the Church. Dürer's work as a whole shows no distaste for saints, the Virgin, or bishops and popes; he had no objection, no scruple apparently, to introducing the notorious Julius II. into his *Feast of the* Rosary, some ten years later. There has perhaps been a tendency to read the intention of these designs too much in the light of after events: and by so doing a great slur is cast on Dürer's consistency; for, had these designs the significance read into them, he must be supposed an altogether convinced enemy of the Church; and the tremendous salaams which he afterwards made to her in far more important works ought, to logical minds, to appear horribly insincere.

Viewed as works of art, one reads about the cut of the four riders upon horses, "For simple grandeur this justly famous design has never been surpassed." One's sense of proportion receives such a shock as gives one the sensation of being utterly outcast, in a world where such a precious dictum can pass without remark as a sample of the discrimination of the chief authority on the life and art of Albert Dürer. Neither simple nor grand is an adjective applicable to this print in the sense in which we apply it to the chief masterpieces of antiquity and of the Renaissance. To say even that Dürer never surpassed this design is to utter what to me at least seems the most palpable absurdity. There is an immense advance in design, in conception and in mastery of every kind shown over the best prints of the *Apocalypse* and *Great Passion*, in the prints added to the latter series ten years later, and still more in the *Life of the Virgin*. And still finer results are arrived at in single cuts of later date, and in the *Little Passion*. If we want to see what Dürer's woodcuts at their finest are for breadth and dignity of composition, for richness and fertility of arabesque and black and white pattern, for vigour and subtlety of form, for boldness and vivacity of workmanship, we must turn to the *Samson* (1497?) (B. 2), the Man's *Bath* (14-?), (B. 128), among the earlier blocks published before the *Apocalypse*, then to those designed in or about the year 1511. The golden period for Dürer's woodcuts, the date of the publication of his most magnificent series, the *Life of the Virgin* and several delightful separate prints. Among these we find it hard to choose, but if some must be mentioned let it be the *St. Joachim's Offering Rejected by the High Priest* (B. 77), the *Meeting at the Golden Gate* (B. 79), the *Marriage of the Virgin* (B. 82), the *Visitation* (B. 84), the *Nativity* (B. 85), the *Presentation* (B. 55), the *Flight into Egypt* (B. 89).

In the glorious masterpieces of this series Dürer has found the true balance of his powers. The dignity and charm of the decorative effect of these cuts has never been surpassed; and to the racy narrative vivacity of such groups and figures as those isolated and enlarged in our illustration there is added an idyllic charm of which perhaps the best examples are the *Visitation* and the *Flight into Egypt*. This sweetness of allure is still more pervasive in the separate cuts that bear this golden date, 1511, that is in the *St. Christopher* (B. 103), and the *St. Jerome* (B. 114). And the *Adoration of the Magi* (B. 3) is much finer than the one included in the *Life of the Virgin*. This idyllic charm had already been touched *upon before* in the *Assumption of the Magdalen* (B. 121) (15?), and in the *St. Antony* and *St. Paul* and the *Baptist* and *St.*

Onuphrius of 1504. It is not felt to lie very deep in the conception of the subject, for all are treated in an obviously conventional manner, the touches of racy realism being confined to subordinate incidents and details. Neither the subjects nor the mood of the artist lend themselves to the dramatic impressiveness of such cuts as the *Blowing of the Sixth Trumpet* or the *St. Michael overwhelming the Dragon of the Apocalypse* (*see* page 262), where the inspiration appears to be Gothic, perhaps developed under the influence of Mantegna's *Combat between Sea Monsters,* of which Dürer early made an elaborate pen-and-ink copy. We find an aftermath of the same inspiration in the engraving on iron, dated 1516, representing a man riding astride of an unicorn carrying off a shrieking woman. Such stormy and strenuous lowerings of the imagination break in upon Dürer's habitual mood as St. Peter's thunders into Milton's "Lycidas," of which the general felicitous mingling of a conventional pedantry with idyllic charm and racy touches of realistic effect is very similar to the general effect of the golden group we have been describing. Among all the work that finds its climax in the beautiful creations of 1511, only in a few prints of the *Little Passion,* published in 1511, do we find any dramatic power or creativeness of essential conception. I may mention the *Christ Scourging the Money-changers in the Temple,* the *Agony in the Garden,* and Judas' *Kiss,* where, though the general effect be rather confused, the central figure is full of appropriate power. *Christ haled by the hair before Annas* (the most wonderful of all), Christ before *Pilate,* Christ *Mocked,* the *Ecce Homo* (a most beautiful composition), the Veronica's napkin incident, *Christ being nailed to the Cross* (a masterpiece), the *Deposition,* the *Entombment:* – several others of the series have idyllic charm or touches of narrative force which link them with the general group, but these alone stand out and in some ways surpass it. After this date Dürer seems in a great measure to have relinquished wood for metal engraving; however, most of his occasional resumptions of the process were marked by the production of masterpieces, if we put on one side the workshop monsters produced for Maximilian – and even in these, in details, Dürer's full force is recognisable. I may mention the *Madonna crowned and worshipped by a concert of Angels*, 1518 (B. 101), which, though a little cold, like all the work of that period, is still a masterpiece; and then, after the inspiriting visit to Antwerp, we have the magnificent portrait of Ulrich Varnbüler, 1522 (B. 155), the *Last Supper*, 1523 (B. 53), and the glorious piece of decoration representing Dürer's Arms, 1523 (B. 160). I have reproduced less of Dürer's wood engravings than would be necessary to represent their importance and beauty, because most, being large and bold, are greatly impoverished by reduction; besides, they are nearly all well known through comparatively cheap reproductions. I have enlarged two details to give an idea of Dürer's workmanship when employed upon racy realism, and when employed in endowing a single figure with supreme grace and dignity.

CHAPTER VI

DÜRER'S INFLUENCES
AND VERSES

I

Before closing this part of my book something must be said of Dürer's influence on other artists. It is one of the foibles of modern criticism to please itself by tracing influences, a process of the same nature as that of tracing resemblances to ferns and other growths on a frosted pane. No one would deny that resemblances are there; it is to distinguish them and estimate their significance without yielding to fancifulness, which is the well-nigh hopeless task. It is often forgotten that similar circumstances produce similar effects, and that coincidences from this cause are very rife. Then, too, it is forgotten that the influence that produces rivalry is stronger, more important, and less easily estimated, than that which is expressed by imitation or plagiarism; besides, it affects more original and fertile natures. The stimulus of a great creative personality often is more potent where discernible resemblances are few and vague, than where they are many and obvious. In Dürer's day the study and imitation of antique art which had brought about the Renascence in Italy was the fashion that in successive waves was passing over Europe and moulding the future. He himself felt it, and welcomed it now as an authority not to be gainsaid, and again as an example to be competed against and surpassed. This fashion, this trend of opinion and hope, was the significance behind the effect produced on him by Jacopo de' Barbari, whose charming but ineffectual originality succeeded merely in creating an eddy in that stream. It was the tide behind him which so powerfully stirred and stimulated Dürer. The resemblances traceable between certain still life studies by the two men, or even in figures of their engravings, is insignificant compared with the fact that through Jacopo Dürer probably first felt the energy and true direction of the great tidal waves which were then rolling forth from Italy. Even Mantegna's influence was probably less the effect of a personal affinity than that through him a power streamed direct from the antique dawn. This great and master influence of those days was more one of hope, indefinite, incomprehensible, visionary, than one of knowledge and assured discovery. Raphael may have received it from Dürer, as well as Dürer from Bellini. Figures and incidents from Dürer's engravings are supposed to have been adapted in certain works, if not of his own hand at least proceeding from his immediate pupils. For Raphael, Dürer was a proof of the excellence of human nature in respect to the arts, even when it could not form itself on the immediate study and contemplation of antiques, and thus added to the zest and expectation with which he improved himself in that direction. These great men did not distinguish clearly between pregnancy due to their own efforts, that of their contemporaries and immediate predecessors, and that due to their more mystic passion for antiquity. Michelangelo, Titian, and Correggio were destined to be the signets by which this great power was to be most often and clearly stamped on the work of future artists. From the unhappy location of his life Dürer was debarred from any such obvious and overwhelming effect on after generations. The influences which helped to shape him were no doubt at work on all the more eminent artists, his fellow-countrymen; on Albrecht Altdorfer, Hans Burgkmair, Lucas Cranach, or Baldung Grien, to mention only the elect. What the stimulus of his achievements, of his renown, meant for these men we have no means of computing; yet we may feel sure that it was vastly more important and significant than any actual traces of imitation or plagiarism from his works, which can with difficulty and for the more part very doubtfully be brought home to them; – vastly more important and significant too we may be sure than his effect upon his pupils and other more or less obscure painters, engravers, and block designers, in whose work actual imitation or adaption of his creations is more certain and more abundant. His pictures, plates, and woodcuts were copied both in Italy and in the North, both as exercises for the self-improvement of artists and to supply a demand for even secondhand reflections of his genius and skill. He was not destined to lend the impress of his splendid personality to the tide of fashion like the great Italians; their influence was to supersede his even in the North.

This is obvious: but who shall compare or estimate the accession of force which the tide as a whole gained from him, or that more latent power which begins to be disengaged from the reserve and lack of proper issue from which he evidently suffered, now that the great tide of the Renaissance has spent its mighty onrush and become merged in the constant movement of life – that power by which he moves us to commiserate his circumstances and to feel after the more and better, which we cannot doubt that he might have given us had he been more happily situated?

II

Only to compare the value of Michelangelo's sonnets with that of
the doggerel rhymes which Dürer produced, may give us some
idea of the portentous inferiority in Dürer's surroundings to those
of the great Italian. Both borrow the general idea of the subject,
treatment, and form of their poems from the fashion around them.
But that fashion in Michelangelo's case called for elevated subject,
intimate and imaginative treatment, and adequacy of form,
whereas none of these were called for from Albrecht Dürer; and if
his friends laughed at the rudeness of his verses, it was not that
they themselves conceived of anything more adequate in these
respects, only something more scholarly, more pedantic. Michelangelo's verse was often crabbed and rude, but the scholarship
and pedantry of Italy forbore to laugh at that rudeness, because a
more adequate standard made them recognise its vital power and
noble passion as of higher importance to true success. Still, in the
following rhymes, Dürer shows himself a true child of the
Renascence, at least in intention; and was proud of a desire for
universal excellence.

When I received this from Lazarus Spengler, I made him the
following poem in reply (Mrs. Heaton's translation):

> In Nürnberg it is known full well
> A man of letters now doth dwell,
> One of our Lord's most useful men,
> He is so clever with his pen,
> And others knows so well to hit,
> And make ridiculous with wit;
> And he has made a jest of me,
> Because I made some poetry,
> And of True Wisdom something wrote,
> But as he likes my verses not,
> He makes a laughing stock of me,
> And says I'm like the Cobbler, he
> Who criticised Apelles' art.
> With this he tries to make me smart,
> Because he thinks it is for me
> To paint, and not write poetry.

But I have undertaken this
(And will not stop for him or his),
To learn whatever thing I can,
For which will blame me no wise man.
For he who only learns one thing,
And to naught else his mind doth bring,
To him, as to the notary,
It haps, who lived here as do we,
In this our town. To him was known
To write one form and one alone.
Two men came to him with a need
That he should draw them up a deed;
And he proceeded very well,
Until their names he came to spell:
Gotz was the first name that perplexed,
And Rosenstammen was the next.
The Notary was much astonished,
And thus his clients he admonished,
"Dear friends," he said, "you must be wrong,
These names don't to my form belong;
Franz and Fritz[80] I know full well,
But of no others have heard tell."
And so he drove away his clients,
And people mocked his little science.
To me that it may hap not so,
Something of all things I will know.
Not only writing will I do,
But learn to practise physic too;
Till men surprised will say, "Beshrew me,
What good this painter's medicines do me!"
Therefore hear and I will tell
Some wise receipts to keep you well.
A little drop of alkali,
Is good to put into the eye;
He who finds it hard to hear,
Should mandel-oil put in his ear;
And he who would from gout be free,
Not wine but water drink should he;
He who would live to be a hundred,
Will see my counsel has not blundered.
Therefore I will still make rhymes
Though my friend may laugh at times.
So the Painter with hairy beard
Says to the Writer who mocked and jeered.

PART IV

DÜRER'S IDEAS

CHAPTER I

THE IDEA OF A CANON OF PROPORTION FOR THE HUMAN FIGURE

Dürer often painted the Virgin's head as a mere exercise or example in those proportion studies with which we must presently deal.

Sir W. M. CONWAY, in "Dürer's Literary Remains," p. 151.

As soon as he comes to speak of the very essence of artistic work, he forgets theories and imitations of the antique; he knows nothing of composition from fragments of Nature, of measurements and speculations. No longer trusting to such aids as these, but launching himself boldly on the broad stream of Nature, he believes that he shall attain to a higher harmony in his work.

THAUSING'S "Albert Dürer," vol. ii., p. 318.

I

The idea of a canon for human proportions has proved a great stumbling-block for so-called classical or academic artists. It is usually taken to mean an absolutely right or harmonious proportion, any deviation from which cannot fail to result in a diminution of beauty. According to their thoroughness, the devotees of this idea seek to arrive at such a scale of proportions for a varying number of different ages in either sex; often even modifying this again for diverse types, as tall or short, fat or lean, dark or blonde, but allowing no excessive variation for these causes; so that abnormally tall people and dwarfs are not considered. This is, I take it, what the great artist Albert Dürer is generally taken to have been aiming at in his books on proportion. It will not be difficult, I think, to show that Dürer had quite a different idea of what a canon of proportion should be, and how it should be applied. And certainly, had it been possible to study Greek practice more closely, and in a larger number of examples, when this idea (supposed to be drawn from that source) was chiefly mooted, a very different notion of the canon of proportion would have been forced on the most academical of theorists. Dürer's great superiority over such academical masters is, that his idea of a canon of proportion and its use agrees far better with what was apparently Greek practice.

Any one who has followed at all the interesting attempts made by Professor Furtwängler and others to group together, by attention to the measurements of the different parts of the figure, works belonging to the different masters, schools, and centres, will have perceived that he is led to assume a traditional canon of proportion from which a master deviates slightly in the direction of some bias of his own mind towards closer knit or more slim figures; such variations being in the earlier stages very slight. Again, it is supposed that from the canon followed by a master, different pupils may branch off in opposite directions according to the leanings of their personal sentiment for beauty. The conception of these ramifications has at least created the hope that critics may follow them through a great number of complications, since a master may modify his canon – after certain pupils have already struck out for themselves, and new pupils may start from his modified canon; and so on into an infinite criss-cross of branches, as any sculptor may be influenced to modify his canon by his fellows or by the masters of other schools whose work he comes across later. In any case, this main fact arises, that the canon appears as what the artist deviated from, not what he abided by: and any one who has any feeling for the infinite nicety of the results obtained by Greek sculptors will easily apprehend that each masterpiece established a new and slightly different canon, and was then in the position to be in its turn again deviated from, as Flaubert says:

> "The conception of every work of art carries within it its own rule and method, which must be found out before it can be achieved."

> "Chayue ceuvre à faire a sa poëtique en soi, qu'il faut trouver."

II

The same thing is asserted by literary critics to have been the cause of the repetition of subjects in Greek tragedy, and to have resulted in the infinite niceties of their forms, which are never the same and never radically new.

The terrible old mythic story on which the drama was founded stood, before he entered the theatre, traced in its bare outlines upon the spectator's mind; it stood in his memory as a group of statuary, faintly seen, at the end of a long dark vista. Then came the poet, embodying outlines, developing situations, not a word wasted, not a sentiment capriciously thrown in. Stroke upon stroke, the drama proceeded; the light deepened upon the group; more and more it revealed itself to the riveted gaze of the spectator; until at last, when the final words were spoken, it stood before him in broad sunlight, a model of immortal beauty.

This passage from Matthew Arnold's deservedly famous preface well emphasises one advantage that a tradition of subject and treatment gave to the Greek poet as to the Greek sculptor: the economy of means it made possible, "not a word wasted, not a sentiment capriciously thrown in," – since every deviation from, every addition to, the traditional story and treatment, was immediately appreciated by an audience thoroughly conversant with that tradition, and often with several previous masterpieces treating it. By merely leaving out an incident, or omitting to appeal to a sentiment, a Greek tragedian could flood his whole work with a new significance. So that the temptation to be eccentric, the temptation to hit too hard or at random because he was not sure of exactly where the mind stood that he would impress, did not exist in anything like the same degree for him as it did for Shakespeare and Michelangelo as it does for romantic and origina natures to-day. The absence of a sufficient body of traditional culture belonging to every educated person tends always to force the artist to commence by teaching the alphabet to his public. As Coleridge so justly remarked in the case of Wordsworth: "He had, like all great artists, to create the taste by which he was to be relished, to teach the art by which he was to be seen and judged." All great artists no doubt have to do this, but the modern artist is in the position of the Israelite who was bidden not only to make bricks, but to find himself in stubble and straw, as compared with a Greek who could appeal to traditional conceptions with certainty. Dr. Verrall is no doubt right when he says:

> Every one knows, even if the full significance of the fact is not always
> sufficiently estimated, that the tragedians of Athens did not tell their
> story at all as the telling of a story is conceived by a modern
> dramatist, whose audience, when the curtain goes up, know nothing

which is not in the play-bill.

This ignorant public, this uncultivated and unmanured field with which every modern artist has to commence, is the greatest let to the creator. What wonder that he should so often prefer to make a gaudy show with yellow weeds, when he perceives that there is hardly time in one man's life to produce a respectable crop of wheat from such a wilderness?

"The story of an Athenian tragedy is never completely told; it is implied, or, to repeat the expression used above, it is illustrated by a selected scene or scenes. And the further we go back the truer this is," continues Dr. Verrall; and the same was doubtless true of sculpture and painting. It is impossible to over-estimate the importance or advantage of this fact to the artist. For religious art, for art that appeals to the sum and total of a man's experience of beauty in life, a public cultivated in this sense is a necessity. Giotto and Fra Angelico enjoyed this almost to the same degree as Æschylus or Phidias; Michelangelo and the great artists of the Renascence generally enjoyed it in a very great degree, and reaped an advantage comparable to that which Euripides and his contemporaries and immediate successors enjoyed. The tradition enabled such an artist to impress by means of subtleties, niceties, and refinements, instead of forcing him to attempt always to more or less seduce, astonish or overawe; strong measures which grow almost necessarily into bad habits, and end by perverting the taste they created. This, it has often been remarked, was the case even with Michelangelo, even with Shakespeare. Yet nowadays, to enable a man to remark this, exceptional culture is required.

III

This idea of the use of a canon may be illustrated in many ways;
for, like all notions which resume actual experiences, it will be
found applicable in many spheres. Thus, on the subject of verse,
the eternal quarrel between the poet and the pedant is, that for
the first the rules of prosody and rhyme are only useful in so far
as they make the licenses he takes appreciable at their just value;
while for the pedant such licenses ever anew seem to imply
ignorance of the rule or incapacity to follow it, – an absurd
mistake, since the power to create and impress has little to do with
the means employed; and if a man builds up for himself a barrier
of foregone conclusions about the exact manner in which alone he
will allow himself to be deeply impressed, it is very certain he
will have few save painful impressions. Or take another
illustration – an artist the other day told me that he had noticed
that one could almost always trace a faintly ruled vertical line on
the paper which the greatest of all modern draughtsmen used.
Ingres, then, with all his freedom, vivacity, and accuracy of
control over the point he employed to draw with, still found it
useful to have a straight line ruled on his paper as a student does,
and may often even have resorted to the plumb-line. It enabled
his eye to test the subtlest deviations in the other lines with which
he was creating the balance, swing or stability of a figure. Rules
of art are, like this straight line, dead and powerless in
themselves: they help both creator and lover to follow and
appreciate the infinite freedom and subtlety of the living work.
The same thing might be illustrated with regard to manners; a
fine standard of social address and receptivity must be established
before the varieties and subtleties of those whose genius creates
beautiful relations can be appreciated at their full value in their
full variety. This dead law must be buried in everybody's mind
and heart before they can rise to that conscious freedom which is
opposite to the freedom of the wild animals, who never know
why they do, nor appreciate how it is done; neither are they able

to rejoice in the address of others; much less can they relish the infinite refinements of exhilarating apprehension, which make of laughter, tears, speech, silence, nearness and distance, a music which holds the enraptured soul in ecstasy; which created and constantly renews the hope of Heaven. And what blacker minister of a more sterile hell than the social pedant who only knows the rule, and mistakes grace and delicacy, frankness and generosity, for more or less grave infractions of it? But the happy critic, free from any personal knowledge of what creation means, or what aids are likely to forward it, is for ever in such a hurry to correct great creators like Leonardo, Dürer, or Hokusai, that he fails to understand them; and when he has caught them saying, "This is how anger or despair is expressed," calmly smiles in his superiority and says,

> "He had a scientific law for putting a battle on to canvas, one condition of which was that 'there must not be a level spot which is not trampled with gore.' But Leonardo did no harm; his canon was based on literary rather than artistic interests."

Analogies with scientific laws have served art and art criticism a very bad turn of late years. Nothing can be more useful to an artist than knowledge of how the emotions are expressed by the contortion of the features; but nobody in his senses could ever imagine that a rule for the expression of anger was rigid throughout and must never be departed from; every one approaching such a rule with a view to practice instead of criticism must immediately perceive that its only use is to be departed from in various degrees. Leonardo's advice for the painting of a battle-piece is excellent if it is understood in the sense in which it was meant, – "everything is what it is and not another thing," as Bishop Butler put it. Be sure and make your battle a battle indeed. It is time we should realise that what the great artists wrote about art is likely to be as sensible as are the works they created. How absurd it is for some one who can neither carve nor paint, much less create, to imagine he easily grasps the rules of art better than a great master! To such people let us repeat again and again Hamlet's impatient: "Oh, mend it altogether!"

IV

Now it will easily be seen that the causes which shape an art tradition may often be independent of, and foreign to, the will that creates beautiful objects. Religious superstition or formalism may often hem the artist in, and hamper his will in every direction; though it is not wholly accidental that the Greeks had a religion the spirit of which tended always to defeat the conservatism and bigotry of its priests. So that their formalism, instead of frustrating or warping the growth of their art tradition, merely served as a check that may well seem to have been exactly proportioned to its need; preventing the weakness or rankness of over rapid growth such as detracts from the art of the Renascence, and at the same time causing no vital injury. The spirit of the race deserved and created and was again in turn recreated by its religion.

Since it is generally recognised that too much freedom is not good for growing life, I think that almost everybody must at this stage have become aware of how immensely stupid the academical idea of a canon appears besides this idea. How suitable both to life and the desire for perfection the Greek practice was! How theologically dense the unprogressive inflexibility of the academical practitioner! And now let us hear Dürer.

But first I will quote from Sir Martin Conway the explanation of what Dürer means by the phrase, "Words of Difference."

These are what he calls the "Words of Difference": large, long, small, stout, broad, thick, narrow, thin, young, old, fat, lean, pretty, ugly, hard, soft, and so forth; in fact any word descriptive of a quality "whereby a thing may be differentiated from the thing (normal figure) first made."

Or, as Dürer says in another place, "difference such as maketh a thing fair or foul."

But further, it lieth in each man's choice whether or how far he shall make use of all the above written "Words of Difference." For a man may choose whether he will learn to labour with art, wherein is the truth, or without art in a freedom by which everything he doth is corrupted, and his toil becometh a scorn to look upon to such as understand.

Wherefore it is needful for every one that he use discreetness in such of his works as shall come to the light Whence it ariseth that he who would make anything aright must in no wise abate aught (that is essential) from Nature, neither must he lay what is intolerable upon her. Howbeit some will (by going to an opposite extreme) make alterations (from Nature) so slight that they can scarce be perceived. Such are of no account if they cannot be perceived; to alter over much also answereth not. A right mean (in such alterations) is best. But in this book I have departed from this right mean in order that it might be so much the better traced in small things. Let not him who wishes to proceed to some great thing imitate this my swiftness, but let him set more slowly (gradually) about his work, that it be not brutish but artistic to look upon. For figures which differ from the mean are not good to look upon *when* they are wrongly and unmasterly employed.

It is not to be wondered at that a skilful master beholdeth manifold differences of figure, all of which he might make if he had time enough, but which, for lack of time, he is forced to pass by. For such chances come very often to artists, and their imaginations also are full of figures which it were possible for them to make. Wherefore, if to live many hundred years were granted unto a man who had skill in the use of such art and were thereto accustomed, he would (through the power which God hath granted unto men) have wherewith daily to mould and make many new figures of men and other creatures, which none had before seen nor imagined. God, therefore, in such and other ways granteth great power unto artistic men.

Although there be such talking of differences, still it is well known that all things that a man doth differ of their own nature one from another. Consequently, there liveth no artist so sure of hand as to be able to make two things exactly alike the one to the other, so that they may not be distinguished. For of all our works none is quite and altogether like another, and this we can in no wise avoid.

We see that if we take two prints from an engraved copperplate, or cast two images in a mould, very many points may immediately be found whereby they may be distinguished one from another. If, then, it cometh thus to pass in things made by processes the least liable to error, much more will it happen in other things which are made by the free hand.

This, however, is *not the kind of Difference* whereof I here treat; for I am speaking of a difference (from the mean) which a man specially intendeth, and which standeth in his will, of which I have spoken once and again....

This is not the aforesaid Difference which we cannot sever from our work, but, such a difference as maketh a thing fair or foul, and which may be set forth by the "Word of Difference" dealt with above in this Book. If a man produce "different" figures of this kind in his work, it will be judged in every man's mind according to his own opinion, and these judgments seldom agree one with another.... Yet let every man beware that he make nothing impossible and inadmissible in Nature, unless indeed he would make some fantasy, in which it is allowed to mingle creatures of all kinds together....

Any one who leads this carefully cannot fail to see that it is not only that Dürer is not "desirous of laying down rules applicable to all cases," or even of "proposing a definite canon for the relative proportions of the human body," as Thausing indeed points out (p. 305, v. 11): but that he does not conceive the proportions he gives as even approximately capable of these functions; and considers it indeed the very nature and special use of a canon of proportions to be wilfully deviated from, pointing out that, though the deviations of which he is speaking are slight and subtle, they are not to be confused with the accidental ones that can but appear even in work done by mechanical processes. Rather they are such variation as a man "specially intendeth, and which standeth in his will;" and again, "such a difference as maketh a thing fair or foul;" for the use of these normal proportions is that they may enable an artist to deviate from the normal without the proportions he chooses having the air of monstrosities or mistakes or negligences. He does not insist that either of the scales he gives is the best that could be, even for this purpose, but that they are sufficiently good to be used; and he would have marvelled at the wonder that has been caused in innocent critical minds that in his own work he adhered to them so little. He never intended them to be adhered to.

V

It may be objected that Dürer certainly sometimes thought of a Canon of Proportion as a perfect rule, because he wrote on a MS. page as follows: –

> Vitruvius, the ancient architect, whom the Romans employed upon great buildings, says that whosoever desires to build should study the perfection of the human figure, for in it are discovered the most secret mysteries of proportion. So, before I say anything about architecture, I will state how a well-formed man should be made, and then about a woman, a child and a horse. Any object may be proportioned out (*literally*, measured) in a similar way. Therefore, hear first of all what Vitruvius says about the human figure, which he

✻ 285

learnt from the greatest masters, painters and founders, who were highly famed. They said that the human figure is as follows.

That the face from the chin upward to where the hair begins is the tenth part of a man, and that an out-stretched hand is the same length, &c.

And again in another place, as Sir Martin Conway points out, he gives a religious basis to this notion,[81] "the Creator fashioned men once for all as they must be, and I hold that the perfection of form and beauty is contained in the sum of all men." In an obvious sense these passages certainly run counter to those which I have quoted (pp. 285-207): but I would like to point out that these are dogmatic assertions about something that if it were true could never be proved by experience (see also pp. 64, 254), those former are Dürer's advice with a view to practice. Men frequently carry about a considerable amount of dogmatic opinion, which has so little connection with actual experience that it is never brought to the test without being noticeably incommoded by it. Yet it is not absolutely necessary to consider Dürer as inconsistent in regard to this matter, even to this degree.

The beauty of form which he held had been Adam's, and which was now parcelled out among his vast progeny in various amounts as a consequence of his fall – this beauty of form doubtless Dürer considered it part of an artist's business to recollect and reveal in his work. This beauty is an ideal, and his canon (or rather canons) were intended as means to help the artist to approach towards the realisation of that ideal. It is obvious also that a man occupied in comparing the proportions of those whom he considers to be exceptionally beautiful will develop and feed his power of imagining beautifully proportioned figures. It would be futile to deny that this is very much what took place in the evolution of Greek statues, or that such works are perhaps of all others the most central and satisfying to the human spirit. The sentences that precede that quoted by Sir Martin are Greek in tendency.

A good figure cannot be made without industry and care; it

should therefore be well considered before it is begun, so that it be correctly made. For the lines of its form cannot be traced by compass or rule, but must be drawn by the hand from point to point, so that it is easy to go wrong in them. And for such figures great attention should be paid to human proportions, and all their kinds should be investigated. *I hold that the more nearly and accurately a figure is made to resemble a man, so much the better the work will be.* If the best parts chosen from many well-formed men are united in one figure, it will be worthy of praise. But some are of another opinion, and discuss how men ought to be made. I will not argue with them about that. I hold Nature for Master in such matters, and the fancy of men for delusion.

And then follows the passage quoted by Sir Martin Conway (see p. 289). It is obvious that, joined with the two preceding sentences, this passage can in no way be made to serve the academical practitioner, as it seems to when taken alone. In the same way, the sentence printed in italics in the above quotation, if isolated, would certainly seem to serve the scientific practitioners and their slavish realism, though in connection with those that follow this is no longer possible. Dürer regards nature as providing raw material for a creation which may not tally exactly with any individual natural object. This was the Greek artists' idea of the serviceableness of nature, as revealed both by their practice and by such traditions as that concerning Zeuxis and his five beautiful models for the figure of Venus. But Dürer does not confine the use of his canons even to this aim, but clearly perceived their utility in regard to quite other aims, as is shown by the passage beginning, "It is not to be wondered at," &c. (see p. 286), in which the imagination of figures not merely intended to embody beautiful or newly assorted proportions is clearly considered; and if we review Dürer's actual work we shall see how much oftener he created figures for picturesque or dramatic effect than he did to embody beautiful proportions in them, though he evidently also considered the last purpose as of the first importance, as we see when he goes on to say:

Let any one who thinks I alter the human form too much or too little take care to avoid my error and follow nature. There are many different kinds of men in various lands: whoso travels far will find this to be so, and see it before his eyes. We are considering about the most beautiful human figure conceivable, but (only) the Maker of the world knows how that should be. Even if we succeed well we do but approach towards it from afar. For we ourselves have differences of perception, and the vulgar who follow only their own taste usually err. Therefore I do not advise any one to follow me, for I only do what I can, and that is not enough even to satisfy myself.

The extreme complexity of Dürer's ideas and their application was a natural result of their having been born of his experience. For excellence is extremely various, and widely scattered through the world. The simplicity of a true work of art results merely from some excellence having been singled out from all foreign circumstances, and presented as vividly as it was intensely apprehended. This excellence may be one of proportion or one of many other kinds. Now, a figure conceived by an artist, whether he value it for its choicely assorted proportions or for picturesque or dramatic effect, may need to be developed before it is serviceable in an elaborate work of art.

Artists who work rapidly, and, whose pictures are dominated by passing moods, have always been in the habit of taking great licences with proportion, and, indeed, with all matters of fact. Dürer's aim is to endow the artist who elaborates his work slowly with a similar freedom. This energy and power in rapid work it is the ever-renewed despair of artists to feel themselves losing in the process of elaboration. And one of the reasons for this is that in larger or more elaborate work, the statement, being more ample, is expected to be also more comprehensive and exhaustive; for the time required begets after-thoughts as to the real nature of the object viewed apart from the mood, which is the only excuse for the work; and so some of the artist's attention is drawn away to facts and aspects which it would have been the success of his work to have ignored. Dürer's object was to help a man to carry out his essential intention, and that alone, in a carefully elaborated picture; the problems faced were precisely similar to those so successfully coped with in Greek statues. In the first place, he would have pointed out that all sketches will not bear elaboration if their merit depends on extreme licence, for instance. Next, that a man who had a standard of proportion could see wherein the deviations of his sketched figure were essential to the effect he wished it to produce, and wherein they were unessential. Then, if he drew the normal figure large, he would be able to deviate from it in exactly the right places and to the right degree to reproduce the desired effect. But to do this he must also have a general notion of how deviations from a normal proportion could be made consistent throughout all the measurements involved not that he would in every case want to make them consistent. Now, there is a class of artists for whom all these suggestions of Dürer's must for ever remain useless, for all science of production is impossible for those whose only success lies in improvisation; such improvisations, however dazzling or however delightful they may be, are, nevertheless, the class of art-works furthest removed in spirit and in method from Greek statuary. I do not say that they need be inferior; I say that they are opposite in method. And, had circumstances permitted, or Dürer's dowry of great gifts been more complete than it was, and enabled him to become as great a creator of pictures as he is a great draughtsman and portrait-painter, no doubt his pictures would have resembled Greek statues both in their effect and their method, however different they might have been in subject and in range. To talk about "beauty" being sacrificed to "truth," with Prof. Thausing; or the ideal of the North being "strength" in works of art as in life, with Sir Martin Conway; – is to confuse the issue and deceive oneself. To have mistaken the proper end of art, beauty, by thinking it was "truth" or "strength," is to have failed to labour in the right direction; that is all-who-ever may condone the failure.

Again, Sir Martin Conway tells us:

> The laws of perspective can be deduced with certainty from mathematical first principles, the canon of proportions' could only be constructed empirically as the result of repeated observations. Nevertheless, once constructed, it can certainly be used as Dürer suggested. Its use has practically been superseded by the study of anatomy.

This last phrase shows us in a flash how far the writer when he wrote it was from apprehending Dürer's meaning. How could the study of anatomy ever do for an artist what Dürer was trying to do? No doubt Sir Martin had Michelangelo in his mind's eye; and it is true that he studied anatomy, and that his influence has been, on the whole, paramount with artists attempting subjects of this kind ever since. Whether Michelangelo studied proportion or not, his practice exemplifies Dürer's meaning splendidly. No anatomical research could have led him to construct figures nine to twelve, or even fifteen to twenty, heads high – to do which, as his work developed, more and more became his practice, especially in designs and sketches for compositions. To arrive at such proportions he followed his imaginative instinct. He found that these monstrous deviations from the normal (which, of course, in a general sense he recognised, whether he gave any study to rendering it precise or not) produced the effect on his mind that he wished to produce on the minds of others – an effect that was emotional and peculiar to his habitual moods. We know that his constitution gave him the staying-power, while his fiery Titanic spirit gave him the energy, to carry out and perfect his mighty frescoes and statues at the same heat that the creative hour yields other men for the production of a sketch alone. This giant son of Time was able to live for days and weeks together in a state of mind two or three consecutive hours of which exhaust the average master even. Considering the rapidity and intensity of his mental process, it is a miracle that, in so many works and to so great a degree, he respected the too much and too little of human reason, and allowed himself to be governed by what the Greeks called a sense of measure, instead of yielding to his native impetuosity and becoming an a-thousand-fold-greater-Blake; and illustrating, to the delight of active and short-winded intelligences, and the stupefaction of slow and dull ones, the futility of eccentricity and the frivolity of passion when unseconded by constancy of character and labour. For futile, in the arts, is whatever the sense of beauty must condemn, however well-intentioned; and frivolous is the passion that forgets the end it would attain, and becomes merely a private rhapsody, however astonishing its develop-ments; slowly but surely it will be seen that such fireworks do not vitally concern us. The proportions of many of Michelangelo's figures are as far removed from any possible normal standard as what Dürer calls "this my swiftness," in the abnormally tall and stout figures among the diagrams illustrating his book.

And this is where Dürer's idea comes nearer to Greek practice. For by letting the striking rather than the subtle govern his departures from the mean, Michelangelo found himself always bound to go beyond himself; as the palate which once has entertained strong stimulants demands that the dose be continually strengthened. Now this is in entire conformity with the impatience which was perhaps his greatest weakness; just as Dürer's too methodical approach is in conformity with that acquiescence in the insufficiency of his conditions which made him in his weak moments swear never again to undertake those better classes of work which were less adequately paid, or made him content to display mere manual dexterity rather than do nothing on his days of darkness, suffering and depression: we may add, which made him choose to live at Nuremberg and refuse a better income and more suitable surroundings at Venice.

It is obviously the more hopeful way to create a beautiful figure first and discover a mathematical way of reproducing its most essential proportions afterwards; and no doubt this is what

Dürer intended should be done; and in consequence he felt a need, and sought to supply it, for mechanical means to simplify, shorten and render more sure that part of the process which must necessarily partake something of the nature of drudgery, if great finish is to be combined with splendid design. The romantic, impulsive *improvisatore* does not feel this need, considers it bound to defeat its own aim; and, given his own gifts, he is right. But none the less, there are the Greek statues elaborated with a thoroughness which, if it ever dims or veils the creative intention, does so in a degree so slight as to seem amply compensated by the sense of ease maintained in spite of the innumerable difficulties overcome; there are besides a score or more of Dürer's copper engravings with their imperturbable adequacy of minute painstaking, never for a moment sleepy or mechanical or lifeless. The one aim need not excommunicate the other even in the same individual; far less need this be so in different artists, with diverse temperaments, diverse aptitudes.

VII

The application of this idea does not end with the simple proportions of measurement between the limbs and parts of the figure; it is also concerned with what is called the modelling, and the treatment of surfaces such as the draperies, the hair, the fleshy portions and those beneath which the bony structure comes to prominence; in painting it may be applied to the chiaroscuro and colour. Reynolds' remarks on the Venetians in his Eighth Discourse well illustrate this fact. He says:

> It ought, in my opinion, to be indispensably observed that the masses of light in a picture be always of a warm mellow colour, yellow, red,

or a yellowish-white; and that the blue, the grey, or the green colours be kept *almost* entirely out of these masses, and be used only to support and set off these warm colours; and, for this purpose, a small *proportion* of cold colours will be sufficient.

   If this conduct be reversed, let the light be cold, and the surrounding colours warm, as we often see in the works of the Roman and Florentine painters; and it will be out of the power of art, even in the hands of Rubens or Titian, to make a picture splendid or harmonious.[82]

Here we see a great colourist attempting to establish a canon for colour. Had he lived at an earlier period, before expression had become generally a subject of criticism, he would have described his discovery in less guarded and elastic language, such as is now applied to scientific laws. And then he might have been as excusably misunderstood as Leonardo and Dürer have been; as it is, the misunderstanding dealt out to him is quite without excuse.

Rembrandt, not only exemplifies the impressiveness of great deviations in structural proportions in much the same degree as Michelangelo, using what the Greeks and Dürer would doubtless have considered a dangerous liberty, however much they might have felt bound to admire the results obtained; not only does he do this when, for instance, he represents Jesus now as a giant, now as almost a dwarf, according to the imaginative impression which he chooses to create; but he follows a similar process in his black and white pattern. For among his works there are etchings, which, though often supposed to have been left unfinished, are discerned by those with a sense for beauties of this class to be marvellously complete, stimulating, and satisfying, and in the nicest harmony with the other impressions produced by the mental point of view from which the subject is viewed, as also by the main lines and proportions of the composition, and to yield the visual delight most suitable to the occasion. Dürer and the Greeks are at one with Michelangelo and Rembrandt in condemning by their practice all purely mechanical application of ideas or methods to the production of works of creative art, such as is exemplified by artists of more limited aims and powers; by academical practitioners, by theoretical scientists calling themselves impressionists, luminarists, naturalists, or any other name. For artists whose temperaments are impeded by some unhappy slowness, or difficulty in concentrating themselves, methods of procedure similar to those elaborated by Dürer in his books on proportion, properly understood, must be a real aid and benefit; as those who are essentially improvisors may help themselves and supply their deficiencies by methods similar to those which Reynolds describes as practised by Gainsborough.

> "He even framed a kind of model of landscapes on his table, composed of broken stones, dried herbs and pieces of broken glass, which he magnified and improved into rocks, trees and water" (Fourteenth Discourse).

This process resembles that of tracing faces or scenes from the life of gnomes in glowing caverns among coals of fire on a winter's eve; it is resorted to in one form or another by all creative artists, but it is peculiarly useful to men like Gainsborough, whose art tends always to become an improvisation, whatever strenuous discipline they may have subjected themselves to in their days of ardent youth.

VIII

Perhaps Dürer's actual standards for the normal, his actual methods for creating self-consistent variations from it, are not likely to prove of much use, even when artists shall be sufficiently educated to understand them; nevertheless, the principle which informs them has been latent in the work of all great creators; is marvellously fulfilled indeed, in Greek statuary. The work of

Antoine Louis Barye, that great and little-understood master – as far as I am able to judge, the only modern artist who has made science serve him instead of being seduced by her – exemplifies this central idea of Dürer's almost as fully as the Greek masterpieces. The future of art appears to me to lie in the hands of those artists who shall be able to grapple with the new means offered them by the advance of science, as he did, and be as little or even less seduced than he was by the foolish idea that art can become science without ceasing to be art, which has handicapped and defeated the efforts of so many industrious and talented men of late years. So truly is this the case that the improvisor appears to many as the only true artist, and his uncontrolled caprices as the farthest reach of human constructive power.

In any case, no artist is unhappy if a docile and hopeful disposition enables him to see in the masterpieces of Greek sculpture the reward of an easy balance of both temperaments and methods, the improvisor's and the elaborator's, under felicitous circumstances, by men better endowed than himself. And this though never history and archaeology shall be in a position to give him information sufficient to determine that his faith is wholly warranted.

> A golden age is a golden dream, that sheds
> A golden light on waking hours, on toil,
> On leisure, and on finished works.

CHAPTER II

THE IMPORTANCE OF DOCILITY

I

I now intend to re-arrange what seem the most interesting of the
sentences on the theory of art which are found in Dürer's MSS.
and books on proportion. He did not give them the final form or
order which he intended, and it seems to me that to arrange the
more important according to the subjects they treat of will be the
simplest way of arriving at general conceptions as to their
tendency and value. We shall thus bring together repetitions of
the same thought and contradictory answers to the same question;
and after each series of sentences, I myself shall discuss the points
raised, illustrating my remarks from modern writers whose
opinion in these matters seems to me deserving of most attention.
I have heard it said by the late Mr. Arthur Strong that Dürer's art
is always didactic; and Dürer as a writer on art certainly has ever
before his mind this one object, to teach others, or, as I should
prefer to phrase it, to help others to learn. For he himself is
continually confessing that he cannot yet answer his own
questions, and it seems to me that the best teacher is always he
who most desires to increase his knowledge, not indeed to hoard

it as some do and make of it a personal possession; intellectual misers, for ever gnashing their teeth over the reputations or the pretensions of others. No, but one who desires knowledge for its own sake and welcomes it in others with as much satisfaction as he gains it for himself. Docility, i.e., teachableness, let me point out once more, seems to be the necessary midwife of genius, without the aid of which it often labours in vain, or brings forth strange incongruous and misshapen births.

Sad is the condition of a brilliant and fiery spirit shut up in a man's brain without the humble assistance of this lively, meek and patient virtue! What unrelieved and insupportable throes of agony must be borne by such a spirit, and how often does such labour end in misanthropy or madness! The records of the lives of exceptionally-gifted men tell us only too clearly what pains those are, and how frequently they have been borne. So I fancy I cannot do better than choose out for my first section sentences which praise or advocate the effort to learn, or attempt to enlighten those who make such an effort on the choice of teachers and disciplines.

II

I shall not hesitate to transpose sentences even when they appear in connected passages, in order, as I hope, to bring out more clearly their connection. For Dürer was not a writer by profession, and his thoughts were often more abundant than he knew how to deal with.

Before starting, however, I must prefix to my quotations some account of the four MS. books in the British Museum from which they are principally taken. Rough drafts in Pirkheimer's handwriting were found among them, but of Dürer's work Sir Martin Conway tells us:

The volumes contain upwards of seven hundred leaves and scraps of paper of various kinds, covered at different dates with more or less elaborate outline drawings, and more or less corrected drafts for works published or planned by Dürer. Interspersed among them are geometrical and other sketches.

He was in the habit of correcting and re-copying, again and again, what he had written. Sometimes he would jot down a sentence alongside of matter to which it had no relation. This sentence he would afterwards introduce in its right connection. There are in these volumes no less than four drafts of the beginning of a Dedication to Pirkheimer of the Books of Human Proportions. Two other drafts of this same dedication are among the Dresden MSS. The opening sentences of the Introduction to the same work were likewise, as will be seen, the subject of frequent revision.

These drafts, notes and sketches date from 1508 to 1523. Some collector had had them cut out, gummed together, and bound without the slightest regard to order, or even to the sequence of consecutive passages. In January 1890 the volumes were taken to pieces and rearranged by Miss Lina Eckenstein, who had previously made the admirable translations of them for Sir Martin Conway's "Literary Remains of Albrecht Dürer," from which my quotations are taken.

The contents of the volumes as rearranged may be roughly described as follows:

Volume 1. Drawings of whole figures and portions of the body, illustrating Dürer's theories of Proportion. Drawings of a solid octogon. Six coloured drawings of crystals. The description of the Ionic order of architecture. Drawings of columns with measurements. A scale for Human Proportions. A table of contents for a work on Geometry. Notes on perspective, curves, folds, &c. The different kinds of temple after Vitruvius. Mathematical diagrams, &c.

Volume II. Draft of a dedicatory letter to King Ferdinand (see page 180). Drafts and drawings for "The Art of Fortification." Drawing of a shield with a rearing horse. Mantles of Netherlandish women and nuns. A Latin inscription for his own portrait. Notes on "Proportion," and on the feast of the Rosenkranz. Scale for Human Proportions. An alphabet. Draft of a dedication for the books on Proportion. Sketch of a skeleton. Studies of architecture. Venetian houses and roofs. Sketches of a church, a house, a tower, a drapery, &c.

Volume III. Drafts of a projected work on Painting and on the study of Proportion. Drafts for the dedication, the preface, and for a work on Esthetics. Drawings of a male body, a female body, and a piece of drapery. Notes and drawings for the proportions of heads, hands, feet, outline curves, a child, a woman, &c.

Volume IV. Proportions of a man, a fat woman, the head of the average woman, the young woman, &c. Short Profession of Faith (see page 130). Scale for Human Proportions, &c. Fragments of the Preface of Essay on Aesthetics, &c. Grimacing and distorted faces. Use of measurements. On the characters of faces, thick, thin, broad, narrow, &c. Sketches of a dragon and of an angel for Maximilian's Triumphal Procession. List of Luther's works (see page 130). Drawings of human bodies proportioned to squares.

See the description in "Dürer's Schriftlicher Nachlass" (Lange und Fuhse), page 263, from which the above abstract is made.

Sir Martin Conway continues:

In these volumes Dürer is seen, sometimes writing under the influence of impetuous impulse, sometimes with leisurely care, allowing his pen to embroider the script with graceful marginal flourishes.

At what period of his career Dürer first conceived the idea of writing a comprehensive work upon the theory and practice of art is unknown. It was certainly before the year 1512. The following list of chapters may perhaps be an early sketch of the plan.

Ten things are contained in the little book.
The first, the proportions of a young child.
The second, proportions of a grown man.
The third, proportions of a woman.
The fourth, proportions of a horse.
The fifth, something about architecture.
The sixth, about an apparatus through which it can be shown that 'all things may be traced.
The seventh, about light and shade.
The eighth, about colours, how to paint like nature.
The ninth, about the ordering (composition) of the picture.
The tenth, about free painting, which alone is made by Imagination without any other help.

III

Glad enough should we be to attain unto great knowledge without toil, for nature has implanted in us the desire of knowing all things, thereby to discern a truth of all things. But our dull wit cannot come unto such perfectness of all art, truth, and wisdom. Yet are we not, therefore, shut out altogether from all arts. If we want to sharpen our reason by learning and to practise ourselves therein, having once found the right path we may, step by step, seek, learn, comprehend, and finally reach and attain unto something true. Wherefore, he that understandeth how to learn somewhat in his leisure time, whereby he may most certainly be enabled to honour God, and to do what is useful both for himself and others, that man doeth well; and we know that in this wise he will gain much experience in art and will be able to make known its truth for our good. It is right, therefore, for one man to teach another. He that joyfully doeth so, upon him shall much be bestowed by God, from whom we receive all things. He hath highest praise.

One finds some who know nothing and learn nothing. They despise learning, and say that much evil cometh of the arts, and that some are wholly vile. I, on the contrary, hold that no art is evil, but that all are good. A sword is a sword which may be used either for murder or for justice. Similarly the arts are in themselves good. What God hath formed, that is good, misuse it how ye will.

Thou findest arts of all kinds; choose then for thyself that which is like to be of greatest service to thee. Learn it; let not the difficulty thereof vex thee till thou hast accomplished somewhat wherewith thou mayest be satisfied.

It is very necessary for a man to know some one thing by reason of the usefulness which ariseth therefrom. Wherefore we should all gladly learn, for the more we know so much the more do we resemble the likeness of God, who verily knoweth all things.

The more, therefore, a man learneth, so much the better doth he become, and so much the more love doth he win for the arts and for things exalted. Wherefore a man ought not to play the wanton, but should learn in season.

Is the artistic man pious and by nature good? He escheweth the evil and chooseth the good; and hereunto serve the arts, for they give the discernment of good and evil.

Some may learn somewhat of all arts, but that is not given to every man. Nevertheless, there is no rational man so dull but that he may learn the one thing towards which his fancy draweth him most strongly. Hence no man is excused from learning something.

Let no man put too much confidence in himself, for many (pairs of eyes) see better than one. Though it is possible for a man to comprehend more than a thousand (men), still that cometh but rarely to pass.

Many fall into error because they follow their own taste alone; therefore let each look to it that his inclination blind not his judgment. For every mother is well pleased with her own child, and thus also it ariseth that many painters paint figures resembling themselves.

He that worketh in ignorance worketh more painfully than he that worketh with understanding; therefore let all learn to understand aright.

Now I know that in our German nation, at the present time, are many painters who stand in need of instruction, for they lack all real art, yet they nevertheless have many large works to do. Forasmuch then as they are so numerous, it is very needful for them to learn to better their work.

Willingly will I impart my teaching, hereafter written, to the man who knoweth little and would gladly learn; but I will not be cumbered with the proud, who, according to their own estimate of themselves, know all things, and are best, and despise all else. From true artists, however, such as can show their meaning with the hand, I desire to learn humbly and with much thankfulness.

A thing thou beholdest is easier of belief than that thou hearest, but whatever is both heard and seen we grasp more firmly and lay hold on more securely. I will therefore do the work in both ways, that thus I may be better understood.

Whosoever will, therefore, let him hear and see what I say, do, and teach, for I hope it may be of service and not for a hindrance to the better arts, nor lead thee to neglect better things.

I hear moreover of no writer in modern times by whom aught hath been written and made known which I might read for my improvement. For some hide their art in great secrecy, and others write about things whereof they know nothing, so that their words are nowise better than mere noise, as he that knoweth somewhat is swift to discover. I therefore will write down with God's help the little that I know. Though many will scorn it I am not troubled, for I well know that it is easier to cast blame on a thing than to make anything better. Moreover, I will expound my meaning as clearly and plainly as I can; and, were it possible, I would gladly give everything I know to the light, for the good of cunning students who prize such art more highly than silver or gold. I further admonish all who have any knowledge in these matters that they write it down. Do it truly and plainly, not toilsomely and at great length, for the sake of those who seek and are glad to learn, to the great honour of God and your own praise. If I then set something burning and ye all add to it with skilful furthering, a blaze may in time arise therefrom which shall shine throughout the whole world.

I shall here apply to what is to be called beautiful the same touchstone as that by which we decide what is right. For as what all the world prizeth as right we hold to be right, so what all the world esteemeth beautiful that will we also hold for beautiful, and ourselves strive to produce the like.

No one need blindly follow this theory of mine as though it were quite perfect, for human nature has not yet so far degenerated that another man cannot discover something better. So each may use my teaching as long as it seems good to him, or until he finds something better. Where he is not willing to accept it, he may well hold that this doctrine is not written for him, but for others who are willing.

That must be a strangely dull head which never trusts itself to find out anything fresh, but only travels along the old path, simply following others and not daring to reflect for itself. For it beseems each understanding, in following another, not to despair of itself discovering something better. If that is done, there remaineth no doubt but that in time this art will again reach the perfection it attained amongst the ancients.

Much will hereafter be written about subjects and refinements of painting. Sure am I that many notable men will arise, all of whom will write both well and better about this art, and will teach it better than I; for I myself hold my art at a very mean value, for I know what my faults are. Let every man therefore strive to better these my errors according to his powers. Would to God it were possible for me to see the work and art of the mighty masters to come, who are yet unborn, for I know that I might be improved upon. Ah! how often in my sleep do I behold great works of art and beautiful things, the like whereof never appear to me awake, but so soon as I awake, even the remembrance of them leaveth me.

Compare also the passages already quoted.

IV

"What an admirable temper!" is the exclamation which expresses our first feeling on reading the foregoing sentences. It renews the spirit of a man merely to peruse such things. Scales fall from our eyes, and we see what we most essentially are, with pleasure, as good children gleefully recognise their goodness: and at the same time we are filled with contrition that we should have ever forgotten it. And this that we most essentially are rational beings, lovers of goodness, children of hope, – how directly Dürer appeals to it: "Nature has implanted in us the desire of knowing all things." It reminds one of Ben Jonson's: –

> It is a false quarrel against nature, that she helps understanding but in a few, when the most part of mankind are inclined by her thither, if they would take the pains; no less than birds to fly, horses to run, &c., which, if they lose it, is through their own sluggishness, and by that means they become her prodigies, not her children.

There is something refreshing and inspiriting in the mere conviction of our teachableness; and when the same author, referring to Plato's travels in search of knowledge, says, "He laboured, so must we," we do not find the comparison humiliating either to Plato or ourselves. For "without a way there is no going," and every man of superior mould says to us with more or less of benignity, "I am the way: follow me." Such means or ways of attainment have been followed by all whose success is known to us, and are followed now by all "finely touched and gifted men." I might quote in illustration of these assertions the whole of Reynolds' Sixth Discourse, so marvellous for its acute and delicate discrimination; but I will content myself with a few leading passages:

> We cannot suppose that any one can really mean to exclude all imitation of others.
>
> It is a common observation that no art was ever invented and carried to perfection at the same time.
>
> The greatest natural genius cannot subsist on its own stock: he who resolves never to ransack any mind but his own will soon be reduced to the poorest of all imitations, he will be obliged to imitate himself, and to repeat what he has often before repeated.
>
> The truth is, he whose feebleness is such as to make other men's thoughts an encumbrance to him, can have no very great strength of mind or genius of his own to be destroyed: so that not much harm will be done at the worst.

Of course, this last phrase will not apply universally; we must remember that the man who sets out to become an artist, or claims to be one by native gift, has made apparent that he is the possessor of no mean ambition. The humblest may see a way of improvement in their betters, and obey the command, "Follow me." Every man is not called to follow great artists, but only those who are peculiarly fitted to tread the difficult paths that climb Olympus-hill. Yet to all men alike the great artist in life, he who wedded failure to divinity, says, "Learn of me that I am meek and lowly of heart, and ye shall find rest to your souls."

He who confines himself to the imitation of an individual, as he never proposes to surpass, so he is not likely to equal, the object of his imitation. He professes only to follow; and he that follows must necessarily be behind.

It is of course impossible to surpass perfection, but it is possible to be made one with it.

To find excellences, however dispersed, to discover beauties, however concealed by the multitude of defects with which they are surrounded, can be the work only of him who, having a mind always alive to his art, has extended his views to all ages and to all schools; and has acquired from that comprehensive mass which he has thus gathered to himself a well-digested and perfect idea of his art, to which everything is referred. Like a sovereign judge and arbiter of art, he is possessed of that presiding power which separates and attracts every excellence from every school; selects both from what is great and what is little; brings home knowledge from the east and from the west; making the universe tributary towards furnishing his mind, and enriching his works with originality and variety of inventions.

In this fine passage we get back to our central idea in regard to the sense of proportion "making the universe tributary towards furnishing his mind"; while in the "discovery of beauties" the complete artist "selects both from what is great and what is little," from the clouds of heaven and from the dunghills of the farmyard.

Study, therefore, the great works of the great masters for ever. Study, as nearly as you can, in the order, in the manner, and on the principles on which they studied. Study nature attentively, but always with those masters in your company; consider them as models which you are to imitate, and at the same time as rivals with whom you are to contend. For "no man can be an artist, whatever he may suppose, upon any other terms."

Yes, an artist is a child who chooses his parents, nor is he limited to only two. Religion tells all men they have a Father, who is God; philosophy and tradition repeat, "man has a mother, who is Nature." These sayings are platitudes; their application is so obvious that it is now generally forgotten. If God is a Father, it is the soul that chooses Him; if Nature is a mother, it is the man who chooses to regard her as such, since to the greater number it is well known she seems but a stepmother, and a cruel one at that. Elective affinities, chosen kindred! – "tell me what company you keep, and I will tell you who you are" (what you are worth). How many artist waifs one sees nowadays! lost souls, who choose to be nobody's children, and think they can teach themselves all they need to know.

I think the very striking agreement between artists so totally different in every respect except eminence, docility and anxiety to further art, as Dürer and Reynolds, ought to impress our minds very deeply: even though, as is certainly the case, the way they point out has been very greatly abandoned of late years, and public institutions in this and other countries proceed to further art on quite other lines; even though critics are almost unanimous in knowing better both the end and the way than the great masters who had not the advantage of a dash of science in their hydromel to make it sparkle, but instead made it yet richer and thicker by stirring up with it piety and religion. I think this "cock-tail and sherry-cobbler" art criticism of to-day is very deleterious to the digestion, and that the piety and enthusiasm which Dürer and Reynolds worked into their art were more wholesome, and better supplied the needs and deficiencies of artistic temperaments.

CHAPTER III

THE LOST TRADITION

I

Many centuries ago the great art of painting was held in high honour by mighty kings, and they made excellent artists rich and held them worthy, accounting such inventiveness a creating power like God's. For the imagination of a good painter is full of figures, and were it possible for him to live for ever, he would always have from his inward ideas, whereof Plato speaks, something new to set forth by the work of his hand.

Many hundred years ago there were still some famous painters, such as those named Phidias, Praxiteles, Apelles, Polycleitus, Parrhasius, Lysippus, Protogenes, and the rest, some of whom wrote about their art and very artfully described it and gave it plainly to light: but their praise-worthy books are, so far, unknown to us, and perhaps have been altogether lost by war, driving forth of the peoples, and alterations of laws and beliefs – a loss much to be regretted by every wise man. It often came to pass that noble "Ingenia" were destroyed by barbarous oppressors of art; for if they saw figures traced in a few lines they thought it nought but vain, devilish sorcery. And in destroying them they attempted to honour God by something displeasing to Him; and to use the language of men, God was angry with all destroyers of the works of great mastership, which is only attained by much toil, labour, and expenditure of time, and is bestowed by God alone. Often do I sorrow because I must be robbed of the aforesaid masters' books of art; but the enemies of art despise these things.

Pliny writeth that the old painters and sculptors – such as Apelles, Protogenes, and the rest – told very artistically in writing how a well-built man's figure might be measured out. Now it may well have come to pass that these noble books were misunderstood and destroyed as idolatrous in the early days of the Church. For they would have said Jupiter should have such proportions, Apollo such others; Venus shall be thus, Hercules thus; and so with all the rest. Had it, however, been my fate to be there at the time, I would have said: "Oh dear, holy lords and fathers, do not so lamentably destroy the nobly discovered arts, which have been gotten by great toil and labour, only because of the abuses made of them. For art is very hard, and we might and would use it for the great honour and glory of God. For, even as the ancients used the fairest figure of a man to represent their false god Apollo, we will employ the same for Christ the Lord, who is fairest of all the earth; and as they figured Venus as the loveliest of women, so will we in like manner set down the same beauteous form for the most pure Virgin Mary, the mother of God; and of Hercules will we make Samson, and thus will we do with all the rest, for such books shall we get never more." Wherefore, though that which is lost ariseth not again, yet a man may strive after new lore; and for these reasons I have been moved to make known my ideas here following, in order that others may ponder the matter further, and may thus come to a new and better way and foundation.

I certainly do not deny that, if the books of the ancients who wrote about the art of painting still lay before our eyes, my design might be open to the false interpretation that I thought to find out something better than what was known unto them. These books, however, have been totally lost in the lapse of time; so I cannot be justly blamed for publishing my opinions and discoveries in writing, for that is exactly what the ancients did. If other competent men are thereby induced to do the like, our descendants have something which they may add to and improve upon, and thus the art of painting may in time advance and reach its perfection.

II

Whether we should exercise our intellects or logical sense alone upon the records and remains of past ages, or whether they may not be better employed for the exercise and edification of the imaginative faculties, would seem to be a question which, though they did not perhaps in set terms put to themselves, modern historians have very summarily answered; and I think answered wrongly. The records of the past, the records even of yesterday, are necessarily extremely incomplete; to make them at all significant something must be added by the historian. The 'perception' of probability is never exact; it varies with the mind between man and man; in the same man even before and after different experiences, &c. But even if the perception of the highest probability were practically exact, it would never suffice; for, as Aristotle says, "it is probable that many things should happen contrary to probability." From these facts it follows that the man who has the most exhaustive knowledge of what has actually survived, and what has been recorded, will not necessarily form the truest judgment on a question of history; it might always happen that the intuition of some unscholarly person was nearer the truth; still no man could ever decide between the two, nor would any sane man think it worth his while to take sides with either of them; such questions are most useful when they are left open. This is the case because the imagination is thus left freer to use such knowledge as it has for the edification of the character; and that model for our example or warning which the imagination constructs may always possibly be the truth. According to the balance in it of apparent probability, with edifying power it will beget conviction. Such a conviction may be doomed to be superseded sooner or later; its value lies in its potency while it lasts. The temper in which we look at our historical heritage is of more importance to us now than the exactitude of our vision; for this latter can never be proved, while the former approves itself by the fruit it bears within us. It is better, more fruitful, to feel with Dürer about the art of Ancient Greece than to know all that can be known of it to-day and feel a great deal less. "Character calls forth character," said Goethe; we may add, "even from the grave." Now that the physical miracle of the Resurrection has come to seem so unimportant and uninteresting to educated men, it might be a wise economy to connect its poetry with this experience, that great and creative characters can raise men better worth knowing than Lazarus from the dead. Nietsche thought that Shakespeare had brought Brutus back to life, (though he knew very little of Roman history), and that Brutus was the Roman best worth knowing. "Of all peoples, the Greeks dreamt the dream of life the best," Goethe said; and again, "For all other arts we have to make some allowance; to Greek art alone we are for ever debtors." To feel the truth of these sayings with a passion similar to that shown in the passages quoted above from Dürer, must surely be a great help to an artist. Such a passion is an end in itself, or rather is the only means by which we can win spiritual freedom from some of the heavier fetters that modern life lays upon us. It freed Goethe even from Germany.

CHAPTER IV

BEAUTY

I

How is beauty to be judged? – upon that we have to deliberate.

A man by skill may bring it into every single thing, for in some things we recognise that as beautiful which elsewhere would lack beauty.

Good and better in respect of beauty are not easy to discern; for it would be quite possible to make two different figures, one stout, the other thin, which should differ one from the other in every proportion, and yet we scarce might be able to judge which of the two excelled in beauty. What beauty is I know not, though it dependeth upon many things.

I shall here apply to what is to be called beautiful the same touchstone as that by which we decide what is right. For as what all the world prizeth as right we hold to be right, so what all the world esteemeth beautiful that we will also hold for beautiful, and ourselves strive to produce the like.

There are many causes and varieties of beauty; he that can prove them is so much the more to be trusted.

The accord of one thing with another is beautiful, therefore want of harmony is not beautiful. A real harmony linketh together things unlike.

Use is a part of beauty, whatever therefore is useless unto men is without beauty.

The more imperfection is excluded so much the more doth beauty abide in the work.

Guard thyself from superfluity.

But beauty is so put together in men and so uncertain is our judgment about it, that we may perhaps find two men both beautiful and fair to look upon, and yet neither resembleth the other, in measure or kind, in any single point or part; and so blind is our perception that we shall not understand whether of the two is the more beautiful, and if we give an opinion on the matter it shall lack certainty.

Negro faces are seldom beautiful because of their very flat noses and thick lips; moreover, their shinbone is too prominent, and the knee and foot too long, not so good to look upon as those of the whites; and so also is it with their hand. Howbeit, I have seen some amongst them whose whole bodies have been so well-built and handsome that I never beheld finer figures, nor can I conceive how they might be bettered, so excellent were their arms and all their limbs.

Seeing that man is the worthiest of all creatures, it follows that, in all pictures, the human figure is most frequently employed as a centre of interest. Every animal in the world regards nothing but his own kind, and the same nature is also in men, as every man may perceive in himself.

Further, in order that he may arrive at a good canon whereby to bring somewhat of beauty into our work, there-unto it were best for thee, it bethinks me, to form thy canon from many living men. Howbeit seek only such men as are held beautiful, and from such draw with all diligence. For one who hath understanding may, from men of many different kinds, gather something good together through all the limbs of the body. But seldom is a man found who hath all his limbs good, for every man lacks something.

No single man can be taken as a model of a perfect figure, for no man liveth on earth who uniteth in himself all manner of beauties.... There liveth also no man upon earth who could give a final judgment upon what the perfect figure of a man is; God only knoweth that.

And although we cannot speak of the greatest beauty of a living creature, yet we find in the visible creation a beauty so far surpassing our understanding that no one of us can fully bring it into his work.

If we were to ask how we are to make a beautiful figure, some would give answer: According to human judgment (i.e., common taste). Others would not agree thereto, neither should I without a good reason. Who will give us certainty in this matter?[83]

II

I have already given what I believe to be the best answer to these questions as to what beauty is and how it is to be judged. Beauty is beauty as good is good (*see* pp. 7, 8), or yellow, yellow; indeed, to the second question, Matthew Arnold has given the only possible answer – the relative value of beauties is "as the judicious would determine," and the judicious are, in matters of art "finely touched and gifted men." This criterion obviously cannot be easily or hastily applied, nor could one ever be quite sure that in any given case it had been applied to any given effect. But for practical needs we see that it suffices to cast a slur on facile popularity, and vindicate over and over again those who had been despised and rejected. What the true artist desires to bring into his pictures is the power to move finely-touched and gifted men. Not only are such by very much the minority, but the more part of them being, by their capacity to be moved and touched, easily wounded, have developed a natural armour of reserve, of moroseness, of prejudice, of combativeness, of pedantry, which makes them as difficult to address as wombats, or bears, or tortoises, or porcupines, or polecats, or elephants. It is interesting to witness how Dürer's self-contradictions show him to be aware of the great complexity of these difficulties, as also to see how very near he comes to the true answer. At one time he tells us:

"When men demand a work of a master, he is to be praised in so far as he succeeds in satisfying their likings ..."[84]

At another he tells us:

"The art of painting cannot be truly judged save by such as are themselves good painters; from others verily is it hidden even as a strange tongue."[85]

Every "finely touched and gifted man" is not an artist; but every true artist must, in some measure, be a finely touched and gifted man. There is no necessity to limit the public addressed to those who themselves produce: yet those who "can prove what they say with their hand" bring credentials superior to those offered by any others, – although even their judgment is not sure, as they may well represent a minority of the true court of appeal which can never be brought together.

No doubt there is a judgment and a scale of values accepted as final by each generation that gives any considerable attention to these questions. Æsthetic appear to be exactly similar to religious convictions. Those who are subject to them probably pass through many successively, even though they all their lives hold to a certain fashion which enables them to assert some obvious unity, like those who, in religion, belong always to one sect. Yet if they were in a position to analyse their emotions and leanings, no doubt very fundamental contradictions would be discovered to disconcert them. Conviction and enthusiasm in the arts and religion would seem to be the frame of mind natural to those who assimilate, and are rendered productive by what they study and admire. Convictions may never be wholly justifiable in theory, but in practice when results are considered, it would seem that no other frame of mind should escape censure.

CHAPTER V

NATURE

I

We regard a form and figure out of nature with more pleasure than another, though the thing in itself is not necessarily altogether better or worse.

Life in nature showeth forth the truth of these things (the words of difference – i.e., the character of bodily habit to which they refer), wherefore regard it well, order thyself thereby and depart not from nature in thine opinions, neither imagine of thyself to invent aught better, else shalt thou be led astray, for art standeth firmly fixed in nature, and whoso can rend her forth thence he only possesseth her. If thou acquirest her, she will remove many faults for thee from thy work.

Neither must the figure be made youthful before and old behind, or contrariwise; for that unto which nature is opposed is bad. Hence it followeth that each figure should be of one kind alone throughout, either young or old, or middle-aged, or lean or fat, or soft or hard.

The more closely thy work abideth by life in its form, so much the better will it appear; and this is true. Wherefore never more imagine that thou either canst or shalt make anything better than God hath given power to His creatures to do. For thy power is weakness compared to God's creating hand.

II

In these and other passages Dürer speaks about "nature," and enjoins on the artist respect for and conformity to "nature" in a manner which reminds us of that still current in dictums about art. Indeed, it seems probable that Dürer's use of this term was almost as confused as that of a modern art-critic. There are two senses in which the word nature is employed, the confusion of which is ten times more confounded than any of the others, and deserves, indeed, utter damnation, so prolific of evil is it. We call the objects of sensory perception "nature" – whatever is seen, heard, felt, smelt or tasted is a part of nature. And yet we constantly speak of seeing, hearing, touching, smelling, and tasting monstrous and unnatural things. And a monstrous and unnatural thing is not merely one which is rare, but even more decidedly one of which we disapprove. So that the second use of the term conveys some sense of exceptionality, but far more of lack of conformity to human desires and expectations. Now, many things which do not exist are perfectly natural in this second sense: fairy-lands, heavens, &c. We perfectly understand what is meant by a natural and an unnatural imagination, we perceive readily all kind of degrees between the monstrous and the natural in pure fiction. Now, this second use of the term nature is the only one which is of any vital importance to our judgments upon works of art; yet current judgments are more often than not based wholly on the first sense, which means merely all objects perceived by the senses; and this, draped in the authority and phrases belonging to judgments based on the second and really pertinent sense.

Whole schools of painting and criticism have arisen and flourish whose only reason for existence is the extreme facility with which this confusion is made in European languages. It sounds so plausible that some have censured Michelangelo for bad drawing because men are not from 9 to 15 or 16 heads high, and have not muscles so developed as the gods and Titans of his creation. And others have objected to the angels, the anatomical ambiguity of their wing articulations. To say that a sketch or picture is out of tone or drawing damns, in many circles to-day; in spite of the fact that the most famous masterpieces, if judged by the same standard, would be equally offensive. This absurdity, even where its grosser developments are avoided, breeds abundant contradictions and confusion in the mouths of those who plume themselves on culture and discernment. I hope not to have been too saucy, therefore, in pointing out this pitfall to my readers in regard to these sentences which I thought it worth while to quote from Dürer, merely because if I did not do so I foresaw that they would be quoted against me.

CHAPTER VI

THE CHOICE OF AN ARTIST

I

In the great earnestness with which the difficulties that beset art and the artist impressed him, Dürer intended to write a *Vade Mecum* for those who should come after him. He has left among his MS. papers many plans, rough drafts, and notes for some such work, the form of which no doubt changed from time to time. The one which gives us the most comprehensive idea of his intentions is perhaps the following.

II

Ihs. Maria

By the grace and help of God I have here set down all that I
have learnt in practice, which is likely to be of use in painting, for
the service of all students who would gladly learn. That,
perchance, by my help they may advance still further in the
higher understanding of such art, as he who seeketh may well do,
if he is inclined thereto; for my reason sufficeth not to lay the
foundations of this great, far-reaching, infinite art of true painting.

Item. – In order that thou mayest thoroughly and rightly
comprehend what is, or is called, an "artistic painter," I will
inform thee and recount to thee. If the world often goeth without
an "artistic painter," whilst for two or three hundred years none
such appeareth, it is because those who might have become such
devote not themselves to art. Observe then the three essential
qualities following, which belong to the true artist in painting.
These are the three main points in the whole book.

  • I. The First Division of the book is the Prologue, and it
compriseth three parts (A, B, and C).

  • A. The first part of the Prologue telleth us how the lad
should be taught, and how attention should be paid to the
tendency of his temperament. It falleth into six parts:
  • 1. That note should be taken of the birth of the child,
in what Sign it occurreth; with some explanations. (Pray God
for a lucky hour!)
  • 2. That his form and stature should be considered;
with some explanations.
  • 3. How he ought to be nurtured in learning from the
first; with some explanations.
  • 4. That the child should be observed, whether he
learneth best when kindly praised or when chidden; with
explanations.

- 5. That the child be kept eager to learn and be not vexed.
- 6. If the child worketh too hard, so that he might fall under the hand of melancholy, that he be enticed therefrom by merry music to the pleasuring of his blood.

- B. The second part of the Preface showeth how the lad should be brought up in the fear of God and in reverence, that so he may attain grace, whereby he may be much strengthened in intelligent art. It falleth into six parts:
  - 1. That the lad be brought up in the fear of God and be taught to pray to God for the grace of quick perception (*ubtilitet*) and to honour God.
  - 2. That he be kept moderate in eating and drinking, and also in sleeping.
  - 3. That he dwell in a pleasant house, so that he be distracted by no manner of hindrance.
  - 4. That he be kept from women and live not loosely with them; that he not so much as see or touch one; and that he guard himself from all impurity. Nothing weakens the understanding more than impurity.
  - 5. That he know how to read and write well, and be also instructed in Latin, so far as to understand certain writings.
  - 6. That such an one have sufficient means to devote himself without anxiety (to his art), and that his health be attended to with medicines when needful.

- C. The third part of the Prologue teacheth us of the great usefulness, joy, and delight which spring from painting. It falleth into six parts:
  - 1. It is a useful art when it is of godly sort, and is employed for holy edification.
  - 2. It is useful, and much evil is thereby avoided, if a man devote himself thereto who else had wasted his time.

- 3. It is useful when no one thinks so, for a man will have great joy if he occupy himself with that which is so rich in joys.
- 4. It is useful because a man gaineth great and lasting memory thereby if he applieth it aright.
- 5. It is useful because God is thereby honoured when it is seen that He hath bestowed such genius upon one of His creatures in whom is such art. All men will be gracious unto thee by reason of thine art.
- 6. The sixth use is that if thou art poor thou mayest by such art come unto great wealth and riches.

- II. The Second Division of the book treateth of Painting itself; it also is threefold.

- A. The first part is of the freedom of painting; in six ways.

- B. The second part is of the proportions of men and buildings, and what is needful for painting; in six ways.[86]
  - 1. Of the proportions of men.
  - 2. Of the proportions of horses.
  - 3. Of the proportions of buildings.
  - 4. Of perspective.
  - 5. Of light and shade.
  - 6. Of colours, how they are to be made to resemble nature.

- C. The third part is of all that a man conceives as subject for painting.

- III. The Third Division of the book is the Conclusion; it also hath three parts.
- A. The first part shows in what place such an artist should dwell to practise his art; in six ways.

• B. The second part shows how such a wonderful artist should charge highly for his art, and that no money is too much for it, seeing that it is divine and true; in six ways.

The third part speaks of praise and thanksgiving which he should render unto God for His grace, and which others should render on his behalf; in six ways.

III

It is in the variety and completeness of his intentions that we perceive Dürer's kinship with the Renascence; he comprehends the whole of life in his idea of art training.

In his persuasion of the fundamental necessity of morality he is akin to the best of the Reformation. It is in the union of these two perceptions that his resemblance to Michelangelo lies. There is a rigour, an austerity which emanates from their work, such as is not found in the work of Titian or Rembrandt or Leonardo or Rubens or any other mighty artist of ripe epochs. Yet we find both of them illustrating the licentious legends of antiquity, turning from the Virgin to Amymone and Leda, from Christ to Apollo and Hercules. By their action and example neither joins either the Reformation or the Renascence in so far as these movements may be considered antagonistic; nor did they find it inconsistent to acknowledge their debt to Greece and Rome, even while accepting the gift of Jesus' example as freely as it was offered.

Not only does Dürer insist on the necessity of a certain consonancy between the surrounding influences and the artist's capacity, which should be both called forth and relieved by the interchange of rivalry with instruction, of seclusion with music or society, but the process which Jesus made the central one of his religion is put forward as essential; he must form himself on a precedent example. I have already quoted from Reynolds at length on this point.

I will merely add here some notes from another MS. fragment of Dürer's bearing on the same points.

He that would be a painter must have a natural turn thereto.

Love and delight therein are better teachers of the Art of Painting than compulsion is.

If a man is to become a really great painter he must be educated thereto from his very earliest years. He must copy much of the work of good artists until he attain a free hand.

To paint is to be able to portray upon a flat surface any visible thing whatsoever that may be chosen.

It is well for any one first to learn how to divide and reduce, to measure the human figure, before learning anything else.

CHAPTER VII

TECHNICAL PRECEPTS

I

If thou wishest to model well in painting, so as to deceive the eyesight, thou must be right cunning in thy colours, and must know how to keep them distinct, in painting, one from another. For example, thou paintest two coats of mantles, one white the other red; thou must deal differently with them in shading. There is light and shadow on all things, wherever the surface foldeth or bendeth away from the eye. If this were not so, everything would look flat, and then one could distinguish nothing save only a chequerwork of colours.

If then thou art shading the white mantle, it must not be shaded with so dark a colour as the red, for it would be impossible for a white thing to yield so dark a shadow as a red. Neither could they be compared one with another, save that in total absence of daylight everything is black, seeing that colour cannot be recognised in darkness. Though, therefore, in such a case, the theory allows one, without blame, to use pure black for the shadows of a white object, yet this can seldom come to pass.

Moreover, when thou paintest anything in one colour – be it

red, blue, brown, or any mixed colour – beware lest thou make it so bright in the lights that it departs from its own kind. For example, an uneducated man regardeth thy picture wherein is a red coat. "Look, good friend," saith he, "in one part the coat is of a fair red and in another it is white or pale in colour." That same is to be blamed, neither hast thou done it aright. In such a case a red object must be painted red all over and yet preserve the appearance of solidity; and so with all colours. The same must be done with the shadows, lest it be said that a fair red is soiled with black Wherefore be careful that thou shade each colour with a similar colour. Thus I hold that a yellow, to retain its kind, must be shaded with a yellow, darker toned than the principal colour. If thou shade it with green or blue, it remaineth no longer in keeping, and is no longer yellow, but becometh thereby a shot colour, like the colour of silk stuffs woven of threads of two colours, as brown and blue, brown and green, dark yellow and green, chestnut-brown and dark yellow, blue and seal red, seal red and brown, and the many other colours one sees. If a man hath such as these to paint, where the surface breaketh and bendeth away the colours divide themselves so that they can be distinguished one from another, and thus must thou paint them. But where the surface lieth flat one colour alone appeareth. Howbeit, if thou art painting such a silk and shadest it with one colour (as a brown with a blue) thou must none the less shade the blue with a deeper blue where it is needful. If often cometh to pass that such silks appear brown in the shadows, as if one colour stood before the other. If thy model beareth such a garment, thou must shade the brown with a deeper brown and not with blue. Howbeit, happen what may, every colour must in shading keep to its own class.

II

The great genius Hokusai, who has obtained for popular art in
Japan a success comparable to that of the best classic masterpieces
of that country and to the drawings and etchings of Rembrandt, a
master of an altogether kindred nature, wrote a little treatise on
the difference of aim noticeable in European and Japanese art.
From the few Dutch pictures which he had been able to examine,
he concluded that European art attempted to deceive the eye,
whereas Japanese art laboured to express life, to suggest
movement, and to harmonise colour. What is meant is easily
grasped when we set before the mind's eye a picture, by Teniers
and a page of Hokusai's "Mangwa." On the other hand, if one
chose a sketch by Rembrandt to represent Dutch art, the
difference could no longer be apparent. If the aim of European art
had ever in serious examples been to deceive the eye, our
painting would rank with legerdemain and Maskelyne's famous
box trick; for it is to be doubted if it could ever so well have
attained its end as even a second-rate conjurer can. I have cited a
passage in which Reynolds confronts the work of great artists with
the illusions of the camera obscura (see p. 237). The adept musical
performer who reproduces the noises of a farmyard is the true
parallel to the lesser Dutch artists; he deceives the ear far better
than they deceive the eye. For every picture has a surface which,
unless very carefully lighted, must immediately destroy the
illusion, even if it were otherwise perfect. Nevertheless, Dürer in
the foregoing passage seems to accept Hokusai's verdict that the
aim of his painting is to deceive the eye; forgetful of all that he
has elsewhere written about the necessity of beauty, the necessity
of composition, the superiority of rough sketches over finished
works.

When a painter has conceived in his heart a vision of beauty,
whether he suggests it with a few strokes of the pen or elaborates
it as thoroughly as Jan Van Eyck did, he wishes it to be taken as a
report of something seen. This is as different from wishing to

deceive the eye as for some one to say "and then a dog barked," instead of imitating the barking of a dog. A circumstantial description in words and a picture by Van Eyck or Veronese are equally intended to pass as reports of something visually conceived or actually seen. Pictures would have to be made peep-shows of before they could veritably deceive; and Jan Van Beers, a modern Dutchman, actually turned some of his paintings into peep-shows. Dürer in the following passage is speaking of the separate details or objects which go to make up a picture, not of the picture as a whole; he never tried to make peep-shows; his signature or an inscription is often used to give the very surface that must destroy the peep-show illusion a definite decorative value. The rest of his remarks have become commonplaces; nor has he written at such length as to give them their true limitations and intersubordination. They will be easily understood by those who remember that art is concerned with producing the illusion of a true report of something seen, not that of an actual vision. Such a report may be slight and brief; it may be stammered by emotion; it may have been confused or tortured to any degree by the mental condition of him who delivers it: if it produces the conviction of his sincerity, it achieves the only illusion with which art is concerned, and its value will depend on its beauty and the beauty of the means employed to deliver it.

CHAPTER VIII

IN CONCLUSION

After turning over Dürer prints and drawings, after meditating on his writings, we feel that we are in the presence of one of those forces which are constant and equal, which continue and remain like the growth of the body, the return of seasons, the succession of moods. This is always among the greatest charms of central characters: they are mild and even, their action is like that of the tides, not that of storms. "If only you had my meekness," Dürer wrote to Pirkheimer (set: p. 85), half in jest doubtless, but with profound truth: – though the word meekness does not indeed cover the whole of what we feel made Dürer's most radical advantage over his friend; at other times we might call it naïvety, that sincerity of great and simple natures which can never be outflanked or surprised. Sometimes it might be called pride, for it has certainly a great deal of self-assurance behind it, the self-assurance of trees, of flowers, of dumb animals and little children, who never dream that an apology for being where and what they are can be expected of them. Such natures when they come home to us come to stop; we may go out, we may pay no heed to them, we may forget them, but they abide in the memory, and some day they take hold of us with all the more force because this new impression will exactly tally with the former one; we shall blush for our inconstancy, our indifference, our imbecility, which have led us to neglect such a pregnant communion. Not only persons but works of art produce this effect, and they are those with whom it is the greatest benefit to live.

It is true that, compared with Giotto, Rembrandt, or Michelangelo, Dürer does not appear comprehensive enough. It is with him as with Milton; we wish to add others to his great gifts, above all to take him out from his surroundings, to free him from the accidents of place and time. In one sense he is poorer than Milton: we cannot go to him as to a source of emotional exhilaration. If he ever proves himself able so to stir us, it is too occasionally to be a reason why we frequent him as it may be one why we frequent Milton. Nevertheless, the greater characters of control which are his in an unmatched degree, his constancy, his resource and deliberate effectiveness, joined to that blandness, that sunshine, which seems so often to replace emotion and thought in works of image-shaping art, are of priceless beneficence, and with them we would abide. Intellectual passion may seem indeed sometimes to dissipate this sunshine and control without making good their loss. Such cases enable us to feel that the latter are more essential: and it is these latter qualities which Dürer possessed in such fulness. In return for our contemplation, they build up within us the dignity of man and render it radiant and serene. Those who have felt their influence longest and most constantly will believe that they may well warrant the modern prophet who wrote:

The idea of beauty and of human nature perfect on all its sides, which is the dominant idea of poetry, is a true and invaluable idea, though it has not yet had the success that the idea of conquering the obvious faults of our animality and of a human nature perfect on the moral side – which is the dominant idea of religion – has been enabled to have; and it is destined, adding to itself the religious idea of a devout energy, to transform and govern the other.

NOTES

1. Swift, "Contests and Dissensions in Athens and Rome."

2. It may be urged that diversities of opinion exist as to what good is. The convenience of the words "good" and "evil" corresponds to a need created by a common experience in the same way as the convenience of the words "light" and "darkness" does. A child might consider that a diamond generated light in the same way as a candle does. He would be mistaken, but this would not affect the correctness of his application of the word "light" to his experience; if he confused light with darkness he must immediately become unintelligible. Good and light are perceived and named – no one can say more of them; the effects of both may be described with more or less accuracy. To say that light is a mode of motion does not define it; we ask at once, What mode? And the only answer is, that which produces the effect of light. A man born blind, though he knew what was meant by motion, could never deduce from this knowledge a conception of light.

3. The Monthly Review, October 1902, "Rodin."

4. "Literary Remains of Albrecht Dürer," p. 177.

5. Ibid. p. 247.

6. "Literary Remains of Albrecht Dürer," p. 252.

7. "Literary Remains of Albrecht Dürer," pp, 244 and 245.

8. "Literary Remains of Albrecht Dürer," p. 180.

9. The Monthly Review, April 1901, "In Defence of Reynolds."

10. Sixth Discourse.

11. Of course all that may have been meant by the phrase "the Evangelist of Art" is that Dürer illustrated the narrative of the Passion; but by this he is not distinguished from many others, and the phrase is suggestive of far more.

12. Froude's "Life of Erasmus," Lecture vi.

13. Wordsworth's Translation,

14. "Literary Remains of Albrecht Dürer," p. 176.

15. Thus far the original is in bad Italian.

16. The retainers of Konz Schott, a neighbouring baron, at one time a conspicuous enemy of Nürnberg.

17. These words are in Italian in the original.

18. Prof. Thausing suggests that this "other *Quadro*" is the "Christ among the Doctors" in the Barberini Gallery at Rome – a picture containing seven life-size half-figures or heads, and dated 1506. The inscription states it to have been *opus quinque dierum*. At Brunswick there is an old copy of it. The original studies for the hands are likewise in existence. In Lorenzo Lotto's Madonna of 1508 in the Borghese Gallery at Rome, the head of St. Onuphrius is taken from the model who sat for the front Pharisee on the left in Dürer's picture.

19. A Nürnberg prison.

20. *The Massacre of the Ten Thousand Saints.*

21. *Supposed to be the Madonna with the Iris.*

22. "Literary Remains of Albrecht Dürer," p. 178.

23. The soil about Nürnberg is sandy.

24. He was one of the leading Humanists of the time. The Madonna referred to was still at Bamberg, at the beginning of the present century.

25. Owing to the existence of some rudimentary form of Zollverein, Dürer's pass not only freed him of dues in the Bamberg district but as far down the Rhine as Köln.

26. Hans Wolf, successor to Hans Wolfgang Katzheimer.

27. There is a portrait drawing of Jobst Plankfelt by Dürer in the Städel collection at Frankfurt.

28. That is the head of the Fuggers' branch house at Antwerp.

29. Erasmus of Rotterdam, the famous Humanist.

30. Holbein also painted a portrait of this man in 1528. The picture is in the Louvre.

31. A pen-and-ink likeness of him by Dürer is in the possession of the painter Bendemann, of Düsseldorf. It bears the inscription in Dürer's hand, "1520. *Hans Pfaffroth van Dantzgen ein Starkmann.*"

32. These were four pictures painted upon linen. They represented *The justice of Trajan, Pope Gregory praying for the Heathen,* and two incidents in the story of Erkenbald. The pictures were burnt in 1695, but their compositions are reproduced in the well-known Burgundian tapestries at Bern. See Pinchart, in the *Bulletins de l'Academie de Bruxelles*, 2nd Series, XVII.: also Kinkel, *Die brusseler Rathhausbilder*, &c., Zurich, 1867.

33. A rapid sketch made by Dürer in this place is in the Academy at Vienna. It is dated 1520, and inscribed, "that is the pleasure and beast-

garden at Brussels, seen down behind out of the Palace."

34. A reproduction of an old view of this house will be found in *L'Art*, 1884, I. p. 188.

35. This picture was painted on four panels and represented the Seven Sacraments and a Crucifix. It is now lost. A similar picture is in the Antwerp Gallery, ascribed to Roger van der Weyden.

36. This is perhaps the drawing in the Bounat collection at Paris; it has been photographed by Braun.

37. It is believed that Dürer here refers to an edition of the satirical tale edited by Thomas Murner, and published at Strassburg in 1519.

38. "He afterwards particularly described to Melanchthon the splendid spectacles he had beheld, and how in what were plainly mythological groups, the most beautiful maidens figured almost naked, and covered only with a thin transparent veil. The young Emperor did not hocour them with a single glance, but Dürer himself was very glad to get near, not less for the purpose of seeing the tableaux than to have the opportunity of observing closely the perfect figures of the young girls." As he himself says, "Being a painter, I looked about me a little more boldly." – See Thausing's "Life of Dürer," vol. ii., p. 181.

39. *Het oud register van diversche mandementen,* a fifteenth-century folio manuscript, still preserved in the Antwerp archives.

40. On April 6, 1520.

41. Tommaso was sent to Flanders in 1520 by Pope Leo X. to oversee the manufacture of the "second series" of tapestries. The painter does not seem to have returned to Italy.

42. Engravings by Marcantonio from Raphael's designs.

43. The picture is lost, but an engraving of it made by And. Stock in 1629 is well-known.

44. The fine monoliths brought from Ravenna and still to be seen in Aachen Cathedral.

45. The confirmation of his pension.

46. Member of a Nürnberg family.

47. The object of the whole expedition was doubtless, that Dürer might see and sketch the whale. In the British Museum is a study of a walrus by Dürer, dated 1521, and inscribed, "The animal whose head I have drawn here was taken in the Netherlandish sea, and was twelve Brabant ells long and had four feet."

48. Gerhard van de Werve.

49. Pupil and afterwards friend of Erasmus.

50. These people were Dürer's principal Nürnberg friends.

51. It is assumed by commentators that *Chapel* means *Altar-piece*, and

it is guessed that the particular altar-piece is the one in the Berlin Museum which Charles V. is reported to have carried about with him, and which belonged to the Miraflores Convent. The guesses are worthless.

52. In St. Jacob's was the *Entombment* by Hugo van der Goes.

53. It is in white marble. It was sculpted about 1501-6. Some critics have refused to accept it as a genuine work. Dürer ought to have been in a position to know the truth.

54. At this time there were plenty of his pictures at Bruges. Dürer doubtless saw his Madonna in St. Donatien's, now in the Academy of the same town.

55. The famous altar-piece painted by Hubert and Jan van Eyck, of which the central part is still in its original place and the wings are divided, two of their panels being at Brussels and the rest at Berlin.

56. This drawing from Dürer's sketch-book is in the Court Library at Vienna.

57. The story is recounted in *Flandria illustrata* (A. Sanderi, Colon., 1641, i. 149.)

58. Gerhard Horeboul of Ghent. Charles V.'s 'Book of Hours' in the Vienna library is his work. He also had a hand in the Grimani Breviary. After 1521 he went to England and entered the service of Henry VIII. His daughter Susanna was likewise in the service of the English King. She married and died in England.

59. Perhaps Jan van den Perre, afterwards goldsmith to Charles V.

60. That is to say, drawings representing *Christ bearing HIS CROSS. Mount of Olives* means the Agony *in the* Garden.

61. The inn-keeper of the *Golden Head* is known to have been a painter. His name was Heinrich Keldermann.

62. Though born at Köln, he was called Hans von Nürnberg. He was cannon-founder and gun-maker to Charles V.

63. Doubtless Dürer's portrait of Maximilian, now in the Gallery at Vienna, dated 1519.

64. Jacopo de' Barbari.

65. Bernard van Orley.

66. The catalogue of this library exists in the inventory of the Archduchess' possessions.

67. This is in the Musée Wicar at Lille; another portrait of Lukas van Leyden by Dürer was in the Earl of Warwick's collection.

68. Hieronymus Imhof.

69. A quarto tract by Luther, printed in 1520 (without place or date), entitled *Von der Babylonischen gefenglnuss der Kirchen.*

70. B. 106, published in 1513. The block is in the Court Library at

Vienna. Thawing says it was designed by Burgkmair or Springinklee.

71. "*Caput argutum*". The phrase is from Virgil's description of the thorough-bred horse (*Georg. iii*). The above passage is introduced (with modifications) into Melchior Adam's *Vitae Germ. Philos.* (p.66). where this sentence runs: "The deep-thinking, serene-souled artist was seen unmistakably in his *arched* and *lofty* brow and in the fiery glance of his eye."

72. In the foregoing quotations the sentences which seem to me most reminiscent of Dürer's ideas are printed in italics.

73. The original, now in the Monastery of Strahow-Prague, is very much damaged, and in part repainted. There are copies in the Imperial Gallery at Vienna (No. 1508), and in the possession of A. W. Miller, Esq., of Sevenoaks. It is to be regretted that the Dürer Society published a photogravure of this latter work, which, though till then unknown, is far less interesting than the original, of which they only gave a reproduction in the text, an exhaustive history of its fortunes from the learned pen of Mr. Cambell Dodgson. This picture, which is so frequently referred to in the letters from Venice, contains portraits of the Emperor Maximilian and Pope Julius II., though neither of them from life, and in the background those of Dürer and Pirkheimer.

74. See what Melanchthon says, p. 187.

75. See the exquisite landscape in the collection of Mr. C. S. Ricketts and Mr. C. H. Shannon, reproduced in the sixth folio of the Dürer Society, 1903. Mr. Campbell Dodgson describes the drawing as in a measure spoilt by retouching, but what convinces him that these retouches are not by Dürer? The pen-work seems to be at once too clever and too careless to have been added by another hand to preserve a fading drawing.

76. XII. Discourse.

77. XIII, Discourse.

78. Ibid.

79. Literary Remains of Albrecht Dürer, p. I 50.

80. Equivalent to our John Doe and Richard Roe.

81. "Literary Remains of Albrecht Dürer," p. 166.

82. See also III Discourse where he defends Dürer against Bacon.

83. "Literary Remains of Albrecht Dürer," p. 244.

84. "Literary Remains of Albrecht Dürer," p. 245.

85. *Idem*. p. 177.

86. The following list comes from another sheet of the MS. (in. 70), but was dearly intended for this place. It is jotted down on a thick piece of paper, on which there are also geometrical designs.

CRESCENT MOON PUBLISHING

web: www.crmoon.com e-mail: cresmopub@yahoo.co.uk

ARTS, PAINTING, SCULPTURE

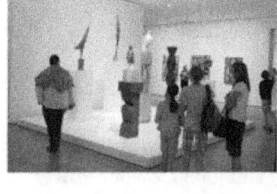
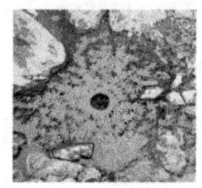

The Art of Andy Goldsworthy
Andy Goldsworthy: Touching Nature
Andy Goldsworthy in Close-Up
Andy Goldsworthy: Pocket Guide
Andy Goldsworthy In America
Land Art: A Complete Guide
The Art of Richard Long
Richard Long: Pocket Guide
Land Art In the UK
Land Art in Close-Up
Land Art In the U.S.A.
Land Art: Pocket Guide
Installation Art in Close-Up
Minimal Art and Artists In the 1960s and After
Colourfield Painting
Land Art DVD, TV documentary
Andy Goldsworthy DVD, TV documentary
The Erotic Object: Sexuality in Sculpture From Prehistory to the Present Day
Sex in Art: Pornography and Pleasure in Painting and Sculpture
Postwar Art
Sacred Gardens: The Garden in Myth, Religion and Art
Glorification: Religious Abstraction in Renaissance and 20th Century Art
Early Netherlandish Painting
Leonardo da Vinci
Piero della Francesca
Giovanni Bellini
Fra Angelico: Art and Religion in the Renaissance
Mark Rothko: The Art of Transcendence
Frank Stella: American Abstract Artist
Jasper Johns
Brice Marden
Alison Wilding: The Embrace of Sculpture
Vincent van Gogh: Visionary Landscapes
Eric Gill: Nuptials of God
Constantin Brancusi: Sculpting the Essence of Things
Max Beckmann
Caravaggio
Gustave Moreau
Egon Schiele: Sex and Death In Purple Stockings
Delizioso Fotografico Fervore: Works In Process I
Sacro Cuore: Works In Process 2
The Light Eternal: J.M.W. Turner
The Madonna Glorified: Karen Arthurs

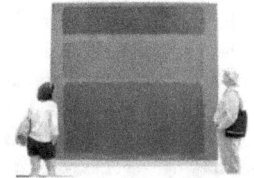
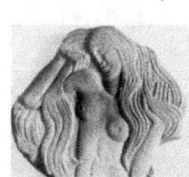
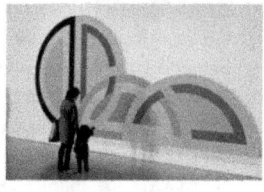
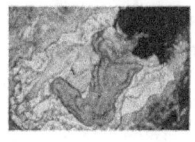
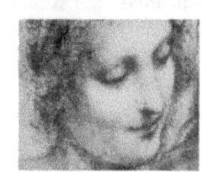
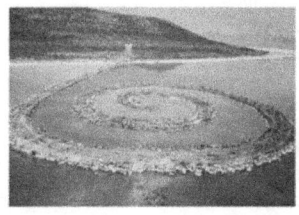

LITERATURE

J.R.R. Tolkien: The Books, The Films, The Whole Cultural Phenomenon
J.R.R. Tolkien: Pocket Guide
Tolkien's Heroic Quest
The *Earthsea* Books of Ursula Le Guin
Beauties, Beasts and Enchantment: Classic French Fairy Tales
German Popular Stories by the Brothers Grimm
Philip Pullman and *His Dark Materials*
Sexing Hardy: Thomas Hardy and Feminism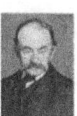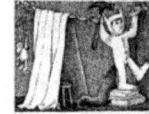
Thomas Hardy's *Tess of the d'Urbervilles*
Thomas Hardy's *Jude the Obscure*
Thomas Hardy: The Tragic Novels
Love and Tragedy: Thomas Hardy
The Poetry of Landscape in Hardy
Wessex Revisited: Thomas Hardy and John Cowper Powys
Wolfgang Iser: Essays and Interviews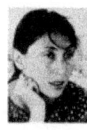
Petrarch, Dante and the Troubadours
Maurice Sendak and the Art of Children's Book Illustration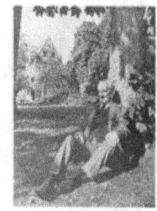
Andrea Dworkin
Cixous, Irigaray, Kristeva: The *Jouissance* of French Feminism
Julia Kristeva: Art, Love, Melancholy, Philosophy, Semiotics and Psychoanalysis
Hélene Cixous I Love You: The *Jouissance* of Writing
Luce Irigaray: Lips, Kissing, and the Politics of Sexual Difference
Peter Redgrove: Here Comes the Flood
Peter Redgrove: Sex-Magic-Poetry-Cornwall
Lawrence Durrell: Between Love and Death, East and West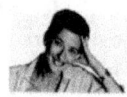
Love, Culture & Poetry: Lawrence Durrell
Cavafy: Anatomy of a Soul
German Romantic Poetry: Goethe, Novalis, Heine, Hölderlin
Feminism and Shakespeare
Shakespeare: Love, Poetry & Magic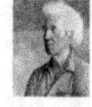
The Passion of D.H. Lawrence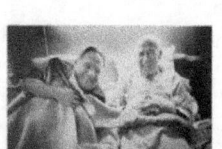
D.H. Lawrence: Symbolic Landscapes
D.H. Lawrence: Infinite Sensual Violence
Rimbaud: Arthur Rimbaud and the Magic of Poetry
The Ecstasies of John Cowper Powys
Sensualism and Mythology: The Wessex Novels of John Cowper Powys
Amorous Life: John Cowper Powys and the Manifestation of Affectivity (H.W. Fawkner)
Postmodern Powys: New Essays on John Cowper Powys (Joe Boulter)
Rethinking Powys: Critical Essays on John Cowper Powys
Paul Bowles & Bernardo Bertolucci
Rainer Maria Rilke
Joseph Conrad: *Heart of Darkness*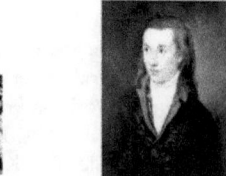
In the Dim Void: Samuel Beckett
Samuel Beckett Goes into the Silence
André Gide: Fiction and Fervour
Jackie Collins and the Blockbuster Novel
Blinded By Her Light: The Love-Poetry of Robert Graves
The Passion of Colours: Travels In Mediterranean Lands
Poetic Forms

POETRY

Ursula Le Guin: Walking In Cornwall
Peter Redgrove: Here Comes The Flood
Peter Redgrove: Sex-Magic-Poetry-Cornwall
Dante: Selections From the Vita Nuova
Petrarch, Dante and the Troubadours
William Shakespeare: Sonnets
William Shakespeare: Complete Poems
Blinded By Her Light: The Love-Poetry of Robert Graves
Emily Dickinson: Selected Poems
Emily Brontë: Poems
Thomas Hardy: Selected Poems
Percy Bysshe Shelley: Poems
John Keats: Selected Poems
Joh n Keats: Poems of 1820
D.H. Lawrence: Selected Poems
Edmund Spenser: Poems
Edmund Spenser: Amoretti
John Donne: Poems
Henry Vaughan: Poems
Sir Thomas Wyatt: Poems
Robert Herrick: Selected Poems
Rilke: Space, Essence and Angels in the Poetry of Rainer Maria Rilke
Rainer Maria Rilke: Selected Poems
Friedrich Hölderlin: Selected Poems
Arseny Tarkovsky: Selected Poems
Arthur Rimbaud: Selected Poems
Arthur Rimbaud: A Season in Hell
Arthur Rimbaud and the Magic of Poetry
Novalis: Hymns To the Night
German Romantic Poetry
Paul Verlaine: Selected Poems
Elizaethan Sonnet Cycles
D.J. Enright: By-Blows
Jeremy Reed: Brigitte's Blue Heart
Jeremy Reed: Claudia Schiffer's Red Shoes
Gorgeous Little Orpheus
Radiance: New Poems
Crescent Moon Book of Nature Poetry
Crescent Moon Book of Love Poetry
Crescent Moon Book of Mystical Poetry
Crescent Moon Book of Elizabethan Love Poetry
Crescent Moon Book of Metaphysical Poetry
Crescent Moon Book of Romantic Poetry
Pagan America: New American Poetry

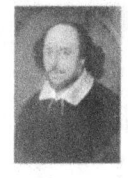
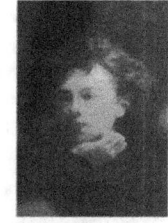
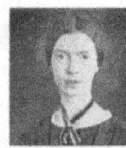
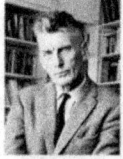

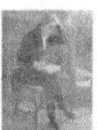
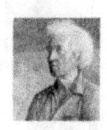
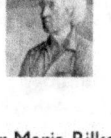
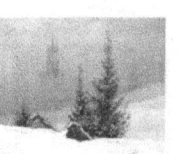
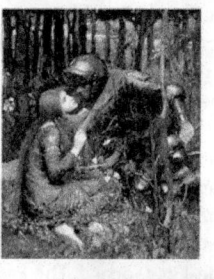
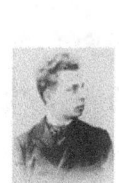
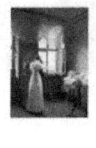
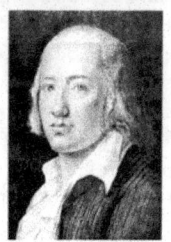
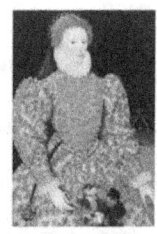

MEDIA, CINEMA, FEMINISM and CULTURAL STUDIES

J.R.R. Tolkien: The Books, The Films, The Whole Cultural Phenomenon
J.R.R. Tolkien: Pocket Guide
The *Lord of the Rings* Movies: Pocket Guide
The Cinema of Hayao Miyazaki
Hayao Miyazaki: *Princess Mononoke*: Pocket Movie Guide
Hayao Miyazaki: *Spirited Away*: Pocket Movie Guide
Tim Burton : Hallowe'en For Hollywood
Ken Russell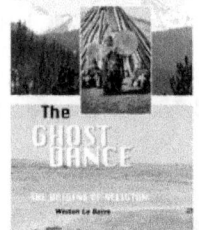
Ken Russell: *Tommy*: Pocket Movie Guide
The Ghost Dance: The Origins of Religion
The Peyote Cult
Cixous, Irigaray, Kristeva: The *Jouissance* of French Feminism
Julia Kristeva: Art, Love, Melancholy, Philosophy, Semiotics and Psychoanalysis
Luce Irigaray: Lips, Kissing, and the Politics of Sexual Difference
Hélene Cixous I Love You: The *Jouissance* of Writing
Andrea Dworkin
'Cosmo Woman': The World of Women's Magazines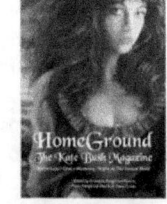
Women in Pop Music
HomeGround: The Kate Bush Anthology
Discovering the Goddess (Geoffrey Ashe)
The Poetry of Cinema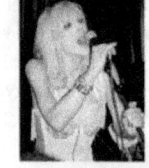
The Sacred Cinema of Andrei Tarkovsky
Andrei Tarkovsky: Pocket Guide
Andrei Tarkovsky: *Mirror*: Pocket Movie Guide
Andrei Tarkovsky: *The Sacrifice*: Pocket Movie Guide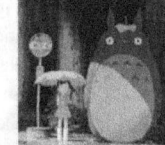
Walerian Borowczyk: Cinema of Erotic Dreams
Jean-Luc Godard: The Passion of Cinema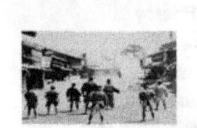
Jean-Luc Godard: *Hail Mary*: Pocket Movie Guide
Jean-Luc Godard: *Contempt*: Pocket Movie Guide
Jean-Luc Godard: *Pierrot le Fou*: Pocket Movie Guide
John Hughes and Eighties Cinema
Ferris Bueller's Day Off: Pocket Movie Guide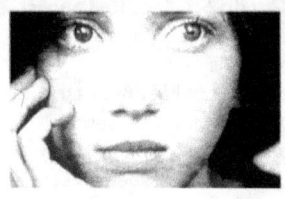
Jean-Luc Godard: Pocket Guide
The Cinema of Richard Linklater
Liv Tyler: Star In Ascendance
Blade Runner and the Films of Philip K. Dick
Paul Bowles and Bernardo Bertolucci
Media Hell: Radio, TV and the Press
An Open Letter to the BBC
Detonation Britain: Nuclear War in the UK
Feminism and Shakespeare
Wild Zones: Pornography, Art and Feminism
Sex in Art: Pornography and Pleasure in Painting and Sculpture
Sexing Hardy: Thomas Hardy and Feminism

The Light Eternal is a model monograph, an exemplary job. The subject matter of the book is beautifully organised and dead on beam. (Lawrence Durrell)
It is amazing for me to see my work treated with such passion and respect. (Andrea Dworkin)

CRESCENT MOON PUBLISHING
P.O. Box 1312, Maidstone, Kent, ME14 5XU, Great Britain. www.crmoon.com

cresmopub@yahoo.co.uk   www.crescentmoon.org.uk

www.ingramcontent.com/pod-product-compliance
Lightning Source LLC
Chambersburg PA
CBHW070216190526

45161CB00002B/92